Introduction to Railway Operations Plannin

Nigel G Harris, Hans Hau
Nils Olsson and Mads Veis

Published by:
A & N Harris
43a Palace Square
London. SE19 2LT. UK.
www.anharris.com

ISBN 978-0-952-9997-6-8

Printed by:
Hobbs the Printers, Brunel Road, Totton, Hampshire SO40 3WX
www.hobbs.uk.com

Introduction to Railway Operations Planning

Nigel G Harris, Hans Haugland,
Nils Olsson and Mads Veiseth

Contents

Introduction to Railway Operations Planning

Preface to the English edition

The focus of other recent books on railway engineering and economics has led to a shortage of material on railway planning topics, with students at many universities looking for something to read which is more comprehensive than can be found in individual articles or conference papers. The resurgence of rail traffic in Western Europe, together with its development in major economies such as China and India, has also meant an increased interest in the basic principles of good railway planning. This is particularly the case as new railway routes are associated with serious cost and project risks, so maximising the use of existing infrastructure is economically-important.

Whilst there are various railway engineering texts (e.g. Profillidis (2014), Lichtberger (2005) or Fiedler & Scherz (2012)) and some providing an overall introduction to railways (e.g. Glover, 2013) or its operation (Pachl, 2009), the key text for railway timetabling and traffic is that by Hansen and Pachl (2008). That addresses the underlying mathematical concepts and analysis in full, and is strongly recommended. However, what seemed to be missing was a book which discussed the practicalities of railway operations and planning on a day-to-day basis.

It was therefore decided to translate Olsson and Veiseth's book into English, a language which has a much wider readership. Whilst doing that, an opportunity has been taken to update and develop some sections of the book, in order to make it of value to a wider international audience, many of whom are facing similar problems. However, we offer no apologies for sharing Nils' and Mads' concerns about actually delivering the plans whose techniques are discussed. We therefore hope that the book will be of interest, not only to students (both within academic institutions and those learning on the job within the industry), but also to managers, civil servants and any others who may need a quick introduction to the types of problems faced in planning the railway.

Acknowledgements

We would like to thank a range of railways around the world which have been our clients, and given us experience and ideas which we have subsequently been able to put together in some sort of order. In addition, there have been students and course attendees who have been the recipients of earlier, less-developed versions of our thoughts, and whose questions have sharpened our ideas. We should also like to acknowledge the technical and moral support given by William Barter, of the IRO. We must also thank our families and immediate colleagues for letting us get slightly distracted from day-to-day work, in order to develop and complete this book. Lastly, we must of course thank Nils Olsson and Mads Veiseth for permission to develop their original text, but any subsequent errors and omissions are ours alone.

Nigel G Harris and Hans Haugland
London SE19/ Oslo, January 2016.

Preface to the Norwegian Edition

The first version of this book was meant to be an introduction to railways and as a supplement to other existing literature in this field, with a special focus on train and crew planning. It was intended to complement other existing literature in the field, and, as railway technology and transport economics are well covered in existing literature, those have therefore just been touched upon briefly. Written specifically for a Norwegian audience, it addressed issues of research and concern in Norway. For instance, railway technology is a specific subject at NTNU with its course literature, whilst punctuality is a field which has had considerable attention in recent years. Generally we have tried to make a text which is readable and understandable without profound background knowledge in technology or economics. The book was based on research and development work within Norwegian railways over the last 10 to 15 years done by SINTEF and NTNU. Such research is generally undertaken in cooperation with the biggest players in the Norwegian railway industry, and was often initiated by NSB.

In general, one can identify three perspectives within railway research:

- Justifying and developing railways. You stress the positive effects of railways, including their positive externalities. Environmental sustainability is often
  a major argument, whilst high speed trains have great importance these days.
- Criticising railways. Here, the focus is on costs, subsidies and the number of travellers. Railways are often presented as "worst case" from this perspective.
- Making railways more effective. Resource management, quality improvement – including maintenance, punctuality, planning, and project management are focused.

This book is first and foremost based on the last perspective: To utilize the present railway in the best possible way. At the same time we are, as most people working with railways, are interested in their further development.

Acknowledgements

This book presents results from a series of railway-related research activities undertaken at the Norwegian University of Science and Technology (NTNU) and the research institution SINTEF over the last 10 years. NSB (Norwegian State Railways) has for many years supported the research of those two institutions in railway traffic, and the commitment of the company has in that way contributed to increasing knowledge about railway operations (traffic) in Norway. Those parts of the book about the planning of railway traffic are mainly based on research supported by NSB.

Jernbaneverket (Norwegian National Rail Authority) has over the last 10 years undertaken several research projects related to railway operations, especially those concentrating on punctuality problems. Among these, Jernbaneverket was responsible for the project PeMRO (Performance Measurement in Railway Operations), which was supported by The Norwegian Research Council (a Norwegian Government research agency). The train operating companies CargoNet, Flytoget and NSB also participated in the PeMRO project, in addition to SINTEF and NTNU. Much of the work on punctuality problems presented in this book is based on results from the PeMRO project.

We would like to thank NSB, Jernbaneverket, CargoNet and Flytoget for contributing to research on railway operations. Their engagement has made the making of this book possible.

Finally we would like to thank all those who have contributed to this book. Special thanks to NSB for the company's financial contribution to making the book. This was decisive. Thanks also to Hans Haugland, others in NSB, and to Per Magnus Heggelund in Jernbaneverket for comments to versions of the manuscript.

This book is published with economic support from NSB.

Nils Olsson and Mads Veiseth
Trondheim /Lommedalen, July 2011

1 Introduction to Railway Operations

Railways are an important part of the transport network in most countries, and are seen as an efficient and environment friendly transport alternative. The basis of rail's advantage is the use of steel wheels on steel rails. Wheels can roll at low friction, which allows for high speed and less energy than transport on wheels on other surfaces: you need 7 times the energy to pull a rubber-tyred lorry on a road compared to pulling a railway wagon with the same weight on railway rails (Lumsden, 1986). To achieve these advantages, an even and good quality track is needed. There are also requirements regarding geometry: curves should not be too narrow, and hills cannot be too steep.

A characteristic feature of railway transport, passenger and freight, is the advantage of traffic density. The costs per passenger or per tonne of freight are reduced with increased number of passengers or volume of goods. As for planning and operations, railways are a tightly integrated system, where all actors are dependent on each other. Railways allow less flexibility than are given by roads, air space or sea: for instance, driving on the pavement to avoid an obstacle is not possible. All railway movements must therefore to a great extent be planned, and traffic must be supervised and coordinated continuously.

The railway is a classic "system" which has been described as a big machine, in contrast to other modes of transportation where every vehicle, plane, boat and infrastructure part are themselves "machines". That the railway is so closely knit together gives also some advantages: in planning you have a good overview of the system, and because railway has its own infrastructure, it is operationally relatively isolated from other transport modes.

The technical apparatus of railway may roughly be divided into rolling stock which runs on the track, and the fixed infrastructure which is needed by rolling stock to run safely. To run trains, you need to have rolling stock and traincrew in place, and a clear signal for departure from the signalling system. Except in automatic railways (of which there are relatively few, and almost all in local urban environments), train crew may consist just of a driver, or may comprise a driver and conductor(s) or guard(s); extra customer service staff may also be provided. In addition, a series of other functions are necessary to run a safe railway operation.

Following policy guidance from the EU, operational control of train production is often split between an infrastructure provider (in Norway, Jernbaneverket,

JBV) and the Train Operating Companies (TOCs). As well as infrastructure maintenance and renewal, companies such as Jernbaneverket are responsible for the operational control of traffic on the railway, either from local, regional or even national train control centres. Operational control of train production demands close cooperation between the control of trains and crew, and several operators in Britain (notably in the South West Trains/Network Rail Wessex "Alliance") have co-located their controls into the same room. Train control is geographically divided between units each responsible for their railway lines or sections of route, whilst the TOCs are responsible for the operational control of rolling stock and train crew, and the scheduled maintenance of rolling stock. On metro railways, the system linkage between trains and infrastructure is also more important, so control of electrical equipment is often also co-located.

1.1 Role of Railways in the Transport System

Traditionally, trains have been understood to have their strengths in three areas:

- Commuting in and out of big cities
- Passenger traffic between big urban centres
- Long distance freight transport

The railway has sufficient capacity to undertake transport in densely populated areas with limited land availability. In Norway railways have recently had a significant role in commuter traffic in the Oslo area, and in container transport between the big cities and to Northern Norway. Elsewhere, medium- and long-distance passenger traffic is significant, for instance in Germany, France and (especially) Japan.

In the passenger market cars dominate over shorter distances up to 300 km. On very long distances air transport is the dominant mode, while trains and buses have low market shares. For commuting in and out of cities, rail's market share tends to rise with city size: rail has a market share of more than 20 % in Oslo but over 80% in London.

In the EU countries there has been an increase in passenger traffic from 1970 to 2007 (Nash and Matthews, 2009). Yet the train market share of passenger transport has been reduced from 10.4 % in 1970 to 6.6 % in 1990 and further to 6.1 % in 2007 (Priemus, 2008, Nash and Matthews, 2009), as the car has increasingly been used for many short- and medium-distance journeys. Internationally, the traffic volumes for local trains have been quite stable over the last 10 years (Schüller, 2001). Even if rail transport and public transport in general have lost market shares over the last 10 years, there have been interesting developments in high speed trains, urban trains and airport express trains. There has been growth within long distance trains, driven by the development in high speed railways in particular. High speed trains accounted for all the increase in rail passenger transport in Europe for 10 years since 1995 (Preston, 2009), but increasingly, changes in society (increasing urbanisation, high petrol costs, and the ability to use technology on the move) mean that car use is now falling (hence rail use rising) amongst young adults in metropolitan areas.

In freight transport, the competitive edge of trains is their economy of scale, which means that you can offer low costs for large quantities of goods (in long trains) over long distances. Wagonload railfreight has generally given way to trainload operation. Within freight transport there has been a concentration of fewer terminals handling more and more goods. Freight transport in Norway is more and more concentrated in the corridors Oslo-Bergen, Oslo-Stavanger (via Kristiansand) and Oslo-Bodø (via Trondheim), in addition to the Østfold line. In these corridors train frequency has increased in recent years.

Figure 1.2 Competition in Rail Freight: Cargolink Class 185 Leaves the Oslo Tunnel with Covered Car Carriers

Combined transport is increasingly the most important mode of freight transport by train in many countries, typically using more than one mode of transport (for example train and lorry) in a freight transport chain, typically to move goods in a container, which is easily transferred between transport modes. Across the EU, the volume of freight transport by train fell from 1980 to 1999, but has since increased a little. The railway market share measured in tonne km has nevertheless been reduced from 12.6 % in 1995 to 10.7 % in 2007 (Nash and Matthews, 2009).

1.2 Organization of the Railway Sector

There are two main models for railway organisation: having a single vertically-integrated company (responsible for everything, but critically both track and trains) and a range of companies specialising in their own activities. Guidance from the European Union in 1991 (directive 91/440) required member states to account separately for infrastructure and train operations, with further legislation in 2001 (directive 2001/14) requiring arrangements for through-running of one railway company's trains on to the network of another to be transparent. These arrangements were enacted into law in the UK by the Railways Infrastructure (Access and Management) Regulations 2005 (SI 2005/3049), although many merely superseded those set out during Britain's 1993 railway privatisation Act. Supporting the separate management of infrastructure and train operations is the need for a regulatory body, to ensure that the infrastructure authority does not unduly favour one company over another; it may also have other roles, for instance in the determination of industry expenditure or charging rates to users (e.g. passenger fares). All of these should be independent of Government agencies which specify or procure rail services.

Unified companies are now predominantly in freight railways (especially those where one customer is dominant), metro railways (where there would not normally be track capacity for another other operators) and in developing countries or other situations where rail is struggling (because there is no commercial incentive for other players to emerge). In both freight and metro examples, the specialist nature of the railway encourages the exact matching of rolling stock and infrastructure, but mixed-traffic railways are more likely to need the disaggregated model. Note that the number of companies is entirely

[1] Preston (1993) analysed the efficiency of different Western European railways, and discovered that economies of scale gave way to diseconomies of complexity at greater sizes; the railways of the Netherlands were considered to be of optimum size. Elsewhere in the world, larger railways (e.g. Russia, India) have often divided themselves geographically into more manageable units.

a different matter from who owns them, although it may make some sense for infrastructure companies to be under Government control (because of the competitive equivalence with the highway network).

Figure 1.1 Unified Railway Operation: (a) industrial freight, Fiji; (b) metro, Chen Sow Lin, Kuala Lumpur, Malaysia

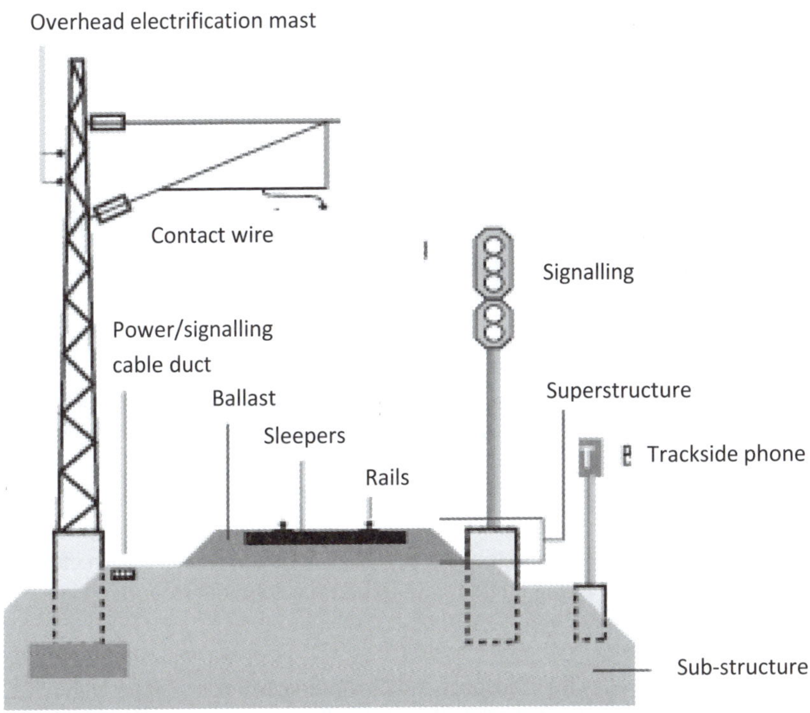

Figure 1.3 Main elements of infrastructure (Jernbaneverket, 2010)

The railway structure in Norway generally has followed EU recommendations. Until recently, the railway in Norway had three different elements: Jernbaneverket (the national railway infrastructure authority), Train Operating Companies (TOCs), and Statens Jernbanetilsyn (SJT, the National Railway Inspectorate), each with different responsibilities. This division in three was carried out in 1996. Until 1996, NSB was a government agency under the Department of Transport responsible for safety, infrastructure and train operation.

Jernbaneverket's mission is to operate, maintain and develop the Norwegian railway network. It is responsible for railway stations and terminals, and for timetable planning giving TOCs track access. Jernbaneverket is also responsible for power supply, signal- and safety installations, and for the control of train traffic on the railway network.

The TOCs transport people and goods across the railway network. Jernbaneverket has track access agreements with the TOCs, determining responsibilities between them, and regulating track usage (in terms of the number of trains that can be run, and at what times, how fast/heavy they may be, and so on). The biggest passenger traffic TOCs are NSB and Flytoget (the Airport Express Train). In freight, CargoNet is the biggest operator, but there are also several smaller TOCs. TOCs are responsible for maintenance of their rolling stock.

Statens Jernbanetilsyn (SJT) supervises safety in the railway, ensuring that those involved in the railway industry fulfil laws and regulations. SJT has a register of approved TOCs and other railway industry businesses. As of 31.12.2015, 11 TOCs (4 passenger and 7 freight) had track access agreements with Jernbaneverket.

A particular feature of the Norwegian system is the existence of Norsk Jernbaneskole (Norwegian Railway School) as a division of Jernbaneverket educating train drivers and train traffic controllers (signalmen). Finishing this education, train drivers get a complementary education and training from TOCs, and will then be authorized as train drivers. The TOCs have their own training of train crew covering safety and service. Signalmen get their training and local competence at the stations where they are serving. Signalmen can have supplementary training for example to be train controllers working in a train control centre.

The Norwegian Ministry for Transport and Communications buys passenger train services that are not economically profitable for TOCs, in order to take advantage of the other benefits the railways bring to societies (externalities such as road congestion relief, time savings, accident savings, less pollution, beneficial impact on the urban environment, tourism etc.). This is called public purchase (offentlig kjøp), and tends to cover local train services in areas where the social benefits are greatest, This is often around bigger cities (where road traffic congestion can otherwise be unacceptable) – for instance in Norway, trains between Oslo, Skien, Lillehammer and Halden. Other areas receiving support from government are often more rural areas, where the importance of maintaining the local economy and avoiding undue unemployment through provision of a basic public transport service may be critical – for instance, on Rørosbanen. However, more generally, subsidizing train services is one of the classical examples in economics where economies of scale make it economically worthwhile to stimulate a higher traffic volume than is profitable for TOCs in narrow financial terms.

Most train operators would expect to pay a track access fee, designed to cover direct traffic costs. The quantity varies very much internationally (depending upon whether a marginal or average cost basis is used for calculation), but fees are particularly low in Denmark and Sweden (Nash and Matthews, 2009). High fees may be found on special infrastructure, as high speed lines, bridges and tunnels. This is the case for example for the Channel Tunnel between England and France.

1.3 Development of Railways in Norway

History plays a huge part in how current railway networks perform. The Norwegian railway network grew slowly during the 19th century, because of the relatively weak economic state of the country. Lines were generally built as single track, and often followed the contours in an attempt to minimise major engineering works; it is said that only 5% of the network is straight track. Therefore there are relatively few parts where the full high speed potential of modern rolling stock can be utilized; only about 30 % of the network is designed for speeds above 100 km/h, and about 3 % for speeds above 150 km/h. Of today's c. 4100 km national railway network in Norway, 94% is single track (Jernbaneverket, 2015), but about 62% of the Norwegian railway network is electrified.

Double track lines are mainly in the Oslo area. Following recent investment in duplicate lines designed for higher speeds, the routes Oslo S – Lillestrøm and Lysaker – Asker now have two double tracks. However, over the last 30 years there has been a continuous development of the road network and airports across Norway. The railway has not generally had a corresponding infrastructure improvement, even if there are on-going developments in the Oslo area in particular. Over the last years, high speed services have frequently been discussed in Norway (where "high speed trains" are those defined as trains doing more than 250 km/h on specially-constructed infrastructure).

Factors influencing the competitive edge of high speed trains are distances between the bigger cities, the demand for long distance travel, and the competitive edge of other modes of transport. Distances between the bigger cities in Norway are within an interval of 250-550 km, which is considered to be ideal for the competitive edge of high speed trains. Compared to countries that have developed a high speed network, however, population density in Norway is low, but at the same time long distance mobility in Norway is high. The competitive edge of other travel modes, like conventional trains, cars and airlines, depends on price, availability and standard. High speed trains in Norway must balance between being a service for end-to-end journeys between the bigger cities and catering for traffic to/from intermediate stops. The failure to date of any high-speed line to be realised is probably a function of the relatively small sizes of Norwegian cities, the difficult terrain between them, and the relative time penalty compared to existing air services.

The railway has been through extensive restructuring since 1996. There are now several players, and Norway is considered to have got relatively far in restructuring railways compared to other European countries (Preston, 2009). The purpose of the divisions has been to clarify the role of different players. At the same time railways are a tightly integrated system demanding close cooperation between participants, so that division may create challenges in taking care of the total perspective. There has been a division between different parts of the railway value chain, e.g. infrastructure (Jernbaneverket), Train Operating Companies (NSB, CargoNet, Flytoget etc.), rolling stock maintenance (Mantena), and services (catering, cleaning etc.), each of whom can develop their own expertise and (ideally) reduce their costs to a greater extent than the profit margin they add to their activities. There has also been competition between businesses within the same activity (for instance, with TOCs and service providers). On the freight side in particular, there is competition with several companies running trains.

One line (Gjøvikbanen) was put out for bidding in 2006, but greater changes have been announced by the Government elected in 2013. These proposals are now (2015) becoming more specific, and all passenger traffic is now due to be opened up for competition, for Norwegian and/or foreign bidders. The railway infrastructure and rolling stock will be state owned, and a Ministry railway directorate shall be responsible for the bidding process, the purchase of train services, and for strategic timetable planning. The private sector will be left to bid only for operating concessions, giving them rather little control over their business. Competition within the freight sector will remain.

Fragmenting the railway means that coordination in the value chain is made through formal contracts, for example between TOCs and service providers. This means that TOCs compete in the market (passengers and freight), and for production capacity (track access). At the same time, the "big railway machine" is split into different areas of responsibility. In a tightly integrated system like railways, it is then a challenge to utilize economies of scale (especially in a country with a relatively small railway sector, like Norway)[1], and it is not always easy to see who is taking responsibility for the total railway system.

1.4 Infrastructure

Like other countries with dominant capitals (such as France), the Norwegian railway network has a "star" shape, with a centre in Oslo. Consequently the bulk of railway traffic is concentrated around Oslo. This means challenges in planning and operation when high frequency local trains must be coordinated with other train types, like regional trains, freight trains and airport express trains. It also is challenging to handle disruptions and to do unscheduled movements of rolling stock. Other countries have a greater portion of double tracks and a more network-like structure (especially Germany, with its greater range of substantial cities scattered across the country).

The traffic load in the Norwegian railway network varies greatly between lines. Parts of the network have only one to two trains a week, while the Oslo tunnel has about 600 trains a day. In 2009 there were 1519 trains a day on Norwegian tracks, of which 827 trains went into or passed through Oslo Central station. Internationally, there are many busy locations with over 1000 trains per day.

The railway infrastructure can be subdivided into

- Tracks, with their supporting formation (in Norwegian, underbygning) and permanent way (overbygning)

[2] An alternative, moving towards the multiple unit concept, is to provide a special vehicle with control equipment ("driving trailer") marshalled at the opposite end of the train from the locomotive.

- Stations and terminals
- Power supply
- Signalling systems
- Communication systems
- Buildings and equipment for operations and maintenance

Figure 1.3 illustrates the main infrastructure elements.

The formation is the foundation/basis of railway tracks, and consists of the mass on which the tracks are resting. The track itself consists of sleepers and rails held to them with ties. The permanent way normally consists of ballast, sleepers, rails and points, although slab track (with the rails set into concrete) is used in certain circumstances (e.g. tunnels with limited clearance). The track gauge in Norway is 1435 mm ("standard gauge"). The power supply gives electrical power to train propulsion on electrified lines.

Key problems in other countries include the loading gauge (the cross-sectional area of the train when stationary, which is small in Britain but particularly generous in Sweden), and the original adoption of a non-standard track gauge (1524mm) in e.g. Spain and Russia.

Stations are also part of the railway, and have four main functions:

- circulatory (for passengers to access and egress from the rail system);
- operational (for ticket selling, and loading catering provisions and traincrew)
- "beacon" (to demonstrate a presence in the high street) and
- commercial (to sell refreshments and other items, and provide retail and office space associated with the connectivity benefit of the adjacent rail services).

Stations are the railway interface to the external world for passengers, and they are an important part of the internal railway logistics. First and foremost it is generally in stations that trains can meet on single track lines, because this is where passing loops are normally located. If appropriate pointwork is provided on double track lines, trains running in the same direction can overtake each other at stations. It is of course also at stations where we allow passengers to interchange, either by their doing this using their own power, or where trains are shunted to provide through carriages to different destinations.

Freight trains are loaded and unloaded in freight terminals, where goods may also be received, sorted, transferred and stored. This can take considerable space and, in particular, length: freight trains are commonly 500m long and may reach several km in length.

The railway system and its subsystems are described in more detail by Pachl (2002) and in the subject Jernbaneteknikk (NTNU, 2009). There are also explanations and much information on the homepages of Jernbaneverket, www.jernbaneverket.no.

In railways, safety is always first priority, even before punctuality. Train movements on the tracks are strictly controlled to avoid collisions. Trains cannot do evasive movements, and they have long braking distances (typically up to 2 km for high-speed trains). It is therefore important for railways to have safety systems to prevent more than one train from getting access to a section of line ("block") at the same time. To attend to safety, train traffic is supervised, and this is done through the signalling system.

The safety system for train traffic in Norway is based on three principles:

- The track is divided into signal blocks
- There can never be more than one train in a signal block in one time
- The order of trains is fixed in the timetable, possibly adjusted by other instructions.

The signalling system ensures safe railway traffic, but it also contributes to an optimal utilisation of track capacity. By using electric or electronic signalling systems, trains can be controlled from train control centres, giving greater opportunities for regulation. However, there are some lines in Norway without a central control system (CTC), where train control is done manually by train despatchers (TXP) on stations along the line; similarly, in Britain, Network Rail is rapidly trying to phase out local signalboxes covering only a few km of route. Communication systems give communication facilities for train traffic, and make sure that that technical installations are functioning properly. Many European countries have done a great deal in developing a separate mobile phone network for the railway (GSM-R).

The railway track is divided in block sections. The signalling and safety systems are based on knowing where a train is, and its direction. Traffic control generally prevents a train entering a track section (a signalled block) where there is already another rolling stock unit. Where no signalling is available, manual control is required, in order to ensure that there is only one train at a time on the defined track section; an in-depth explanation of this is given in Grande and Nilsson (1989).

Remote train control means that the signalling equipment of a line is typically controlled from an electrically or electronically-operated signalbox or central control centre. The two rails are electrically insulated from each other, and the track block is seen to be occupied when a wheel axle is connecting the two rails. This enables control staff to be sure that the block up till the next station or block post is free from other trains. Access of trains to the block can therefore be controlled remotely by a train controller. Remote control enables more flexible train traffic, and reduces demand for personnel. Remote control makes it possible for trains to meet in stations not manned by a train despatcher (TXP) or, indeed, at passing loops in the middle of the countryside.

Automatic train control (ATC) is a system braking trains automatically to avoid dangerous situations. The train brakes if the speed is too high, if the driver is braking too late, or if the train passes a signal at stop. The ATC system consists of transmitters and receivers in trains and tracks. Transmitters and receivers in the tracks are called transponders (balises). The transponders have an interface to the signalling system.

ERTMS (European Rail Traffic Management System) is a standardized European system being introduced for signalling and traffic control using GSM-R for communication. GSM-R is an extended and specially adapted mobile phone network used by the railway. It is used for communication between train controllers, train drivers and those working in or by the tracks. With the full ERTMS system, physical signalling equipment along the tracks is no longer needed. All signal images are moved into the driver's cabin in the train. Jernbaneverket is planning a line-by-line renewal of the signal system, in combination with a step-by-step implementation of ERTMS. The first line, Østfoldbanen Østre linje, is now (2015) in operation, and a corresponding number of trainsets are equipped for ERTMS.

Importantly for the train planner, all this infrastructure needs maintenance, and it is not practical or safe for all this maintenance to be undertaken when trains are running. Taking into account when tracks are planned to be closed for maintenance, and adapting to situations when emergency maintenance is required, are therefore key problems.

In addition to track, stations and signalling, there is a need for buildings and equipment for the operation and maintenance of infrastructure and rolling stock. That is generally beyond the scope of this book, except to note that major service changes (especially those involving the introduction of new train fleets) will need to consider these wider implications – in particular, trains have to be ordered well before they are scheduled to run, and need to have maintenance facilities established equally early in the process.

1.5 Rolling Stock – Trains

Coaches, wagons, motorized carriages and locomotives are often put under the general heading of "rolling stock". Locomotives are separate units pulling passenger carriages or freight wagons, and are commonly available either diesel and/or electric-powered. Electric locomotives have a higher maximum speed, are stronger, accelerate quicker, are cheaper to operate and maintain and are more environmentally friendly than diesel locomotives. However, the advantage of diesel locomotives is that they can be used on non-electrified lines. In addition to locomotives used for pulling carriages and wagons, there are shunting locomotives and rail tractors used for splitting and joining trains and for moving trains and carriages within an area or a station. Norwegian rolling stock is described in Sando et al. (2008).

A motor carriage is a railway carriage with motor(s). A multiple unit train set usually consists of several cars with or without motors, with cabs at both ends of the set, and various facilities for passengers in the cars; there have also been experiments with freight multiple units. In either type, more train sets may be coupled together. Because a multiple unit can be operated from both ends, you do not have to turn the whole train around at terminals. This is a distinct advantage compared to trains operated with a locomotive, where either the locomotive must move from one end of the train to the other, or it must be replaced by another locomotive, or there need to be separate locomotives at both ends of the train[2].

Trains are designed with different purposes in mind, in terms of the level of comfort and facilities provided, the layout of seats and doors (1/3: 2/3 spacing is common for suburban trains, in order to minimize egress time, but end doors provide more comfort for inter-city passengers), acceleration and maximum speed (for mechanical reasons, trains with higher maximum speeds tend to have poorer acceleration). Lastly, of course, trains are not all of the same size and capacity, with passenger trains having between 1 and 24 carriages, and the length of freight trains ranging from 20m to 2km. This all matters to the planner, since the constraints of the network will apply differentially to different trains, whilst a lack of interchangeability makes matters more complicated and/or may require changes to the infrastructure.

Some choices of the technical characteristics of rolling stock are strategic in nature. Rubber-tyred stock has been used for metros (mainly in France) and does permit faster acceleration and hence more closely-spaced stations, but at the expense of more complicated equipment and the (time and maintenance) costs of more stations. Articulated rolling stock shares bogies between adjacent carriages, but this may require more complicated equipment within depots, for maintenance.

For safety and operational reasons all rolling stock must be maintained at regular intervals. Historically, distance based intervals have used i.e. accumulated kilometers since last maintenance determine when rolling stock is due for maintenance. Typically, light maintenance is done every 10 000 km for older rolling stock and 20 000 km for newer ones. Modern asset management systems incorporate greater knowledge of assets and likely failure modes, and may be supplemented by information gathered in real time from the train as it moves around the network. In addition to light maintenance, there is, at longer intervals, a need for heavy maintenance, when larger replacements and repairs are carried out. The operations planner must then not forget the impact of train maintenance.

1.6 Summary

Railways are classic 'systems' involving fixed and movable infrastructure, a wide range of systems and processes designed to provide transport services safely and cost-effectively, and a multiplicity of types of customer all having to be serviced simultaneously. The railway also has to cope with the fact that its customers are physically located within the area of production, so it is extremely visible to them, and a degree of political interference. As a result, the railway planner has to understand a wide range of trade-offs, and we have tried to describe many of these in the following chapters.

2 Strategic Planning

2.1 Introduction

Good railway planning needs to be linked to the planning of other transport modes and, indeed, the various transport needs of the country it is trying to serve. Many countries achieve some success in the former of these (perhaps through a multi-modal government Department of Transport), and some make links with the land-use/development process of town planning, but few maximize the potential for the joint development of transport and logistics with larger employers and manufacturers. We would, however, encourage railway managers to do all of these, since it is much too easy to attempt to provide enhanced services for existing customers, without realizing that a far greater potential exists with markets not currently being served.

Strategic planning for railway networks may need to be done by a number of organizations, with different perspectives. In Norway, long-term planning is undertaken both by Train Operating Companies (TOCs) and in Jernbaneverket (JBV). To achieve a common and long-term perspective, the-long term plans are merged into a National Transport Plan (Nasjonal Transportplan, NTP) covering all transport modes. The plan is revised every 4 years, and presents the long- term guidelines for transport policy. NTP used to cover a 10-year period, but this has now been extended to 12 years. The plan for 2018 to 2029 now underway also includes a 50-year perspective. However, discussions between transport directorates (including JBV) about the draft NTP, the budget for it, and political influences mean that some major projects in the NTP have not been carried out, whilst other activities (e.g. the extension of Nationaltheatret Station in Oslo in 1999) have been taken forward without being in the NTP.

Long-term planning should include an evaluation of the effects of management decisions. Effects can be positive and/or negative, and they may be expected or unexpected (Samset, 2001). Most methods of evaluation include an analysis of both positive and negative effects, and strive to include all effects. Another key issue is who is affected. The identification of stakeholders is important because the effects of a project may be positive for some groups and negative for others. Common trade-offs in railway planning include passenger v freight, and long-distance v local passenger transport. Whilst it is accepted that there will be some political input, many of these decisions can be aided by proper planning techniques and principles – for instance, multi-criteria analysis based on generalized cost theory.

2.2 The Demand for Rail Transport

The relative volume of expected demand should be the main determinant of the type of technology used in a rail system. There is a range of types of technology designed for different purposes, with capacities ranging between 6,000 pphpd (passengers per hour per direction) (certainly within the capacity of bus operations) and 60,000 pphpd (certainly not). However, many systems are designed to carry more passengers than they actually do, either because demand is expected to grow in the future, or because that level of capacity is required elsewhere on the network. For instance, segregated metros may have branches with only 4 or 6tph (trains per hour), because these link with other branches to provide a 30tph service in the core part of the network. Similar principles apply to mainline rail.

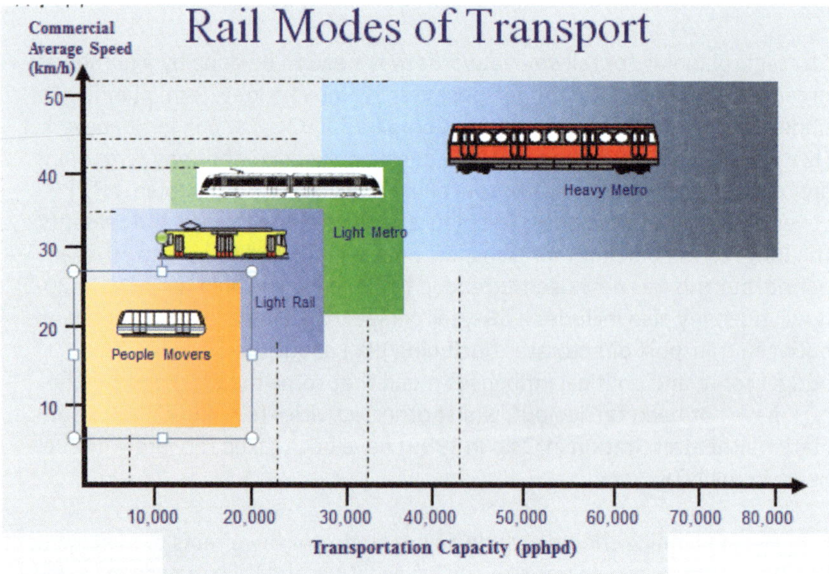

Figure 2.1 Capacity Levels of Different Railway Technologies
Source: University of Birmingham (with permission)

Other systems fail to achieve the potential capacity of that technology, owing to other constraints. These include limited loading gauge (London Underground is a prime example) and the impacts of junctions and inadequate terminal capacity. Especially in the developing world, however, a lack of investment resources may simply mean that too little transport capacity is provided, and this creates problems for operational planners, who have to deal with the consequences e.g. the impact of overcrowding on station stop times. Elsewhere, pressure groups may request the carriage of bicycles on trains, which has obvious consequences for the capacity for passengers.

The demand for passenger rail services is affected by many factors (e.g. see Wardman, 2006) and, if they are to be successful, railway companies need to plan their services taking all these factors into account. These factors may be grouped into two types.

Exogenous factors are those outside the control of the railways, including:

- personal income;
- population, and its distribution;
- employment, and its distribution;
- car ownership;
- driving licence and car parking availability;
- road journey speeds, congestion levels and reliability;
- bus/coach journey times, frequencies and fares;
- air journey times, frequencies and fares;
- the urban realm, including abilities to walk and cycle to/from stations.

Figure 2.2 Dadar, Mumbai: Too Little Capacity

Even offpeak loadings lead to significant crowding

Figure 2.3 Section of Copenhagen S-Tog train with Bicycle Space

Any assessment of railway performance or formal benchmarking work comparing the relative performance of railways also needs to take into account a wide range of other, rather more hidden, external factors which impact on its ability to produce output through a planning process. These include:

- background geography (e.g. borders and crossing points; orientation of hills and rivers; location within a wider continent, enabling transit traffic);
- geological conditions providing gradients, minerals for transport, or the stability to provide support for high-speed operation;
- the background levels of technology available in areas such as signalling;
- railway company structure, objectives, vision, power (i.e. money) and the type/level of political interference;
- laws concerning minimum wages, terms and conditions of employment, town planning processes, consumer protection etc.;
- management style and workforce culture, including the level of unionisation and the approach taken by unions; and
- (dis)economies of scale and economies of traffic density.

Endogenous factors are those factors within the control of the railways which impact on the cost of using the service. But how do we measure this cost? There is clearly a range of attributes which are important, with fare and journey time being critical. However, demand can clearly be manipulated by altering other journey aspects e.g. increased frequency also increases the demand for travel. We therefore need to develop a measure which includes all these attributes, and this is now conventionally understood to be generalised cost (gc), which may be understood as an index of the hassle associated with travel. It is conventionally measured in units of (perceived) minutes.

2.3 Generalised Cost Theory and its Implications

Generalised cost is usually defined as a linear sum of relevant terms e.g.:

$$gc = F + b_1 \cdot A + b_2 \cdot W + b_3 \cdot R + n \cdot I + b_0$$

where F = fare (converted into minutes using an appropriate Value of Time)
b_1,b_2 & b_3 are weightings
A = access time
W = waiting time
R = running (in-vehicle) time (although some of this may also be used for other activities such as working or eating)
n = number
I = interchange

b_0 represents a residual error term for various measures which are unquantified. It may be seen to comprise some elements which are related to running time (e.g. seat comfort), some which are related to the number of journeys undertaken (e.g. time to gather information about the service), and yet others which are related to the fare (e.g. ease of buying a ticket). The (small) value of these can be determined through market research (e.g. see Australian Transport Council, 2006, pp. 48–49).

Generalised cost may be understood as an index of hassle or, in economists' terms, an index of utility. It enables us to quantify the difficulty of travel and, through the application of elasticities (response rates) understand to what passengers might respond, and by how much. Strictly speaking, it should be thought of as an index of *dis*utility, given that it encompasses various activities which are not enjoyed. These disutilities are suffered only because the benefits of the trip (e.g. getting paid for going to work) outweigh them; if they do not, the trip may be forfeited altogether.

Generalised cost is generally considered in relation to the in-vehicle time, to which the other elements are compared (note that, as all people have the same amount of time, and not money, standardising for time is behaviourally-preferable, although some authors (e.g. Pienaar, 1997) give the formula standardised for money). An area in which the railway perhaps under-sells itself is in the fact that one can often use parts of a rail journey for other purposes (e.g. working on the train); this 'useful' time may therefore be understood to be subtracted from the in-vehicle time. This issue has come to recent prominence in the debate about HS2 in Britain, where journey time savings are likely to reduce the amount of work undertaken on the train by businessmen travelling from Birmingham and Manchester to London.

On-train crowding affects many urban railways and is perceived by passengers through a greater response to the journey time: 10 minutes in a crowded train may feel like 11 or 12 minutes. The valuation of journey time (the b_3 parameter) may therefore be 1.1 or 1.2 in those cases, but it rises exponentially with the levels of on-train crowding. This emphasizes the fact that passengers respond to their perceptions of rail service, not its actual characteristics. Interestingly, the impact of crowding begins before all the seats have even been taken, as passengers do not always want to sit next to a stranger.

Delays cause significant annoyance to passengers, and this is reflected in their weighting (typically 3 times in-vehicle time). However, there is usually a small threshold (5 minutes?) below which weightings are lower.

Rail managers often forget the importance of access and egress time, since these occur away from the railway. In fact, passengers typically weight these double in-vehicle time (i.e. $b_1 = 2$, reflecting the physical nature involved in walking (especially with luggage, and exacerbated by infirmity) and the potential for the weather to influence trips. Values of rise with increasing effort – for instance, potentially reaching $b_1 = 4$ for climbing stairs, hence the benefit in providing escalators and lifts. Where more passengers access stations by car, however, average values are slightly lower.

Waiting time is similarly disvalued, again with a typical parameter weighting of 2. Here, the behavioural explanation is that waiting time is unproductive (one is not moving), and again weather influences comfort. The provision of facilities at stations (e.g. shops, pubs) can, however, fulfil the same role as being able to work on the train i.e. reducing the apparent loss of time whilst travelling. Here, however, there is an additional benefit: the railway receives rents from retailers, and the extra footfall also improves feelings of personal safety.

Interchange is significantly disvalued, especially by unfamiliar travellers. There is a specific interchange penalty which reflects worries about forgetting to get off, or being disrupted from work/reading/sleeping when it is necessary to alight; the penalty can therefore be instead regarded as an alighting penalty. For the avoidance of doubt, the penalty is in addition to the extra walking around the interchange station and waiting time for subsequent services, so it still remains, even when perfect cross-platform interchange is provided, which is best practice.

In urban areas, regular commuters may only feel that provision of a through service is worth 5 minutes' travel time: changing lines on metro systems is an understood part of the mode. However, for irregular older travelers (for instance, grandparents taking Christmas presents to grandchildren), the interchange penalty may be as much as an hour, emphasizing the importance of through services. Nevertheless, this is somewhat cultural: the emphasis that the Swiss put on providing connections within their 'Taktfahrplan' strategy (see section 3.3) will reduce the value of the interchange penalty there.

Figure 2.4 Cross-Platform Interchange between London Underground and Mainline Rail Services at Stratford

The fare paid is also, of course, a key part of the overall 'cost' of travelling but is measured in different units (e.g. £ or €, not minutes). It is converted into time units using the Value of Time. Passengers' Values of Time reflect their income and journey purpose. The current average for rail passenger travel in

Britain is about £7/hour, but this reflects a weighted average between leisure trips (perhaps £4/hour) and business trips (perhaps £40/hour), with the key commuting market being close to the average. A £14 return fare would therefore be equivalent to 60 minutes' worth of generalized cost in each direction, for an average passenger[1].

Fares policy is an important part of railway planning, in ensuring that sufficient income is received to cover as much of the costs as possible, in using differential pricing to encourage passengers to travel in offpeak periods (where there is spare capacity) and in using market segmentation to encourage those with lower willingnesses-to-pay to travel more. In particular, the use of train-specific Advance-purchase tickets is theoretically interesting, as passengers are offered cheaper fares if they forego some of the choice of departure times (and so therefore increase their average likely waiting time). People with lower incomes/Values of Time are likely to find this an attractive offer, whilst the requirement to travel on a specific train enables the railway to yield-manage demand by train, which is particularly useful for longer-distance operators.

In some countries, including Norway, season cards are heavily subsidized for political reasons, so that commuters in peak periods pay a very low fare compared to occasional travelers, despite their higher ability to pay and the higher costs of providing peak rail services.

Although generalized cost was first mentioned by Warner in 1962 as a way of understanding travel behaviour, and has become commonplace in urban and regional multi-modal planning, many railway staff have been trained separately from the mainstream of transport planning and are unaware of either the theory or the valuable implications it has for railway planning.

Its implications for rail planning are, however, profound. For instance, it might seem to the uninitiated that, if one branch line had twice the number of passengers as another, it would merit twice the number of trains. However, that is not necessarily the case. The proper objective of transport planning is to minimize the total weighted generalized cost of everyone who wants to travel i.e.

$$\min \sum_{i=1}^{n} \sum_{j=1}^{n} \sum_{p=1}^{p} (Pij \ x \ Gij)$$

[1] £14/2 = £7; £7/(£7/hour) = 60 minutes

where
Gij = generalised cost of travel from i to j (n origins and destinations)
Pij = number of passengers between i and j, summed across all passenger types p

However, because the relationship between waiting time and service frequency is not linear (see Figure 2.5), then that between passenger volume and headway need not be either. At low frequencies each extra train provides a very substantial reduction in waiting time. However, for metro services operating at 20tph, the waiting time benefit of the 21st train is almost zero – the train is provided almost entirely for its additional passenger-carrying ability. This is really important when considering service changes on national rail networks: the per-passenger benefit of having two services running hourly is much greater than having one. This benefit remains important up to c. 4tph. This is because, up to about that frequency, many passengers will seek to arrive at the station in time to catch a specific train whilst, for more frequent trains, they may simply "turn up and go" – which is a considerable marketing appeal for such services. Typical waiting time curves are therefore non-linear, and may be represented by two elements, as shown in Figure 2.6.

A second example of the importance of generalized cost theory is what it can tell us about the requirement to provide through services. Here, however, market research is needed into local conditions, in order to understand how passengers respond to interchange: generally, when facilities are of high quality, and connections are held in the case of late-running, passengers' perceptions are less negative.

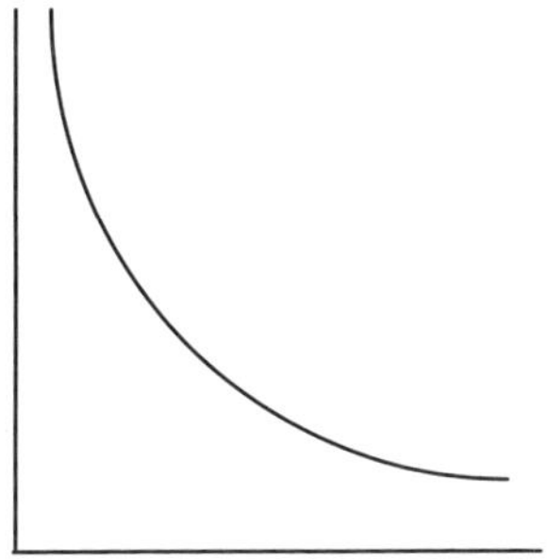

Frequency

Figure 2.5 Relationship between Waiting Time and Headway/Service Frequency
Headway is the inverse of service frequency (e.g. 15 minutes as the inverse of 4 trains per hour)

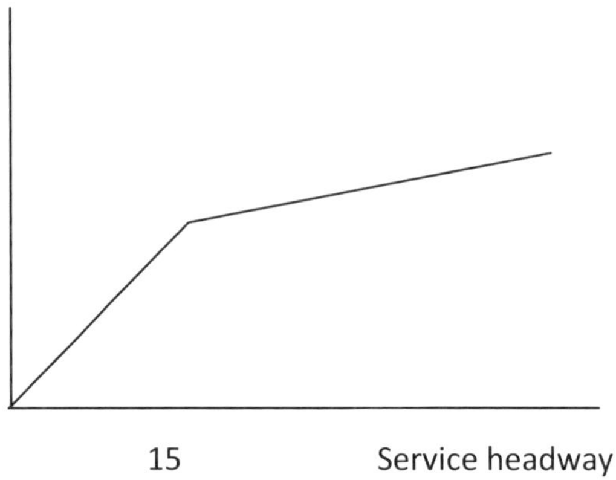

Figure 2.6. Impact of Headway on Waiting Time

Thirdly, generalized cost should encourage planners to consider which elements of the journey are proportionately largest, and to which passengers are most responsive, on a per-minute basis. This tends to lead to improvements in journey time and reductions in fares for longer journeys but (importantly) to improved access and frequencies for urban railways, where line-haul speeds may actually be relatively slow (e.g. the Overground services in London).

However, especially at lower frequencies, detailed market understanding of local conditions will be required, in order to make services as useful as possible. For instance, in one example in England, the franchise specification for the Northern franchise used to require bidders to provide a train arriving in Barrow before 09:00, so one was provided arriving at 08:40. From an office-based culture from London, this appeared to satisfy a purpose. Unfortunately, Barrow is predominantly an industrial town, where the majority of jobs start work at 08:00, making this train almost useless.

As well as deductions we can make directly from generalized cost theory, there are other elements of guidance which are consistent with it, but for which there is little direct proof. For instance, some practitioners advise against running any train services which call at more than 10 stations, as passengers are thought to find this unduly tedious. Passenger behaviour is certainly determined by the perception of time and not actual time.

The differing responses of different market segments to elements of generalized cost should also be taken into account. For instance, because of their infrequency of travel (hence unfamiliarity with the service) and luggage, passengers travelling to/from airports are particularly sensitive to interchange and (because of the need to catch flights) sensitive to delays, whilst the potential to carry visitors with a poor understanding of the local language means that complicated service patterns (including splitting and joining) are also not recommended. Munich S-Bahn's use of portion working on the S1 to Friesing and the airport is therefore not best practice, even if multiple announcements during the prolonged station stop at the junction at Neufahrn mitigate many difficulties.

Moreover, there remain trade-offs within railway planning which will require political understanding, if not particular input. For instance, it is common to find that urban areas have MPs of a different political party to suburban and rural areas, so a decision made entirely on the basis of minimizing overall generalized cost may not initially be popular. Nevertheless, an underlying independent logical framework can be useful in minimizing the tensions and arguments about the provision of costly railway resources.

Generalised Cost for Freight?

The conceptual understanding of the requirements of rail freight has a strong equivalence to those of passenger rail, albeit applied to materials and containers and not people. With freight, the competitor modes may of course including shipping as well as road, but air is only a relevant competitor for small high-value cargo.

In terms of access, high-capacity transport feeders remain critical – but here we are talking about the proximity to junctions on motorways and other major road roads.

Journey times for freight can be needlessly extended, if trains are recessed awaiting a driver change, or delayed at national frontiers awaiting border clearance and/or a change of personnel and/or locomotive; reducing the latter of these has been a focus of EU rail policy. Many freight trains are capable of 100kmh running, so achieving end-to-end averages of less than half that should not be regarded as acceptable. Speeding up freight trains, to make them less different to passenger trains in operational terms, has both capacity and commercial benefits. Freight traffic is often (although not always) less time-critical; even for Just-In-Time processes, a delivery window of 30 minutes may be fine. On the other hand, since many freight trains have a single customer, it may be possible to cancel them completely without penalty if there is no traffic to convey.

Waiting times for trainload freight are often irrelevant, since trains for one customer should be timed for their convenience. However, the low frequency (e.g. 2 tpd) of wagonload freight trains (designed to carry a variety of traffics) does reduce rail's ability to compete against the lorry – especially for flows which can be carried in a one day "out & back" trip[2].

"Hub and spoke" operation can maximise the efficiency of operations, with longer-distance faster-speed services between hubs, and local 'trip' working providing access to/from particular factories and sidings. However, research many years ago highlighted the economic problem: the former of these uses perhaps only 20% of the costs, with the trip workings (slower and of shorter length) adding disproportionately to the costs.

The equivalent of passenger interchange is the transhipment of traffic between one mode and another (potentially even rail:rail, where different gauge systems meet). The time taken for this (and the potential for delay or damage) again makes this a significant deterrent from using rail for freight. This also emphasises why railfreight can do relatively well at ports, where goods are loaded to/from ships anyway: rail is at no comparative disadvantage compared to road. Elsewhere, however, carrying loads to/from customers by road, and transferring them to rail later on, is a significant deterrent, and a key reason why rail can struggle in a competitive environment.

As with passenger services, however, pricing is crucial, although finding out willingness-to-pay can be very difficult. Other 'quality' elements can also be important in mode choice, with security and real-time tracking important for freight.

2.4 Project Goals and Evaluation

Having a good analytical framework is necessary, but insufficient; railways also need to understand carefully their objectives, as these vary widely.

Railways may be intended to:

- maximize profit;
- maximize traffic;
- minimize costs;
- maximize road congestion relief or other environmental benefits;
- maximize time savings to passengers;
- provide access to employment;

---

[2] At greater distances, road hauliers need to start swopping drivers between lorries (a logistical problem for which the railway is arguably much better-prepared) or pay for lorry drivers to sleep overnight

- support economic development, either at the micro- (specific site), urban (town centre) or regional level; or
- provide military or strategic links.

Although, in theory, any railway may be given any objective, it is perhaps more usual for inter-city railways to have profit targets, as many governments believe that inter-city transport should be self-supporting. National railways may be required to provide some sort of service across the entire network, within which providing connections can be a key element. Suburban railway objectives are often about maximizing peak capacity and minimizing journey times to the city centre, whereas rural railways are often charged with minimizing costs (and hence minimizing subsidy). The suburban policy can lead to trains missing out minor stations, whereas the rural one is likely to lead to trains calling at all stations (even very small ones), thereby becoming very slow, in order to try to pick up all the potential traffic. The relative balance between profit and traffic maximization will also have impacts on what the railway is supposed to do in the offpeak: continue running the trains (to provide some marginal benefit or find extra sources of traffic) or keep the trains in sidings (in an attempt to minimize costs).

However, objectives are also often conflicting. For some years, London Transport's objective was to "maximize net social benefit within a defined gross margin." The first part of this is about providing time savings, and the latter about limiting (un)profitability. This clearly provides mutually-incompatible advice in some circumstances, which had to be worked through with civil servants. Figure 2.7 highlights potentially-conflicting objectives for railway planning, with trade-offs between different goals: for instance, one can have higher frequencies normally only by making trains more similar (i.e. less heterogeneous).

Whilst a railway can be made to address any particular objective, they often struggle when objectives are changed abruptly by government. For instance, the Beeching report of 1963 in Britain cast off some of the 'common carrier' obligations of the past but required efficiencies to be made across the network, the extent of which was at the time seen as unsustainable. A somewhat-rushed process led to errors in network rationalization and trains being ordered for lines which were being closed.

However, if Governments and railway managements realise that objectives for a particular part of the network are very conflicting, then decisions can be made to provide separate networks. Although railways exhibit economies of density (more traffic on a given network size is generally more efficient),

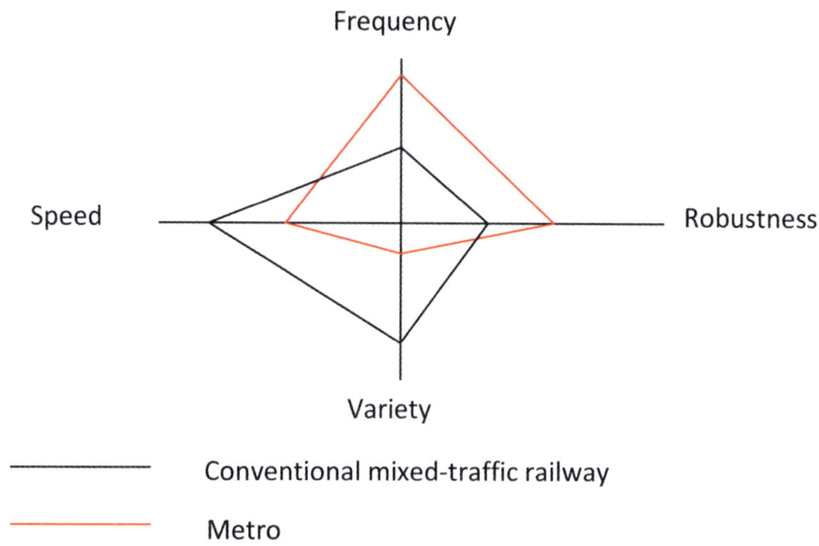

Figure 2.7 Star Diagram showing Conflicting Timetabling Requirements
Source: derived from UIC (2004), Figure 1.

sometimes the characteristics of different types of trains are so different as to prevent this. Lightly-used lines in urban areas may be converted to tram operation (as in Manchester), whilst DB Netz has taken some steps to separate freight and passenger traffic (e.g. on the lines on either side of the Rhine).

Specific railway projects are normally based on one or more of the following goals:

- increasing demand and hence revenue;
- reducing (operational) costs;
- providing economic or other wider benefits as noted above.

However, it is appropriate to differentiate between result goals, effect goals and public (community) goals (see Figure 2.8). Result goals are related to the project itself, for example the construction of a new double track. Result goals are often about completion, cost and fulfilling specifications. Effect goals are about consequences of a project from the users' point of view. We can therefore differentiate between the *efficiency* of railways (which may provide intermediate outputs, such as train-kms, or construction of a bridge) and their *effectiveness* (e.g. in enabling passenger journeys to be made, or tons of freight carried). Although the word 'efficiency' is more commonly used in English, project goals should be about trying to establish effective outcomes.

Irrespective of the structure of the railway industry in any particular country, it is common for some companies and projects to work towards (narrow) financial goals, although railways often have to take into consideration wider socio-economic factors too. Public goals are about the more long-term effects of a project as seen from the commissioner or owner of the project. The effect concept goes further than the concerns of the project owner. An example of this might be the environmental effects of new transport infrastructure projects. In Norway, the commissioner or owner could be the Ministry of Transport or its directorates, while other parts of government (i.e. the Ministry for Environment and its directorates) have their primary interest in environmental effects.

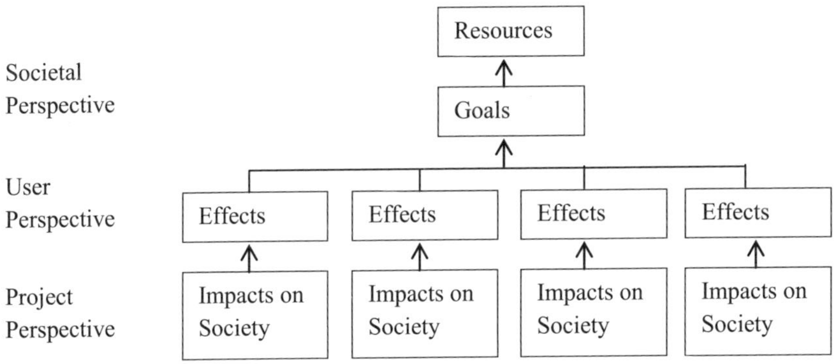

Figure 2.8 Hierarchy between public goals, efficiency goals and result goals, and where these goals originate
Source: Norwegian Ministry of Finance, 2008

Quality control procedures may be an important element of project evaluation (as in Norway), in order to obtain an independent review of projects before budgets are set. Quality control may relate both to the conceptual development of new plans (quality assurance stage KS1 in Norway), and/or to the documentation, costings and levels of certainty (KS2).

Other countries have slightly different ways of assessing project worthwhileness. Following a number of cost overruns on major projects, as noted by Flyvbjerg (2007), the British government applies cost mark-ups ("optimism bias") to projects. These reduce as work is refined, with initial estimates of costs increased by up to 60%, which is progressively lowered to 6% as construction is about to start.

Bertolini (2008) discusses two different approaches to planning of public transport. Stockholm, Copenhagen, Munich, Tokyo and Singapore are examples of long term and coordinated planning and completion of public transport, often with local trains and metros as main arteries in the transport systems. In Stockholm the long term strategy covers a 60-year period. Stockholm city centre was a natural hub in the network, and organizational structures have paved the way for a coordinated strategy implementation.

Another approach has been used in cities like Karlsruhe, Naples and Rotterdam. These cities did not have a tradition for centralized planning, and were characterized by a spread-out city structure. Yet there was a demand for coordination and improvement of public transport, which was achieved by linking existing networks together. Even if the long term perspective has advantages, Bertolini (2008) shows that it also has challenges. In Stockholm, for example, the strength of the transport system lies in transport from surrounding cities and municipalities and into the city centre. Direct transport opportunities between surrounding cities and municipalities are less developed. For cities that did not have a long term plan, the example of Karlsruhe shows that improvement in public transport can be achieved without necessarily having a 60-year perspective. As shown by Boge (2006), there is a stronger tradition for long term planning in the transport sector in Sweden than in Norway. However, in recent years, the Ruter organization has made good progress in reducing previous planning fragmentation in the Oslo region (Central Østlandet).

Where the future is uncertain, scenario planning can be helpful in assessing whether plans are robust to possible events. Network Rail, for instance, recently undertook long-term market studies for rail demand in Britain, examining the likely impacts on rail demand of two levels of national economic performance and two levels of interaction between Britain and the rest of the world (Network Rail, 2013).

A particular problem can arise when infrastructure and train operations are managed separately, as has been encouraged by the European Union. With infrastructure authorities staffed largely by engineers, it is not surprising that their objectives can be the maintenance, renewal and replacement of key assets – obviously major structures, but also existing tracks and track layouts. That may constrain the timetables that can be operated reliably, prevent the operation of new services, or merely add cost to the operation of existing services which may not be maximizing traffic. For instance, a train planning solution of splitting and joining services might enable a reduction in overall train frequency which otherwise required the construction of new tracks.

Nevertheless, there are several examples showing that infrastructure and rolling stock plans can and should be based on strategic timetables. Switzerland is, in many contexts, brought up as a pioneer in planning infrastructure and timetables in a long-term perspective, linked to its Taktfahrplan timetabling concept (see chapter 3). In 1982 they started a long term process to develop their rail infrastructure based on a strategic timetable. "Bahn 2000" has been supplemented by subsequent initiatives, with funding agreed through referenda, since it was established (Avelino et al. 2006). Van den Berg and Odjiik (1994) describe how Dutch railways around 1994 similarly set up strategic timetables for the period 2010 to 2015. They wanted a timetable and infrastructure plan in order to, among other things, minimize the number of transfers for passengers.

Another approach can be successful if the infrastructure authority is given overall responsibility for train performance, as in Britain. Network Rail's analysis of delays on the East Coast Main Line enabled them to provide a business case for grade segregation of junctions at Hitchin and Doncaster during 2014.

2.5 The Current Position

From one perspective one can argue that there has been a dynamic development of many railways over the last 15 years. A whole new generation of railway routes has been constructed (for instance in high-speed lines and connections to airports), whilst new trains have been delivered. Some train operators have made gains in efficiency and customer service, either in-house, or by franchising/ contracting-out (e.g. cost reductions of 20% have been reported from German franchising), or the threat of doing so. Freight transport is more focused and made more effective, and there has been an increase in rail freight volumes e.g. in Britain.

However, the success of some projects and market segments often disguises other problems. Asset management regimes are weak in many railways: despite international recognition of its TGV services, ¼ of the French railway network was suffering from speed restrictions – or even complete "bustitution"[3]. Speed reductions caused by inadequate track maintenance,

[3] "Bustitution" is a term sometimes used to refer to the situation where rail services are suspended, and replaced by bus transport, either to cover short-term engineering work, or even if rail services no longer run. This latter situation has currently lasted for seven years, in respect of train services to Barlaston and Wedgwood stations in Britain.

or traffic disruption caused by line renewals undertaken at commercially-inconvenient times, can lead to an irreversible deterioration in traffic. Britain has been very fortunate in that the economic regulation role of ORR requires the network to be maintained to a given (fairly high) quality level, and the government to fund this.

Problems with maintenance of infrastructure and/or rolling stock can lead to poor punctuality, which can either be a direct problem, or made to be an image issue when repeatedly reported in the media. Strikes can cause long-term damage to customer relations, leading to the loss of traffic: SNCF's railfreight volumes have been falling at a rate of c. 1% per month for several years, because of this. Failure to manage budgets has left many railways with significant debts (c.10% of the entire costs of running Britain's national railways are in servicing Network Rail's debts) or pension fund deficits.

It is all too easy for politicians (and railway managers?) to crave the publicity associated with the development of high-profile new high-speed lines. A commitment for railways is needed, aiming to:

- reduce travel time
- increase frequency
- improve reliability

whether in the historic network or any new routes. A long term and consistent focus on maintenance and availability is essential, and elsewhere has been neglected over many years. The really successful railways (such as MTRC in Hong Kong) achieve their success through attention to the detailed asset management of both obvious assets such as the train fleet and often-hidden items as drains and lineside vegetation clearance.

2.6 IT Support in the Planning Process

From mainly being a manual process, there has been a development in recent years towards a greater proportion of the planning process having IT support. This is often undertaken separately within each planning element (for example, timetable planning, rolling stock planning and personnel planning), using IT tools that support the planners in their work e.g. by providing train timings, drawing train graphs or identifying conflicts automatically. Sometimes optimization is used, where an IT system suggests plans based on a set of input criteria. The railway industry has therefore matured in its use of IT through the steps shown in Figure 2.9.

There are established interfaces between the various planning systems, but optimization is often only made within each planning stage. The main reason for this is that to optimize for example timetables and rolling stock plans together is relatively complex, even for traffic in the Oslo area, which in international terms is not very big.

Optimization is commonly used for rolling stock-, personnel-, and maintenance planning. Simulation is used for the simulation of timetables (especially to evaluate punctuality and delays) but also for the impact of infrastructure interventions and changes. Transport demand models may be used for estimating the number of passengers resulting from various changes in train service.

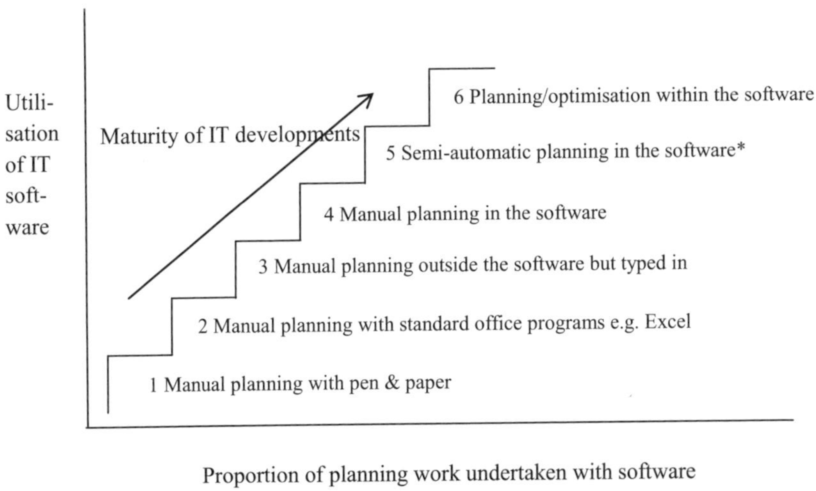

Figure 2.9 Illustration of how much of planning is supported by IT tools at different steps. A higher step means that more of the planning is done with IT support.
* e.g. software generates possible solutions, but these have to be selected manually

2.7 Requirements for Planning

Having realistic prerequisites for planning and abiding by them are key success factors for train service quality. Plan requirements may be decided by government or the infrastructure authority before the planning process, but "planning prerequisites" include more than what is formally defined in the timetable process. For example, a maximum train length for passenger services may be defined by, among other things, platform lengths, whereas those for freight may be based on the length of signalling sections or typical passing loops. On the other hand, minimum train length is also an important prerequisite for local trains during peaks (because shorter trains may cause longer station dwell times) and for some high-speed services (in order to ensure sufficient braking power).

Many delays are caused by breaches of plan requirements. In Norway, the Track Access Agreement section 9 -1 states that "The railway network shall be in order so that traffic can be carried out according to the at any time valid timetable and/or the at any time valid planning prerequisites". Correspondingly, section 8–1 states that "Rolling stock must be in a condition so that it can be run according to any time-valid timetable".

Planning processes in railways, and also in other transport modes, are in practice projects, and they are often done through a project organization. It is an established practice to make a project plan and define resources for the planning processes. The format of the final product (the plan) is often presented as construction plans, timetable plans, rolling stock plans etc. What is challenging to define and evaluate/follow-up, however, is the prerequisites which are the basis of these plans.

Good projects are marked by a clear strategic direction, but a tactical flexibility as to how the goal is to be achieved. Another hallmark of successful projects, and of successful project management, is that a clear "base line" is defined, against which you measure progress, cost and delivery development. A clear reference point should thereafter be a guideline and basis for assessments of projects proceeding as planned.

Experience shows that if the basic requirements for a project are changed, execution of the project as planned does not guarantee that the project result is as good as expected. The realism of a proposed project may be assessed by checking if the basic requirements are consistent between them. Here it is important to assess prerequisites when seeing them together.

Another part of quality assurance is control of the project's requirements. These requirements may be explicit, or more implicit ones. This check is important for two reasons. The project may hang on to requirements that have become outdated (we are aware of a new rail line being planned on the basis of a potential flooding risk, even though the Environment Agency had recently completed a major scheme to deal with that risk), or the project may have made new requirements. The project may still operate based on the original requirements (or the projects' interpretation of the original prerequisites). In such cases, the projects' own requirements "lag behind" the actual ones. In other cases, projects establish new requirements, and make them a basis for the project. This may happen before project owners and decision makers are fully aware of these new requirements.

In both cases there will sooner or later be a moment of truth, when a possible deviation between the projects' requirements and those of the project owners or other stakeholders, are made visible. In the worst case, this happens after the project is finalized. Conflicts resulting from gaps between the requirements of different stakeholders will typically increase, the longer these deviations have existed. An objective of risk assessments of the basic requirements is therefore to identify such gaps as early as possible.

Table 2.1 illustrates how different aspects of planning requirements may be put together, whilst the concretization of assumptions, and quality assurance about which planning requirements really are used in the planning process are illustrated in Figure 2.10.

Subject for measurement	Background		Specific Plan Requirements for future		Plan Requirement Follow-Up	
	Basis of current timetable	Measurement of current situation	Requested level of new plan	Accepted criteria	Status as of today	Expected out-turn
Availability of drivers	53	52	59	>60	56	60
Hallmarks of robust plan	55		62		56	

Table 2.1 Example of Changing Requirements during the Planning Process

It is important to ensure that those making plans do not make up their own requirements. There must be a check that the requirements worked with in the project are in line with the original ones.

With a structured follow-up of planning requirements during the planning process, a list of actual requirements can be put together, and later risks may be developed on the basis of identifying and following-up possible deviations. A follow-up of risks based on fundamental requirements may, in its simplest form, be put together in a table as shown in Table 2.2; the use of infrastructure examples is deliberate, as train planners are often dependent upon physical works having been completed.

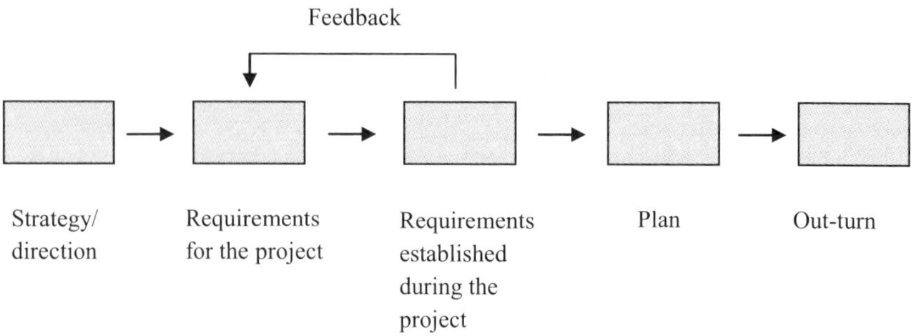

Figure 2.10 Development and Feedback of Project Assumptions

Requirement	Status	Deviation
A	B	A – B = C
5 platforms	4 platforms	1 platform
New signal	Not yet installed	Awaited
2 platform extensions	1 platform extension	1 platform extension
16 depot sidings	14 depot sidings	2 depot sidings

Table 2.2 Follow-up of Planning Requirements

This type of follow-up was used in the preparations for the strategic timetable changes in Norway in 1998/1999. However, this needs to be updated across several areas, and as plans change; Table 2.3 gives a simple illustration by rolling stock volume.

How serious, then, is a deviation between original and observed plan requirements? Earlier it was argued that deviations are themselves indicators of risk. Greater deviation can be assumed to mean greater risk, but it is often difficult to say how robust plans are to a deviation in any particular requirement. Yet it is important to be able to prioritize risk management towards the possible deviations expected to have the greatest influence on the robustness of the plan.

A high risk may result if there is a major deviation from original planning principles in an area where there is low robustness to any deviations. For punctuality, for example, robustness can be maintained by having generous turnround times at terminal stations, so that trains can recover from any delays. If run times and turnround times are reduced too far, there is a great risk for delays, both for trains arriving at the terminal station, and for their subsequent departure.

Rolling Stock Type	Plan requirement	Latest plan version	Deviation
A	34	55	21
B	12	36	24
C	8	15	7
D	16	16	0
E	34	64	30
F	13	99	86

Table 2.3 Follow-up of planned requirements for rolling stock

To prioritize between risks, they can be quantified so that the highest risks may be identified. Deviations are measured relative to the original value (0 to 1). Robustness is also measured on a scale from 0 to 1, where small numbers indicate high robustness to deviations in plan requirements.

Plan requirement	Status	Deviation	Robustness	Risk = Deviation*robustness
A	B	(A-B)/A=C	D	C*D

Table 2.4 Theoretical Development of Risks within the Planning Process

Basic information on train planning rules and infrastructure limitations (for instance, Network Statements) should be available at the beginning of the timetabling process. However, changes may need to be made, for instance in the descriptions of the infrastructure actually available (e.g. once the plans for new works have been finalised), and these may need to be summarized at the end of the timetabling process, together with their impact (e.g. expected loss of time). Changes may include:

- Timetable assumptions e.g. % slack to be assumed;
- Infrastructure availability (e.g. details of engineering possessions);
- Changes to working procedures on the railway (perhaps derived from safety and/or regulatory bodies);
- Any changes to contingency planning or for restoring the service after disruptions;
- Knowledge of recent changes in market conditions (e.g. of major sports events).

These processes are represented in Figure 2.11.

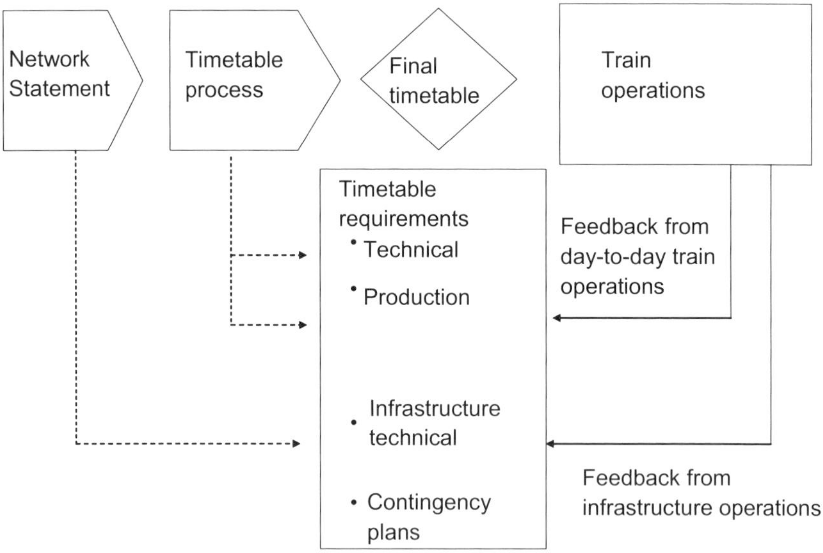

Figure 2.11 Plan prerequisites as seen by the Train Operating Companies Illustration from the timetable change 12.06.2006.

In principle, train operators base their plans on prerequisites defined by the infrastructure authority (Figure 2.11). Yet TOCs often make their own (more restrictive) prerequisites for their own plans (typically to ensure plan robustness), and there are also many things not defined by the infrastructure authority (or only at a very high level) e.g. the availability of rolling stock, maintenance depots and personnel.

A list of plan prerequisites for a TOC may look like this:

Infrastructure

- Infrastructure activities, including track development and other improvements
- Locations for service reversal
- Capacity limitations in general, and especially in defined bottlenecks
- Capacity to store rolling stock (off-peak, overnight)

Timetable

- Timetable-technical prerequisites, as defined by the infrastructure provider
- Run time calculations
- Technical properties of the rolling stock, including maximum speed, acceleration, seat capacity and traction power
- Turnround times
- Number of train calls per station
- System crossings on single track lines, including length of passing loops
- Additions to run times because of infrastructure or other

Train service

- Commuter traffic: relative peakiness
- Capacity (seats or freight volume) on different routes, perhaps distributed over day or week
- Extra peak trains
- Daily operation length/off-peak traffic

Rolling stock and maintenance plans

- Rolling stock availability, including total and planned in diagrams
- Maintenance, interval between maintenance breaks and requirements for maintenance and cleaning for each train type
- Maintenance depots for each train type

Personnel plans

- Existing personnel resources for each depot
- Competence profile for personnel resources
- Planned training and recruitment
- Existing agreements and laws, including possible exceptions

One particular issue is worth mentioning here: *turnround times* are a vital element of the planning process: How much time should be allowed at the end of a line, before a train is timetabled to come back again? Whilst this issue is discussed more fully in section 3.7, the key point to note is that there is a minimum time actually required for passenger movement and operational functions, but extra time is allowed to provide some ability to recover from delays.

This therefore means that the length of layovers is something of a judgment. Where costs are dominant (for instance in the rural rail sector), the fleet requirement is determined by the turnrounds; on a more profitable (e.g. inter-city) route, the commercial consequences of knock-on delays are much greater, and (despite pressures to use assets efficiently) turnround times are correspondingly longer.

So turnround times are a key determinant of railway planning. Long turnrounds lead to (potentially-costly) poor utilisation of rolling stock and crew (although there can be an opportunity for the crew to take their required breaks during the layover) but also provide the possibility of recovery from disruption. The relative importance of these criteria will determine the exact response of a railway to its choice of turnround times, although specific constraints (such as of units of a particular train type, or platforms at key stations) may be the defining rationale in certain circumstances.

2.8 Route Planning

Like many aspects of railway planning, route planning also requires trade-offs. On the demand side, longer routes may be able to serve more settlements or factories directly, but increase end-to-end journey times, so that increasing market share in one market may lead to decreased market share in another. Any judgment about which option to choose needs not only to take into account the relative market share of each, but the railway's competitive situation (how much market share will be lost, if services are not direct?) and the costs of serving off-line centres through different technologies. For instance, one might use shuttle train services, shuttle bus services, the splitting and joining of rail services ("portion working"), or other modes such as light rail shuttles (at airports) or (for freight) conveyor belts, or merely hope that people will bring themselves and their goods to the nearest railhead (as opposed to using the competing road network for their entire journey).

Good route planning also takes into detailed account the likely use of the line once built. On double-track lines, decisions on signalled headways and the type of junctions need to be made in conjunction with operational planners. On new single-track lines, it is worth evaluating where trains are expected to pass, before finalizing the locations of passing loops. If h is the planned headway, loops need to be at h/2 minutes' running time apart, if trains are to pass without unnecessary delay (actually, slightly less than h/2, to allow for signal sighting and route set-up time at those loops). Problems arise, however, if h changes over time, other than by a factor of 2. For instance, it would be impossible to increase service frequency from an even 3tph to an even 2tph on a line designed for the former; alternating 20- and 40-minute headways would be the only way of running 2tph.

On the cost side, any longer routes are likely to require more maintenance (simply because they are longer), but they may be cheaper to build if they follow contour lines more closely. That can have eternal consequences: a key reason for buying tilting trains for Britain's West Coast Main Line in the 1990s is that the line was built "on the cheap" by the London & Birmingham Railway in 1838. On the other hand, a shorter route (such as the Köln – Frankfurt Neubaustrecke in Germany) may require major engineering works, such as bridges and tunnels; these are not only expensive to construct, but can also have ongoing operational consequences: rolling stock may have to sustain higher pressure resistance as trains enter and leave tunnels.

Especially for high-frequency railways, it can be helpful to construct an alignment which is not flat but which rises up to platforms, and falls away from them again. Whilst more complicated (although not necessarily much more expensive) to construct, this substantially adds the acceleration of trains out of stations, and aids braking when approaching them. This therefore also saves energy consumption – see section 10.2.

The choice of line speed is a specific key decision to get right, and requires a number of trade-offs between engineering, maintenance and commercial issues. Engineering issues include the limitations on gradient (especially if freight trains are to be operated) and the wider curves needed at higher speeds (e.g. radii of 5km are common on high-speed lines). As we have already seen, passengers value shorter journey times although, as these become a smaller component of generalized cost, extra journey time reductions become less important. Once any 'kinks' in the demand curve relating to the generalized cost of competitive modes have been undercut, the demand and revenue benefits of going ever faster may be relatively small; the important step is getting average speeds (including stops) above typical motorway speeds.

Some costs rise substantially with increasing speed. Indeed, it has been reported from France that the maintenance costs of operating TGVs at 360kph

Figure 2.12 Cheaply-built but Ultimately Uncompetitive: Original Narrow-Gauge Djibouti – Addis Line, Ethiopia

are double those of running at 300kph, whilst energy costs rise exponentially, as air resistance increases. However, other operational costs fall. For instance, rolling stock can make more journeys per unit time. If inter-city trainsets cost c. £25m each, then such savings matter. As an example, broadly 55 steam locomotives were used to ply the London – Edinburgh route, which fell to 22 'Deltic' diesels in the early 1960s and 15 HSTs in the 1980s.

Perhaps one of the key lessons to emerge from the planning of a proposed maglev system linking London and Scotland was that, at higher speeds, it is possible to have a longer route connecting more places, without losing undue market share. At 400kph, it appeared possible to run London – Birmingham – Manchester – Leeds – Newcastle – Edinburgh – Glasgow on one core route, rather than having to have separate branches (as the 300kph HS2 network is to have). The real benefit of that is that the total amount of route could have fallen substantially, emphasizing rail's economies of density i.e. that railways become more economic/efficient/profitable if more traffic can be achieved on a smaller network.

2.9 Summary

Railway planning needs to be undertaken within the wider context of strategic planning of transport, land-use planning and economic development. Planners need to understand the drivers of demand, including those which they cannot control. They should remain focused on delivering against the objectives set, using relevant IT support and ensuring that they continue to meet specific outputs e.g. number of trainsets. Route planning at the strategic level, as well as the more detailed planning discussed in later chapters, is usually a matter of trade-offs.

3 Train Service Planning

3.1 Introduction: Timescales and Hierarchies

Unlike other transport modes, train movements are restricted to a line. Put another way: trains have only one degree of freedom. This implies that train movements must be planned, and they must be planned in great detail.

Usually planning is split into a strategic/long-term, a tactical/medium-term and an operational/short-term level. The different stages are organized by decreasing length of planning horizon, and mostly with an increasing level of detail.

The planning of railway operations is done in different time perspectives, as shown in Figure 3.1. From experience, infrastructure requires the longest time perspective. In Britain, Network Rail has just electrified the line between Liverpool and Manchester which was opened in 1830, whilst tilting trains were chosen for the West Coast Main Line in the 1990s because of the curvaceous nature of the line, built cheaply also in the 1830s. Planning of railways also requires a lot of time; how much varies, but can be particularly significant in democracies with high environmental values. London's Crossrail project (due to open in 2018) was first discussed in 1949, whilst, in Norway, new double track between Asker and Sandvika was proposed in the National Transport Plan (NTP) in 1999, but opened in 2005, largely because of its underground nature not having significant public impacts. New structures would normally be planned with a design life of 60-100 years.

Rolling stock has somewhat shorter lifespans and decision times. NSB decided in 2008 to order 50 new "Flirt" trainsets from Stadler, and the first ones were delivered in 2011. The life time of a trainset may be illustrated by NSB Type 68 local trains, which had 45 years in service, between 1956 and 2001 (some of them were then used by Ofotbanen AS). The oldest current train sets used by NSB are some Type 69s built in 1970, whilst in Britain, ex-London Underground 1938 stock has been re-used to provide a shuttle service on the gauge-restricted Isle of Wight line. These examples emphasise the need for a long-term perspective when planning railways. We also see that the lifespan of trains and infrastructure are considerably longer than the lifespan of any plans for using them. Timetables, plans for rolling stock operation and personnel plans may change twice per year, but trains and infrastructure last longer. Infrastructure and trains may therefore need to be used in other ways than planned for at the time of acquisition, so flexibility and adaptability become important. The "passive provision" of equipment, enabling them to be adapted to future needs without undue difficulty, is good practice.

Long-term planning is about bigger changes to timetables, normally about every 5th year, and often connected to rolling stock acquisition or larger changes to infrastructure. In this phase high level production plans are constructed.

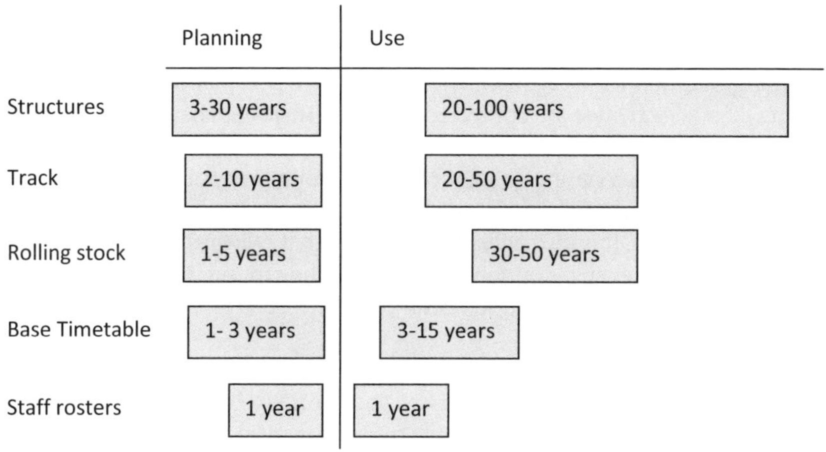

Figure 3.1 Time Perspectives in Railway Planning

3.2 Constituents of the Planning Process

In railway operations a lot of factors have an impact on each other, and these must be coordinated for the operation to work: railways are classic systems. This leads to a high complexity in the planning process. Train service planning starts with planning the infrastructure you want or expect. This is followed by a timetable, which lays the foundation for rolling stock planning, and enables traincrew and vehicle maintenance planning. In addition, marketing and sales need to be organised. Even if there is a clear sequence in planning, there are often several rounds (iterations) of planning, with increasing level of detail – or fewer contradictions to resolve (particularly for timetable planning). There may also be several alternatives, which are then evaluated and developed further. As an extreme example, a 2007 re-write of the timetable for Britain's CrossCountry franchise, which covers long-distance services via Birmingham and interacts with many other train companies, took 85 iterations.

There are many restrictions to consider. Restrictions include:

- highly utilized infrastructure;
- the laws of physics for accelerating, braking and curvature;
- rolling stock type, performance and capability (e.g. length, comfort levels and seating capacity);
- physical limits for personnel
- labour rules legislation
- health and environment regulations; and
- union agreements.

Planning should be an interactive and iterative process, where all departments in the organization work together. Theoretically the best plan should come about when all activities are optimized together. This could have been made when all framework conditions are put up against all market related requirements, and an optimum solution found. Complexity and a lack of development of powerful decision support tools are reasons why this cannot be made in real life. It is also only quite recently that railways have used optimisation tools even in the separate steps of the process, but it is also common that the 'perfect' solution is simply impossible.

Strategic planning sets the long term course. It is often characterized by being top-down and made by top management and centrally-based staff. A strategic plan is superior and influences decisions made in tactical and operational planning. It may effectively be determined by Government in terms of specifics (in terms of an output specification e.g. journey time or frequency aspiration) or something broader. For instance, the British Government issues a High-Level Output Specification to Network Rail, together with the Statement of Funds Available (SoFA), leaving NR to respond as to the deliverability (or otherwise) of this, and the ORR to regulate/intervene to come to a consensus.

Typical subjects at a strategic level of planning are:

- Major new infrastructure investments (routes, junctions)
- Timetable principles
- Line frequencies
- Rolling stock allocation
- Investments in new and upgraded rolling stock
- Distribution of manpower between organization units
- Demand for train drivers and conductors
- Broad targets for cost recovery

Ideally the result of a good consequence analysis and decision support should include:

- Incomes, by service
- Costs, by input
- Description of production (including frequency, rolling stock and personnel requirements, number of seats, rolling stock quality, service level etc.)
- Description of expected market consequences (development of customer satisfaction indexes, market share etc.)
- Link to superior goals and plans
- Risk profile and uncertainty

Figure 3.2 shows a typical sequence of evaluation and planning. Often business plans are made first (at a strategic level), followed by specific evaluations of alternatives (the tactical plan), which is a basis for the detailed plan made later on. Finally, operational planning is undertaken when production plans are changed during the timetable period. In practice, each step will have moreorless the same functional steps: timetable, rolling stock and personnel plans as shown in Figure 3.3, which is also in several iterations.

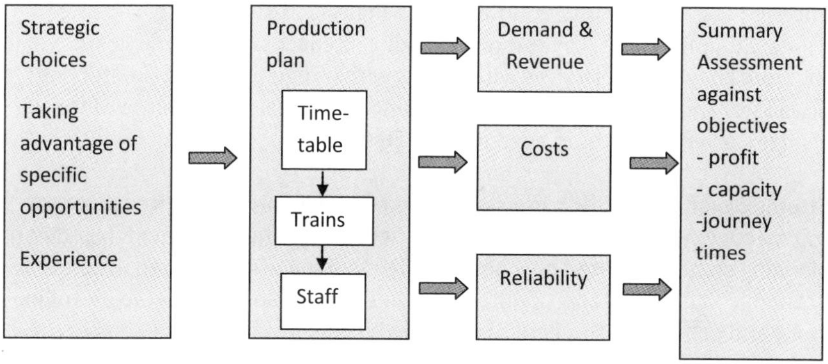

Figure 3.2 Elements in a consequence analysis

In tactical planning deadlines are linked to deadlines from infrastructure managers for timetable slots. For the European railway network the main annual timetable change is in December, but this requires initial concepts to have been developed perhaps one year earlier. For really significant changes, timescales will need to be even longer, if plans are to be robust: initial train service planning for the London 2012 Olympics started in 2006, not only because the event was very high-profile, but also because infrastructure works and new trains were also part of the package.

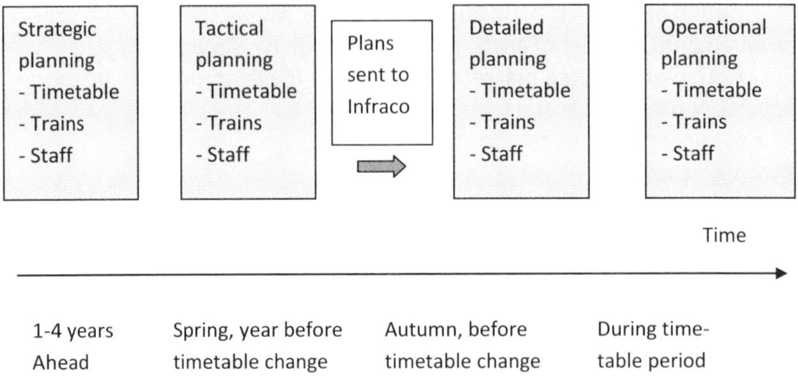

Figure 3.3 Simplified illustration of timetable process seen from a train operating company

But even apparently-simpler timetable changes are likely to take a couple of years to implement, key reasons including the lack of spare rolling stock, the need to link train services with others within regulatory and timetabling processes, and the need to provide staff and passengers with details of the changes several months in advance (see Figure 3.4).

Strategic planning is often top-down. The people involved are often close to top management, which means that connections to them are good. Top-down planning should be based on a broad understanding of the market, accurate economic figures and appropriate strategies when planning timetables, rolling stock and personnel. This kind of planning is usual in a long-term perspective and should be linked to company-wide strategies.

However, final plans for timetables, rolling stock and personnel are made at a tactical level. These plans firm up and elaborate the guidelines from strategic plans. For the TOCs what is here called tactical planning is the basis for ordering timetables (slots) from the infrastructure authority. This may be undertaken collaboratively at some form of timetabling conference, or TOCs can merely submit their plans independently.

Detailed plans have a bottom-up approach and are designed for use by operational personnel. Typically, planning is based in the operating and

- get safety management system & banking facilities (a prerequisite for the whole process)
- develop a business case for a particular service frequency (T-72 to T-60);
- persuade a ROSCO to acquire appropriate rolling stock (T-60 at the latest);
- get formal approval (by the TOC board and/or government (T-56);
- recruit and start to train relevant staff (T-52);
- bid for slots at timetable conference (T-48);
- negotiate with infrastructure authority about access charges, performance regime and detailed timings (T-34 to T-26);
- send draft track access contractor to regulator (T-20);
- market service/create fares and seat reservations (T-12);
- public timetable produced (T-12);
- lease rolling stock and finalise staff training (maintenance staff, driver route knowledge) (T-8);
- create staff rosters (T-8);
- create rolling stock diagrams/platform working (T-4);
- get access contract approved (T-2);
- start service on timetable date T

Figure 3.4 Timetable Planning Process Flowchart

production departments, and includes the detailed allocation and timing of rolling stock, personnel and maintenance in the medium- and short-term perspective. Today's IT tools are mainly adapted to this planning tradition. Although these plans are more detailed than top-down plans, they often do not visualize (e.g. commercial) risk, and may not properly consider interactions with other parts of the business (e.g. marketing). Train service performance risks may be modelled through simulations, but strategic issues such as unexpected demand growth are difficult to handle in this context. If platform allocation is left until this stage (which it often is), it may be too late to avoid conflicts in the working of trains in the station throat occurring every hour, with consequent impacts on train service performance.

There are two common steps in all rolling stock and personnel planning. First, a general plan is made, where the rolling stock individual or the individual person assigned to the work task is not defined. This type of plan can be made for one general week, and then rolled out for every week in the planning period. The next step is to define which individual trainsets or drivers shall perform the different parts of the plan.

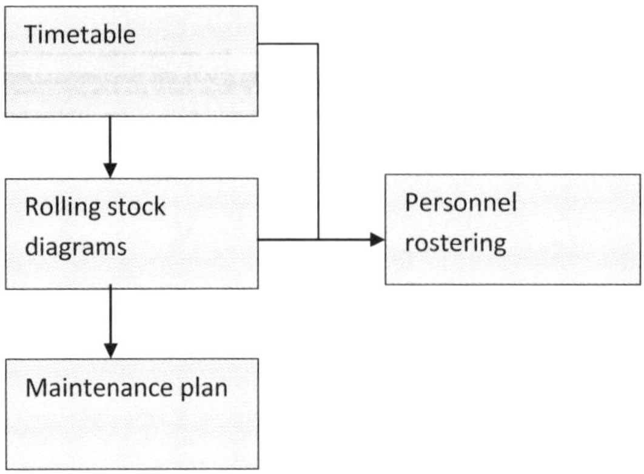

Figure 3.5 Functional split of production plans

The two steps are illustrated in Figure 3.6, which shows that the personnel plan is done in three steps, while rolling stock plans more often are done in two steps (maintenance plans are added here, but not shown in the Figure).

In the medium term (between one year and two weeks before the plans are put in operation), the high-level plans are detailed. The goal of planning at this level is the best possible utilization of resources. The final timetable for the next term will be decided at this planning stage.

During the tactical planning stage, the process of making detailed plans for rolling stock, personnel and maintenance is undertaken, after the main timetable requirements are dealt with by the infrastructure operator, and the timetables are defined.

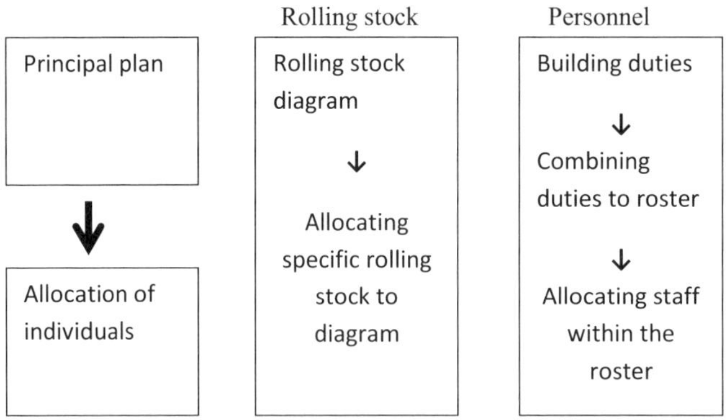

Figure 3.6 Basic steps in the planning process, with examples from rolling stock and personnel planning

Operational planning is planning during the timetable period i.e. plans made after the current timetable is in operation. At this level, there is a continuous quality assessment and updating of plans to handle changes and disturbances. Here the main purpose is to allocate resources to tactical plans, so that they may be carried through as planned.

As shown in Figure 3.5, development of timetables, rolling stock plans and personnel plans are connected. It is difficult to make a rolling stock plan without a timetable, and it is difficult to plan maintenance and train crew without doing both timetable and rolling stock plans. The process is basically sequential, but there should be iterations between separate activities. For instance, it may be more cost-effective in overall terms to adjust a timetable to allow better access to a maintenance depot, or for staff overtime not to be required, even if this makes the public timetable less than perfect.

3.3 Timetable Planning

Key aims

A timetable holds information on planned departure and arrival times, and places and routes for trains. Timetable planning means making a satisfactory train service for both the customers and for the operator (through intensive usage of rolling stock and personnel assets), but "satisfactory" tends to require trade-offs between variables and desired outcomes, as discussed above. According to Pachl (2008), timetable planning has the following functions:

- To coordinate train services for the good utilization of infrastructure
- To ensure the predictability of train service
- To produce information to customers
- To be a basis for train control and the planning of rolling stock and personnel

Minimum requirements for a timetable are that it should:

- Fulfil safety regulations
- Provide sufficient capacity
- Be executable in theory, i.e. be without internal conflicts between trains
- Be executable in practice, i.e. prepare for punctual train service under normal conditions
- Be able to recover when disturbances occur

The timetable should also, as far as possible, satisfy market demands for frequency and travel time.

However, we posit that an even wider range of issues have to be considered, including demand from competing groups of customers (not least passenger and freight), providing links with other public transport modes in order to provide a door-to-door journey, access to the network for maintenance, rolling stock availability, guidelines from public authorities, and marketing the railway: the timetable offer is what the railway sells.

Timetable proposals are evaluated as to safety, compliance with operating parameters, customer satisfaction, punctuality and cost recovery/profitability. No plan is optimal with regard to all requirements; you have to balance and try to prioritize.

Taking each issue in turn: **safety** is an absolute requirement that always has to be satisfied: for instance, one cannot plan on exceeding the speed limit of the line, or for two trains to be in the same place at the same time. The rules of physics (combined with the technical performance of the train) limit its likely acceleration and deceleration rates: 0.5 and 0.7 m/s^2 are typical respectively in practice, but clearly vary considerably depending on the conditions: freight trains (and also passenger trains at higher speeds) accelerate more slowly (perhaps $0.3m/s^2$), whilst "full service" and emergency braking rates are perhaps 0.9 and 1.1 m/s^2.

Many railways have detailed **operating parameter** rules[1] for timetabling, reflecting strategic decisions made by senior managers. For instance, the signalling system may enable a train to run every 3 minutes, but doing so would inevitably lead to delays, so it may be decided that trains should not be planned at headways less than every 4 minutes. This can itself cause problems, as a line may not have consistent headways: for instance, at the timing of writing, for trains travelling between Reading and Birmingham in England, there are currently sections of line with 3- (Aynho – Birmingham), 4- (Reading – Oxford), and 6- (Oxford – Aynho) minute headways, dependent upon the length of the track sections. This means that two trains running sequentially with no problem in one area will require the second to be delayed on the approach to the line section with 6-minute headways.

More detailed operating rules may also cause problems for planners: for instance, it may be policy that level crossing gates are raised and lowered again between trains (in order to minimise the risk of users attempting to cross

[1] For a number of years, Network Rail in Britain subdivided these into "Rules of the Plan" (which set out timetable policy rules) and "Rules of the Route" (which spelt out the capabilities of the network, and when it was open)

anyway), but this effectively increases the required time separation between trains, if delays are not to occur.

Customer Satisfaction for rail users depends of course on the service they actually receive, not that which is planned, but the planned service has to be of high quality if the actual service is to work well. Competing requirements here include:

- faster journey times v many stops at which passengers can access the service;
- a wide range of departure times v departures at the most-desirable times (e.g. 17:30); and
- passenger v freight.

Punctuality is one of the key measures against which many railways are judged. Although many of the root causes of delays are nothing to do with the timetable (rolling stock, infrastructure condition, passengers and even events external to the railway), timetables can be constructed to maximise the chance of service recovery. For instance, more slack can be put into train timings, although that often has a contradictory impact: traincrew may not hurry about their tasks if they believe there is plenty of time. Where to put a given amount of slack time matters, since it can either improve the likelihood of punctual connections – or effectively provide an obstruction to the planning of other trains. It is better to consider the slack between trains on the train graph. The UIC recommend that not more than 75% of line capacity is used (but perhaps 85% in the peak hour), in order to minimise the knock-on delays from one train to another, and to enable extra train movements (e.g. of recovery vehicles) to be possible. The way in which timetables degrade in operation when there is a delay is often described in terms of the ratio between secondary (output) and primary (input) delay: what is the total delay to all trains if one train is delayed by one minute? A reasonable target would be that the secondary delay was not greater than the original delay, but in intensively-used systems with many conflicting train movements, secondary:primary delay ratios of 10, 100 or even 1000 are known.

Cost recovery and profitability are important timetable criteria, especially in railways operated by the private sector. Running trains at times when they are little-used may not provide Value for Money (even when that is measured more widely, in social cost:benefit terms, with time savings providing significant benefits). Of course, timetable planners do not set out to run trains when they are not going to be used, but policy may dictate that a regular service has to be provided, the 'ideal' slot may already be filled by another service, and trains have to return to depots at some stage. More subtly, the characteristics of the train should ideally fit the demand, but railway demand is characterised by significant peaks: we may need a 10-car train to run into an urban area in the peak, but we have to get it to its origin first, and perhaps only a handful of people want to go there at that time.

Peakiness

The peakiness of passenger demand is a function of the economic geography of the area, and the relative distribution of population and employment. The biggest cities can have huge numbers of jobs focussed in under-populated Central areas (Central London, for instance, has c. 1 million jobs located within the Circle line, but perhaps only 100,000 residents). The ratio of peak:offpeak demand in London is often 4:1, and is as high as 12:1 on lines originating from dormitory towns with little of their own employment. Considerable costs (e.g. in rolling stock purchase, infrastructure capacity and staff numbers) are incurred in meeting the peak, and assets may not be used at other times of day. C2C (who run trains between London and Southend) currently has a peak vehicle requirement of 73 4-car trainsets (out of a fleet of 77) but only needs 37 of them offpeak; the other 36 (at an annual leasing cost of c. £500,000 per trainset) are parked in sidings in the inter-peak, when they earn no income. It is very difficult filling the peak service so much as to be able also to pay for these offpeak costs. On the other hand, as offpeak demand rises, the costs of servicing it are absolutely marginal (e.g. in fuel); even the traincrew cost may be zero, if they have been employed for a full shift but only operated one peak train (hence the desire of railway managements to have shifts of variable lengths, which can be better matched to requirements).

Much effort is also made by timetable planners to try to match train lengths to the likely demand – but this goes much further, too: Chiltern Railways deliberately moved their main depot out from London to Aylesbury, since the majority of their demand is into London in the morning and out again in the evening, so having a depot at the 'country end' minimises the amount of empty running required.

Trade-offs

The above factors usually conspire to be mutually-incompatible, so that the timetable planner spends much time undertaking trade-offs. Some of the more important of these are discussed here.

There is an innate balance to be struck between the (cost of) service provision and the resulting demand for it, triangulated by the level of service reliability. The non-linearity of passenger response (dependent upon the impact of waiting time, as shown in Figure 2.5) is but one element of this, but leads to diminishing marginal returns of service frequency enhancement. In other cases, it might be cheaper to run a railway with shorter turnround times, or short workings just on the busiest part of the line, but that can lead to a lack of robustness when anything goes wrong. A famous example of this was Northern line timetable 42 on London Underground, when the turnback sidings at Archway and Golders Green were fully-used in the offpeak periods, in order to concentrate the service where passengers wanted it, namely in the Central area. However, this prevented service controllers from undertaking one of their most effective strategies to limit disruption, which is to turn some trains short of their destination, enabling them to regain their slot in the timetable in the reverse direction. As a result, timetable 42 was replaced by a timetable with greater train mileage (and hence cost) but improved reliability.

Capacity can be provided in different ways. Customers would generally prefer higher-frequency services, since this minimises waiting time, which is (dis) valued more highly than in-vehicle time. However, running more trains uses up more track capacity and requires more train drivers. Operators would therefore like to run fewer, longer trains, but that may cause problems: most railways have maximum train lengths for planning purposes, related to the signalled headway and/or the capacity of typical passing loops. Whilst station platform lengths can prove a constraint with older rolling stock, many modern multiple-unit trains have a 'selective door opening' facility, so that doors beyond platforms cannot be opened. This has safety benefits, otherwise passengers could fall onto the trackside. In countries where railway authorities

Figure 3.7 Train Length Exceeding Platform Length, New Delhi, India

are struggling to cope with the level of demand (e.g. China and India), however, running long (up to 25-coach) passenger trains is not uncommon, but this does create problems at stations, where passengers land up having to cross tracks, a safety issue which is not considered acceptable in Western Europe.

Capacity for passengers can also be provided for them to be either seated or standing. Obviously, passengers much prefer[2] having a seat but, in urban conditions, an attempt to provide seats for all passengers may mean that some are unable to board at all. This is because the space taken by up a seated passenger (including the seat, and their legs (which protrude)) is typically up to 0.5m^2, whereas passengers will stand at densities of 4/m^2 (in Europe) or even 8/m^2 (South America, SE Asia).

Once train length is at its maximum (usually that of the platform), train planners need to take into account what sort of rolling stock would be most appropriate. The provision of a seat is more important for longer journeys (and, indeed, is regulated to be so in Britain, where the target is that no one should have to stand for more than 20 minutes). Where trainslots are scarce, and many passengers travel longer distances and therefore need a seat, double-deck stock can be considered (see Johnson, 2015 for a detailed discussion). Unfortunately, the extra stairs in double-deck stock take up quite a lot of room so that such vehicles typically only seat 100-120 passengers/vehicle, only 30-50% more than single-deck stock. Moreover, the ability to provide only two vestibules per carriage means that the number of passenger boarding and alighting movements per door rises significantly, and so station stop times with double-deck stock can become unacceptably high. Double-deck stock is used on the Paris RER, but timekeeping in the peak periods is poor; the service in the central area often runs (up to 20 minutes) late, as trains cannot disgorge their load at Chatelet quickly enough, despite the provision of two platforms.

A completely different approach to maximising rolling stock capacity is to remove most of the seats. The epitome of this are probably some of the 25m-long vehicles in Hong Kong, with only 40 seats and 5 doors per side, but London Overground have adopted a similar policy, with 20m vehicles and only 36 seats; the rest of the carriage is effectively a box with handrails. Even within the restricted British loading gauge, longitudinal seats and large vestibules enable up to 200 passengers to be carried per carriage, compared to a crush load of about 150 in conventional British suburban trains.

---

[2] The weighting of in-vehicle time for passengers in congested conditions rises exponentially, but would often be 2 for those passengers standing, and even 1.1 for those with a seat

Figure 3.8 Double-Deck Stock at Versailles Chantiers, France

Figure 3.9 Interior of Class 378 London Overground Stock, Britain

Another trade-off is that between train stopping patterns and travel times. End-to-end passengers typically want shorter travel times and therefore fewer stops on their journey. At the same time, you reach a larger customer market with more stops. From a market point of view it is desirable that departure times from a station have the same fixed times during the hour: so called "fixed-minute" patterns. A fixed pattern will have regular departure times like 8:45, 9:45, 10:45 etc. during the whole day for a station, which is easy to remember for passengers. For production, this has some advantages and some disadvantages. As for planning, fixed patterns mean a good general view, because all hours are "the same". As for capacity, this may create problems in areas of high capacity utilization of infrastructure, because fixed slots from different train services may not mesh properly. If you have various fixed pattern services on the same line, you may not have an optimal utilization of track capacity.

Because demand typically falls off with distance from major urban areas, train service frequencies might also be expected to do so. However, this can cause problems. Short-distance services from A might terminate at H, with longer-distance commuter trains continuing to M. If all trains call at all stations, then all passengers can board the trains to M, but only travellers for the inner suburbs can use the short-turning trains. A disparity in loadings is likely, with the M trains more heavily-loaded. Removing stops from the M trains reduces the crowding but running faster then generates more demand again. Moreover, at more significant suburban stations served by both types of train, passengers will preferentially board the faster trains, again leading to an imbalance in loadings. An iterative process adjusting stopping patterns for several timetable periods may be needed, before train operators are able to equalise loadings between trains.

A better way of matching demand with supply can be to use different services to provide capacity over the core section of the route, with branches (with inherently-lower demand) receiving lower frequencies, as occurs on London Underground's Central line.

However, the number of branches can lead to capacity problems. Where there are many branches, each requiring a basic level of service (e.g. the Munich S-bahn has 7 branches at its Western end, each looking for 4tph, or the London – Brighton corridor, with 8 branches, each looking for at least 2tph), rail planners can have difficult choices to make. Pressure to increase core line capacity may require very significant capital expenditure, which is only warranted when a range of train service planning techniques have been used to ensure that this is the only option left. Maximising train length, and using

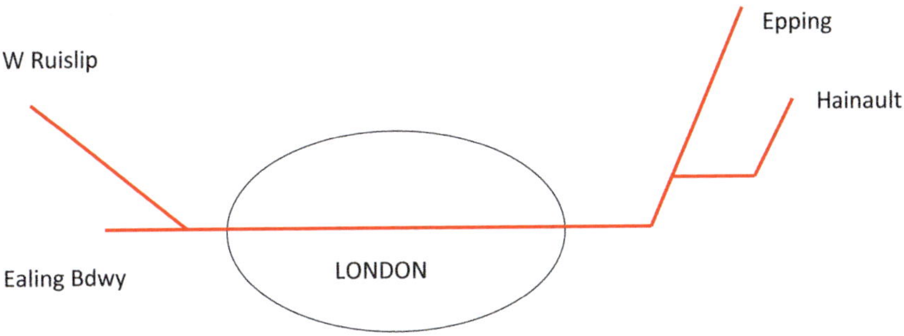

Figure 3.10 Generic Route Diagram of LUL's Central Line
N.B. Woodford – Hainault service excluded, as generally run as a separate shuttle

splitting & joining to provide as many through services as possible with as few on the core as possible, are both important strategies.

However, the detailed implications of generalised cost theory do need to be understood here. Because the value of additional frequency falls with each extra train (as explained in section 2.3), it may be better to run an even split of train service between two branches, even if the proportions of demand are not very even. This is especially the case because diverting one train in every three to a branch tends to mean that the service to the other branch is uneven, which disproportionately increases waiting time and congestion levels.

Political considerations can also come into play when the planner is considering such trade-offs. For instance, it is not uncommon for inner-suburban areas to vote for different political parties than outer-suburban areas.

Type of Timetable
In principle, the timetable may either be based on a fixed pattern or on a pragmatic adaption to practical and market situations. The pragmatic approach (referred to as "market driven" by Ford and Haydock, 1992) means that trains are put in to suit market requirements (passenger and freight), subject to railway network limitations and restrictions. One might, for instance, want to time a two trains-per-day service with trains in the morning and afternoon peaks, to make them as attractive as possible to potential passengers (see Figure 3.11).

Alternatively, it might be desirable to timetable a daily long-distance passenger service aimed at the leisure market to depart at 09:30, convenient for a leisurely morning departure. However, network limitations may be

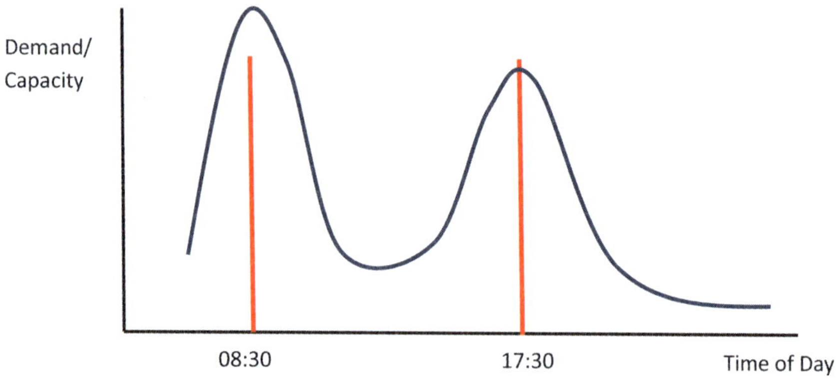

Figure 3.11 2tpd Service Matched Against Typical Rail Demand by Time of Day

severe: crossing patterns on single track lines, in particular, give restrictions, sometimes very far away; for instance, Network Rail decided to double a section of line across a viaduct in Cornwall, when this became the limiting factor in service planning at the major hub at Birmingham New Street, 300kms away.

A low-frequency service timed to coincide with peaks in demand may be appropriate for serving some markets, but may not be very efficient in its use of resources. As demand rises for such services, so does the need to provide a wider range of departures. However, on many sections of railway the demand for paths is reaching or has exceeded realistic capacity. It is well-established that a carefully-constructed sequence of trains running to repeating patterns ensures optimal use of that capacity (until such time as new signalling technology or new build becomes feasible). Non-standard paths, or any not used every hour, reduce effective capacity.

An alternative, production-driven approach, is therefore to make regular patterns with so called fixed-interval or fixed pattern timetables, where trains are planned at regular intervals (see Figure 3.12). However, in more recent years, other advantages of regular-interval timetables have become appreciated. For instance, regularity (and hence the memorability of times) is an important element in the offer of service marketed to potential travellers. In busy areas and on busy corridors frequency is equally significant for rail's competitiveness, especially against the ever-flexible car. And given that not every place-pair can be provided with a through service it is essential to minimise the time lost in interchanging between trains.

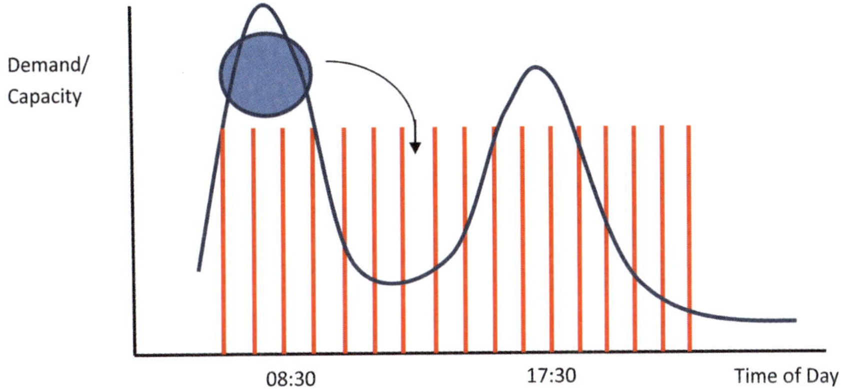

Figure 3.12 Hourly Service Matched Against Typical Rail Demand by Time of Day

Because greater overall capacity is being provided, it is possible for each trainset to be shorter. It may be possible to make up any shortfall in capacity in the peaks by using pricing policy to transfer non time-sensitive traffic to offpeak periods. Alternatively, it may be necessary to strengthen trains (e.g. by providing two trainsets), or to insert extra trains or extend their route length in order to serve demand levels associated with the height of the peaks. Several of these techniques are used by Dutch Railways (NS) to supplement the fixed hourly-repeated timetable patterns (van den Berg and Odiijk, 1994).

There are also different approaches to the practicalities of timetable planning. Sone (1994) describes a Japanese technique for timetable planning based on differences in run times and stopping patterns. However, in the Netherlands, the structure of fixed timetable patterns and provision for passenger interchanges at junctions was established as long ago as 1938 (Avelino et al., 2006). den Brok and Vissers (1994) describe the Dutch practice of timetable and production plan in five steps:

- Establishing a required time table pattern for every main line for a normal hour
- Expanding the pattern to a normal day. This is done for train service to be put in production in two years' time
- Completion of a comprehensive timetable, rolling stock plan and general personnel plan. This is done for production to be in service in one year's time
- Adaptations for moveable holidays etc., for the present year
- Operational adaptations

Timetable planning is commonly seen as adapting to infrastructure, because infrastructure is assumed to have a longer life than the timetable. However, the planning of timetables and infrastructure in Switzerland demonstrates that this may be done the other way around. Here, a required timetable is taken as the basis, and this timetable provides the guidelines for infrastructure development. As travel times between major cities were about one hour, timetables and infrastructure could be adapted so that train arrive at major stations (hubs) five minutes before the hour, and leave five minutes after every hour (Avelino et al., 2006). On the busiest lines, frequencies are increased to half-hourly. Where travel times are not just under an hour, infrastructure development has occurred (e.g. through the "Bahn 2000" works programme) to reduce journey times to fit, even if this has involved expensive works such as the provision of new tunnels. Principles of this "Taktfahrplan" process have been applied in the Netherlands (where the ideas were first formulated) and in the German Länder networks, and are shown in Figure 3.13 and Box 3.1. However, it is in Switzerland that these principles have been taken furthest, and the concepts are now applied across the whole system of public transport. (see Figure 3.14). *Takt* has been approved in referendums, become embedded in Swiss life and influenced high modal shares for trains and buses.

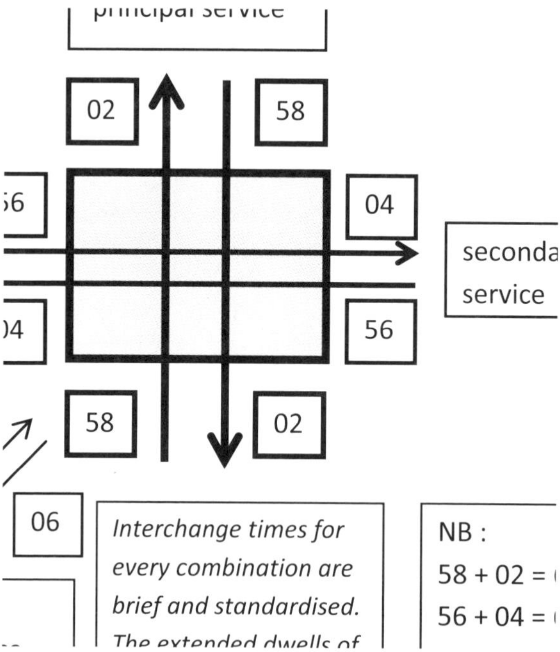

Figure 3.13 Principles of Taktfahrplan Timetable

Box 3.1. Taktfahrplan

Considerations of good capacity use, regularity to enable marketing, and a combination of frequency and good interchange underpin the *Taktfahrplan* ('rhythmic timetable') whose concepts have determined the systematic development of the Swiss timetable since 1982. Its key features are:

* identification of the nodes of the network at which the majority of interchanges naturally take place (including those with other public transport services);
* arrangement of paths (and provision of sufficient tracks) so that groups of trains arrive at those nodes just before xx:00 or xx:30 and depart just after, where xx represents every hour (for opportunities for interchanges, see diagram);
* enhancement of infrastructure and/or traction capabilities so that inter-node running times are reduced to about 54 or 24 minutes in order to fit into the 00/30 scheme at every node;
* acceptance of the maxim that sector timings should be "as fast as necessary, not as fast as possible", i.e. securing connectivity is normally preferred to reducing running times further, since the latter does not benefit anyone interchanging or journeying across a node;
* services running at 120 / 60 / 30 / 15 / 7.5 minute intervals, so that connections always take the same time (a half-hourly inter-city service meeting 20-minute regional services lengthens alternate journey-times);
* rigorous application of the 'mirror-image' rule whereby timings in one direction are reflected in the other, e.g. arrival at A from B at xx:58 is matched by departure from B for A at xx:02 (this ensures that travellers have the same experience of type of train, intermediate stops and connections in both directions);
* appropriate frequencies for every traffic flow, including alternating through and one-change options every hour where half-hourly through trains cannot be justified;
* repetition of the pattern every hour without variation throughout the day, except for judicious thinning of frequency at start and close of service;
* continuity of the pattern through the peak periods, with trains lengthened and some superimposition of extra services; and
* standard paths for freight trains within the hourly sequence that can be offered on a 'catalogue' basis to operators.

Jonathan Tyler, PTN

It is doubtful whether a 'perfect' solution can ever be found, given the huge range of factors – geography, infrastructure constraints, resource utilisation, multiple flows, disparate customer requirements. Compromises are inevitable, but the coherent network-planning process in Switzerland ensures that decisions are as objective as can be. Moreover, Switzerland has shown that it is possible to follow an evolutionary path of improvements, and it has yielded improvements in phases: *Taktfahrplan* was initiated in 1982 and has been revised every two years, with 'big-bang' changes accompanying the opening of the Alpine base tunnels.

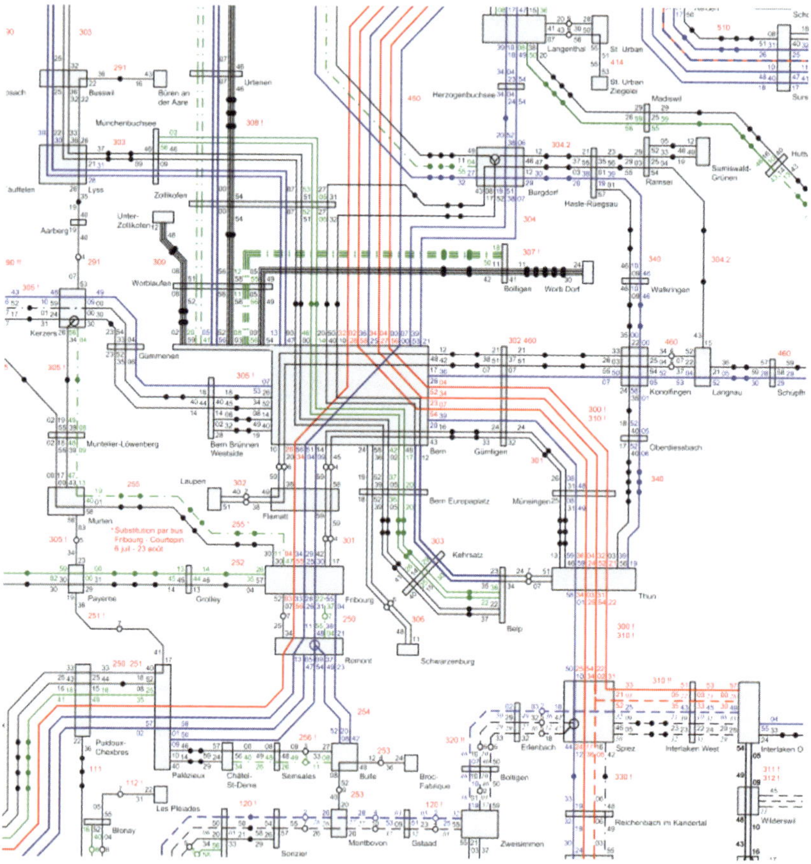

Figure 3.14 Extract of Swiss National Taktfahrplan
Source: Timetable data: SBB Infrastruktur / Concept and design: SMA und Partner AG, Zürich. Reproduced with permission

To be taken to their logical conclusion, Taktfahrplan timetables should also provide linkages between the rail network and other public transport services, if public transport is to provide a door-to-door service. However, there can be disadvantages to this: local bus services may unnecessarily be amended to suit a few longer-distance trips whilst not optimising conditions for the majority of local passengers. It can also tie in bus service planning to the rather more rigorous longer-term necessities of developing the rail network. Nevertheless, linking other modes into the Taktfahrplan, as is done in Switzerland, can provide a high-quality national transport system including people living far from the rail network, who may otherwise feel excluded. There may also be other necessities for rail services to link more closely within a Taktfahrplan network to other modes: Figure 3.15 shows a German inter-city service to Kobenhavn actually on board the train ferry between Puttgarden and Rødby.

Figure 3.15 Part of the Timetable: DB Service on the Puttgarden–Rødby Train Ferry

Although Taktfahrplan principles have primarily been focussed on passenger operation in a few Western European countries, elements of them are demonstrated around the world. There have even been proposals for using them for freight services – see Figure 3.16.

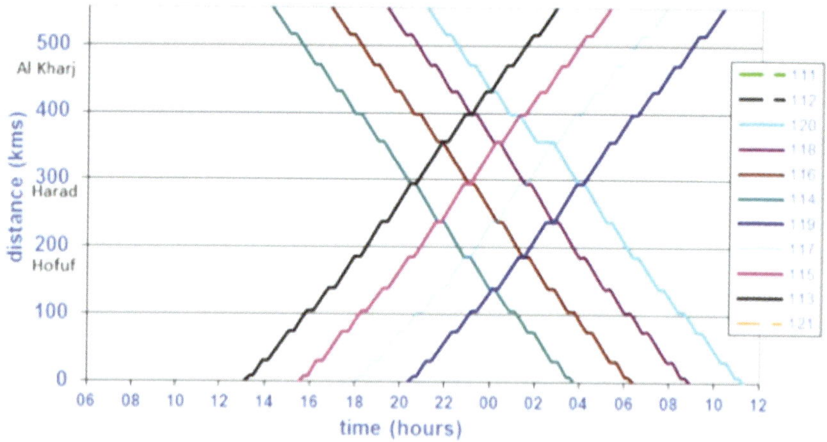

Figure 3.16 Standardised Freight Paths on Dammam – Riyadh corridor, Saudi Arabia

Lower-level decisions also have to be taken, balancing the needs of different groups of customers. At quiet stations in rural areas (see Figure 3.17), one has to decide whether to attempt to offer an attractive service or not. If every train calls there, but often no-one either alights or boards, the journey times for all passengers already on board the train are extended (and (at the margin) demand will be lost, which can be evaluated by assessing the impact on generalised cost, and applying an appropriate elasticity). In addition, costs will accrue to the operator: typically, the cost for stopping a local train is of the order of €1 in extra fuel and another €1 in extra maintenance (e.g. brake wear and tear).

On the other hand, only providing a couple of trains a day can make it impossible for willing potential travellers to make the journeys they need. One potential solution to this problem is that of 'request stops', in which the train slows down to c. 30kph, and any passenger wishing to board signals the driver (as you might when wishing a bus to stop); any passenger wishing to alight should already have made their intentions known to on-board staff. Unfortunately, this solution is not as good as it seems. In any peak periods, when more people would benefit if the train did not stop, it is more likely to do so. In quieter periods, when it is unlikely that anyone would want to use the station, the time to do so cannot be omitted from the timetable, in case someone does, so the train may have to wait time at the next station anyway. There is also a danger of trains running early, if they do not call at several successive request stops.

Figure 3.17 A Classic Rural Location for a Request Stop: Cilmeri, Wales

The train is arriving (and unfortunately left) early, following no need to call at the previous station

3.4 The Timetable Process

More comprehensive (strategic) timetable changes are done at intervals of several years. A strategic timetable is a fixed "core/pattern" lasting over several years. They may be designed to address lines with very high capacity utilization (for instance, the cross-Oslo tunnel in Norway) (Jernbaneverket, 2005), or to underpin major route upgrades or new commercial contracts/franchises. The strategic timetable is therefore a basis for all other timetable planning.

In recent years, strategic timetable changes in Norway have been made in 1994, 1998/1999 and 2013. This is not a formalized process, but has been carried out on demand depending on changes in major framework conditions example e.g. new infrastructure, rolling stock or marketing strategies. In countries with more extensive railway networks, planning resources preclude developing a new strategy for the whole country at once, so specific corridors (e.g. main lines) or regions are likely to be considered. One of these may be undertaken every year, on a rotating basis, keeping central resources fully-occupied, and effectively leading to a new plan every 5-10 years for any particular service (although minor 'tweaks' may be needed in intervening years). In some ways, this is what happens by necessity with Britain's franchised railway, as it is not possible organisationally to let all franchises at once.

Until 1996, when NSB (as national railway operator in Norway) was responsible for both infrastructure administration and train operations, it also had responsibility for practical timetable planning. Since then, infrastructure manager Jernbaneverket (JBV) plans and distributes railway network capacity for fixed periods, in a process with equivalents in most other railway systems where operations and infrastructure are managed separately. In Norway, the timetabling periods are for 12 months, with 6-month part-terms (Jernbaneverket, 2009); this means that major changes to the timetable can only be done once a year. Yet the yearly changes may only be seen as minor changes to an existing strategic timetable ("grunnrute"). In Norway all train service is in principle based on a timetable. There are, however, examples of train services not following an established timetable. According to Pachl (2008), there are several train operating companies running trains based on an operative, priority based train service. This train service mode is common on freight railways in the US and in mining railways around the world.

Basically, the timetable repeats itself every week, but varies over the day and between weekdays. Train services are reduced in parts of the week and on days when demand is lower. Variations are mainly about train service reductions in evenings/nights, Sundays and holidays because of fewer customers and increased train services in peak hours. Service may also be reduced somewhat during major holiday periods, if leisure traffic is not expected to fill the void created by fewer work trips. Infrastructure work may require timetable changes. Besides passenger train services the timetable also has empty train movements for passenger rolling stock[3], as well as ensuring that freight traffic can continue to operate.

Timetable planning is traditionally done by using train graphs (Pachl, 2008). According to Ford and Haydock (1992) it was previously usual to put the fastest trains in first, and then add local trains and freight trains. Later on local trains and freight trains have had more weight in timetable planning, not least in a franchised railway environment, where the operators of such trains have equal legal rights to access to the network.

[3] These are movements without passengers in order to get trains to/from maintenance depots or for positioning trains for later services.

The timetable planning process in TOCs follows the infrastructure authority's periods for distributing capacity, with TOCs applying for capacity for their train services in advance. Usually the marketing/planning departments of TOCs will present suggestions for the new timetable based on requirements from their customers. However, operators may agree that a previous timetable is not working properly and needs to be re-written, or an infrastructure authority may need the timetable to be re-written, in order to match changes to the infrastructure.

The timetabling process should be iterative, with links made between these. For instance, market-led timetables should be checked against rolling stock and personnel capacity before timetable requirements are decided and the main order is sent over to the infrastructure authority. Operator/infrastructure-led timetables should be checked for their convenience for passengers. Arguably, the commercial imperative should have precedence if railways are to succeed in the future. Infrastructure authorities will give feedback on what is feasible and not, and this forms the basis for making a final order. Capacity distribution is often done in two main processes: tactical and operational capacity distribution (e.g. Jernbaneverket, 2005). All fixed train paths must be allocated in the tactical stage, but extra trains may also be ordered at this stage.

Freight presents a particular challenge since freight trains may not run every day of the week, which can lead to unused capacity on the other days. Moreover, in order to provide a flexible service to major customers, it may be necessary to add extra services with only a couple of day's warning (for instance, if a container ship arrives at a port), described as Short Term Planning (STP) or even at almost no notice (on the day, Very Short Term Planning (VSTP)). In some countries, freight train punctuality is very poor, so that multiple paths may have to be provided, in order to ensure the timely passage of a train through a busy or complex area. However, there is a developing agreement about best practice on mixed-traffic railways, which is to provide fixed (e.g. half-hourly) slots for freight services within an overall timetable (Morvant, 2015). This enables freight trains to take up a different slot if running late (or early) and/or for extra trains to run, without compromising the performance of the whole railway.

According to Hansen and Pachl (2008) the following success criteria are valid for developing good timetables:

- Good general view of all parts of railway infrastructure, including lines, stations and depots
- Detailed general view of design and functionality of signal equipment

- General view of network capacity, based on modern methods
- Good run time calculations
- Established standards for energy efficient train service
- Active use of robustness analyses, specially focused on points of conflict and bottlenecks
- Use of different types of simulation
- Follow-up and analysis of punctuality information and other train service information

To these we might add an accurate estimation of likely station stop times, and a good understanding of the long-term value of punctuality for both users (passengers and freight) and operators.

One might start the timetabling process by trying to develop a set of times for the first train of the day, using appropriate parameters, and subjecting it to all the relevant constraints, margins, connections etc. One could then either continue with the expected work for that trainset, or to replicate the initial times in a repeating pattern throughout other hours of the day. Services which connect or inter-work may need to be dealt with simultaneously, as may trains in the opposing direction on single lines, in order to ensure that they pass at passing loops. Alternatively, one might back-time an important train from a desired key arrival time (e.g. at a major station during the morning peak), and do the whole thing in reverse.

However, the development of timetables often starts with setting up a base hour timetable ("grunnrute" in Norwegian). The "grunnrute" is independent of variations in passenger flow during the time of the day when the service is operated. In this approach, peak hour variations are dealt with by inserting additional trains and/or extending or lengthening "grunnrute" trains. Ideally, in order to get an easily understandable timetable, and to split the passengers evenly between two departures, the extra trains should be timed midway between two "grunnrute" departures. In this way an hourly frequency can be extended to a half-hourly one in the morning and evening peak. During peak hours, demand is so great that infrastructure and rolling stock tend to limit production. There may also need to be changes to the basic timetable at the beginning and end of the traffic day, for instance to ensure that trains and traincrew start from/end up at appropriate locations e.g. stations with sidings and traincrew depots.

Whilst initial efforts are likely to concentrate on developing a standard off-peak timetable, and sufficient capacity for the peak periods, consideration also needs to be made about other times of day. Good practice is to try to continue to run the off-peak standard timings in the peak period too, but either with longer and/or with extra trains. Service strengthening, however, depends upon having appropriate infrastructure and train services at key nodes, where attaching/detaching (or the replacement of a long train with a short one) can occur. This can be difficult to achieve at major urban termini, where capacity may be under severe pressure: dividing a long train into two at 09:00 creates the problem of needing two drivers and two separate slots for departure; before that, the platform remains half-occupied, but there may still be any other trains arriving. Even worse, trying to join trainsets at key locations at 16:30 can lead to severe delays, should any problems emerge. Despite the extra energy incurred, many train operators therefore do not attempt to shorten train lengths during the inter-peak, because of the potential impact on p.m. peak operations. However, they would expect to provide shorter train lengths at weekends, if demand was expected to be significantly less, which would normally be the case.

The beginning and ends of the traffic day bring both problems and opportunities. It is not desirable for trains to start from/end up at very minor locations, at the ends of branch lines. Either services will have to be run empty to/from a larger centre with train and crew depots, or local arrangements will be needed. As outstabling trainsets makes them unavailable for maintenance but potentially available for vandals, this is not ideal. Furthermore, small traincrew depots attract significant overhead costs: in order to ensure service reliability, the ratio of spare staff needed at small traincrew depots is necessarily higher than at large ones, thereby increasing costs.

Nevertheless, this does afford opportunities to provide through services at the ends of the traffic day which are marginal in cost terms but can be a major boon to passengers. The ends of routes are not so likely to be commercially-worthwhile to run, but demand is typically peaky, and (if the train planner is particularly skilled or simply fortunate), it can be possible for these end-of-day extensions to coincide with local peak demands. For instance, Britain's East Coast franchise had to pull out of the market between Glasgow and Edinburgh because it had insufficient rolling stock for its core routes in England; many local services were still available to provide the Glasgow-Edinburgh connection. However, it has proved possible to provide an early morning train from Glasgow to London via Edinburgh (because that trainset was not required to provide a 02:00 London – Edinburgh), and that train conveniently passes through Edinburgh in the morning peak, where the extra capacity afforded by a full-length InterCity train provides significant capacity. It is also possible to do this in the evening peak, but the poorer punctuality of long-distance services may make this a less-attractive option: CrossCountry provides an evening peak departure out of Edinburgh to Dundee, but this is formed of a train which originated in Plymouth, 8 hours earlier.

Eventually, a timetable may need to be checked against the rights that a train operator has to run on the network, as changes to train paths may have flexed the path into times or even places that the operator is not supposed to run. Harris & Cooper (2000) presented results of a British system, ARDV, which was set up to help Railtrack assess capacity sold and used.

3.5 Background Information Required

Before a timetable is written, there are two types of rail industry information which need to be agreed in advance. The first of these relates to the available infrastructure (this was, for a time, called "Rules of the Route" in Britain) and the second to the timetabling practices ("Rules of the Plan").

A document setting out Rules of the Route needs to explain such things as:

- when a route is normally open (signalboxes may not be open 24/7, or engineering work may be scheduled overnight[4]);
- if major line closures are to take place at particular times (e.g. weekends within the forthcoming timetable period);
- maximum line speeds;
- platform lengths;
- the capabilities and limitations of specific tracks e.g. regarding electrification, axle weight or structure gauge;
- if particular types of train are prevented from running at particular times (e.g. freight is often banned in commuter peaks).

Infrastructure authorities such as Britain's Network Rail often provide network maps indicating the characteristics of each route, for reference by potential train operators.

Ideally, there should also be a document setting out timetable policy, including such things as:

- methods for the calculation of train running times;

[4] As an example, the 3-track section of Britain's Midland Main Line between Bedford and Kettering has all trains scheduled to use the single line normally allocated to freight during the night, to enable maintenance work to be undertaken on the two main lines. As will be seen in section 4.2, use of a single line substantially reduces capacity and imposes significant restrictions on train movements.

- policies for energy-efficient driving[5];
- policies for adding slack time;
- policies for the timetabling of successive trains (headways derived from the signaling system);
- policies for the timetabling of conflicting train movements (the junction margins that should be applied[6]);
- allowances for specific tasks e.g. train preparation, changing locomotives and drivers, loading particular goods, customs checks at borders etc.

If a schedule implies splitting or joining of trainsets, it is important to ensure that there is enough allowance for the time this will take (in terms of coupling/

Figure 3.18 Class 377 EMUs Immediately after Splitting at Haywards Heath, Britain

---

[5] For instance, inter-station timings may assume that trains accelerate as hard as possible to their maximum speed, then coast towards their destination before brakes are applied to ensure an accurate stopping position; this enables some time to be recovered in practice if trains are run for a greater time at their maximum speed, and full service braking applied to bring the train to a stand.

[6] Note that these should (but often don't) vary by train length as well as train speed: longer, slower freight trains take longer to clear points of conflict

uncoupling, brake tests, passenger announcements etc.), and that this is planned for in places on the network where such operations can be done (in terms of pointwork, platform length etc.). The relevant locations and appropriate allowances would normally be decided in advance, and taken as a constraint by the train planner.

According to the Institute of Railway Operators, the fundamental components of the timetable, with which the train planner works, are:

- Sectional Running Times (SRTs) – the point-to-point timings that trains can achieve;
- Allowances – extra time to be added on top of SRTs for contingencies;
- Line headways – the minimum time interval between trains that the signalling (or other control arrangements) can offer en route;
- Margins – the minimum time interval between trains that the signalling (or other control arrangements) can offer at junctions and stations;
- Station dwell times – the minimum time that trains must stand at stations on route and between trips at terminals.

More detail on the calculation and use of train running and station stop times is set out in section 3.7 below. But, even before we reach that detail, some problems may immediately become obvious. Whilst line closures for maintenance are normally scheduled so as to minimize disruption for passenger services, they can cause severe problems for freight operators wanting to run 24/7 services. Long-distance freight operations cannot avoid peak periods in all the urban areas they may wish to traverse, whilst international services may also have to change drivers and/or locomotives and/or be subject to customs inspections at borders.

3.6 Methods of Providing Timetable Information

There are four main methods through which we can share information about the desired operation of railway services, namely:

- timetables;
- train graphs;
- capacity use figures; and
- simulations.

Timetables

Timetables are for Train Operating Companies (TOCs) to plan their production, and for travellers to know when the trains run. These were the original way in which railways presented information, although this is no longer the case, as most passengers now access a summary of this information through some form of website or mobile app. Timetables may appear in various formats, depending on who is the user – users or staff.

Timetables for passengers (Figure 3.19 is an example) show departure times from stations for trains, and in some cases also arrival times. Traditionally these have been provided on paper, but now internet based versions are taking over. They may also include information about services offered to passengers in the trains, for instance the provision of catering facilities. Repeating train service patterns clearly reduce the quantity of description required, and simplify things for passengers. Greater use of IT means that many passengers may not actually be able to understand a full timetable well enough to derive all the information they need from it, so 'tailor-made' versions for a particular passenger's needs are increasingly available from websites.

11.06.06-06.01.07	Første avg.					Deretter min. over hel time		Til	Siste avg.			Ekstra rushtidstog		
Drammen	0448		0547		0647						0022			
Brakerøya	0450		0549		0649						0024			
Lier	0454		0553		0653						0028			
Asker	0503	0536	0606	0636	0706	36	06	2136	2236	2336	0036			
Høn	0505	0538	0608	0638	0708	38	08	2138	2238	2338	0038			
Vakås	0506	0539	0609	0639	0709	39	09	2139	2239	2339	0039			
Hvalstad	0508	0541	0611	0641	0711	41	11	2141	2241	2341	0041			
Billingstad	0511	0544	0614	0644	0714	44	14	2144	2244	2344	0044			
Slependen	0513	0546	0616	0646	0716	46	16	2146	2246	2346	0046			
Sandvika	0516	0548	0618	0648	0718	48	18	2148	2248	2348	0048			
Blommenholm	0518	0550	0620	0650	0720	50	20	2150	2250	2350	0050			
Høvik	0521	0553	0623	0653	0723	53	23	2153	2253	2353	0053			
Stabekk	0523	0555	0625	0655	0725	55	25	2155	2255	2355	0055			
Lysaker	0526	0557	0627	0657	0727	57	27	2157	2257	2357	0057			
Skøyen	0531	0601	0631	0701	0731	01	31	2201	2301	0001	0101	1517	1549	1617
Nationaltheateret	0535	0605	0635	0705	0735	05	35	2205	2305	0005	0105	1521	1553	1621
Oslo S	0538	0608	0638	0708	0738	08	38	2208	2308	0008	0108	1524	1556	1624
Oslo S	0540	0610	0640	0710	0740	10	40	2210	2310	0010	0110	1525	1558	1625
Bryn	0544	0614	0644	0714	0744	14	44	2214	2314	0014	0114	1529	1602	1629
Alna	0547	0617	0647	0717	0747	17	47	2217	2317	0017	0117	│	│	│
Nyland	0550	0619	0649	0719	0749	19	49	2219	2319	0019	0119	│	│	│
Grorud	0552	0621	0651	0721	0751	21	51	2221	2321	0021	0121	1534	1607	1634
Haugenstua	0554	0623	0653	0723	0753	23	53	2223	2323	0023	0123	1536	1609	1636
Høybråten	0556	0625	0655	0725	0755	25	55	2225	2325	0025	0125	1538	1611	1638
Lørenskog	0558	0627	0657	0727	0757	27	57	2227	2327	0027	0127	1540	1613	1640
Hanaborg	0600	0629	0659	0729	0759	29	59	2229	2329	0029	0129	1542	1615	1642
Fjellhamar	0602	0630	0700	0730	0800	30	00	2230	2330	0030	0130	1543	1616	1643
Strømmen	0604	0632	0702	0732	0802	32	02	2232	2332	0032	0132	1545	1618	1645
Sagdalen	0606	0634	0704	0734	0804	34	04	2234	2334	0034	0134	1547	1620	1647
Lillestrøm	0609	0637	0707	0737	0807	37	07	2237	2337	0037	0137	1549	1623	1649

Det stopper flere tog ved Drammen, Brakerøya, Lier, Asker, Sandvika, Lysaker og Lillestrøm enn hva som er vist her - se eget rutehefte »NSB Lokaltog Kongsberg-Asker-Lillestrøm-Eidsvoll« for alle tog til og fra Oslo for disse stasjonene.

Merknader:
Vær oppmerksom på at det kan bli endring i togtrafikken ved høytider Drammen-Asker-Oslo S-Lillestrøm, se side 20.

Sommerinnstillinger:

I perioden 24.6-20.8. innstilles følgende togavganger:
Fra Asker kl. 1906, 2006 og 2106, til Lillestrøm, samt ekstra rushtidstog fra Skøyen kl. 1517, 1549 og 1617 til Lillestrøm.

Ekstratog:
I perioden 24.6.-20.8. kjøres følgende ekstratog.
Fra Drammen kl. 1922, 2022, 2122, 2222 og 2322 til Asker med stopp i Brakerøya og Lier.
Togene fortsetter som lokaltog fra Asker til Lillestrøm.

Figure 3.19 Example of timetable for passengers
Source: NSB. Trains shown in yellow do not operate all the time, some (centre column) not being operated during the Summer holiday period, or added during peak hours (right-hand columns)

However, this is insufficient information for railway staff to be able to run the railway, so staff have their own timetables, Service or Working Timetables

(Figure 3.20). These may still be available on paper, but are increasingly being provided on hand-held devices or on cab screens.

the Summer holiday period, or added during peak hours (right-hand colun

Pt. 1120. Moss - Spikkestad
Alle dager
Hast. 130

2	3	4	5	6	7	Kjør fo
asjoner mv.	Spor	Til	Merkn.	Fra	Krysser	
.... K+	3			**11.14**		
ukta	2			**17**		
kk Bp B.....						
ɔ	2		■	**19**		
rud Bp B...						
sveien.......			■	**22**		

Figure 3.20 Example of Service or Working Timetable
Source: Jernbaneverket

Additional information in the service timetable may include:

- train characteristics (e.g. length, weight and maximum speed);
- distance travelled;
- timings at intermediate places where the train does not stop;
- which tracks and platforms are to be used, where there is a choice;
- notes about stops (if it is an ordinary station stop or a stop on demand);
- passings of/connections with other trains, especially on single lines;
- other times/locations which may be important (e.g. the limits of different railway companies' infrastructure, or international borders).

Usually the different types of timetables have the same times. However, Hansen and Pachl (2008) recommend differentiating between public timetables and internal timetables. First, many railways calculate times quite accurately (e.g. to the nearest half-minute, or even 10s), and presenting this to passengers would not be helpful. Announcing a train as the "16:56 and 20s" is not really practical.

Secondly, there will be occasions when local stations are spaced in such a way that only operating to the nearest whole minute would lose unnecessary time. For instance, in South London, the actual times required when leaving Crystal Palace at xx:00 are xx:02½ at Gipsy Hill and xx:05 at West Norwood. Allocating three minutes to each of these inter-station pairs would be too generous, whilst only two minutes is insufficient. Instead, two minutes can be allocated as far as Gipsy Hill; this is too little, so all trains will be slightly late upon departure, but the three minutes apparently allowed to West Norwood makes this up. Note that the strategy of providing three minutes to Gipsy Hill does not work, since most trains would be expected to achieve this and, since early departures are to be avoided, would then wait until xx:03 before departing to West Norwood, where they would be late, since 2 ½ minutes is needed for that inter-station segment.

Thirdly, this opens up opportunities to use times to manipulate passenger behaviour. We would probably tell passengers that the train noted above leaves at 16:56, which gives us a recovery margin of 20s before we are actually late.

Lastly, timetables should include some slack time (which clearly does not need to be in whole minutes), which enables the railway to recover from delays without having to promise to deliver unrealistic "lucky day" times. Wien (2006) had similar thoughts as a method of adaptation for saving energy during off-peak periods.

Train Graphs

Train graphs are a useful tool in the development and presentation of timetable material, and as a basis for rolling stock and personnel plans, and for service operation. They are a graphical representation of train service in a time-distance diagram (see Figure 3.21). In most countries, time (as the independent variable) is shown on the X axis, with distance on the Y-axis. Stations, stops and sidings are indicated, and stations are marked with a horizontal line.

In train graphs every train is represented by a line. The line shows where the front of the train is planned to be at any moment. Line gradients show the train speed; a steep line indicates a faster train compared to a slacker line, as shown in Figure 3.23, because it covers the same distance in less time. Horizontal lines may represent stationary trains, so that stopping trains are normally shown as a "staircase" although, in reality, as trains accelerate and brake, the edges of the "stairs" should be shown rounded (see Figure 3.22).

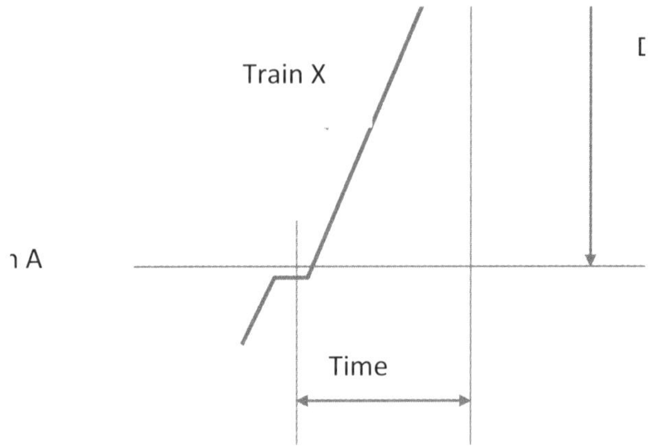

Figure 3.21 A train graph shows the time a train uses from Station a to Station B.

Train graphs can help us to realise that the (average) characteristics of stopping passenger trains are not actually too dissimilar from those of continuously-moving freight trains (see Figure 3.22). Instead, what creates real problems for timetable planners are trains which are of markedly-different speed to the 'normal' speed of trains on that line. Depending upon how the latter are defined, different trains may be understood to be a 'problem': high-speed passenger trains fit poorly in suburban rail services, whilst slow freights fit poorly on inter-city main lines.

:r-city main lines.

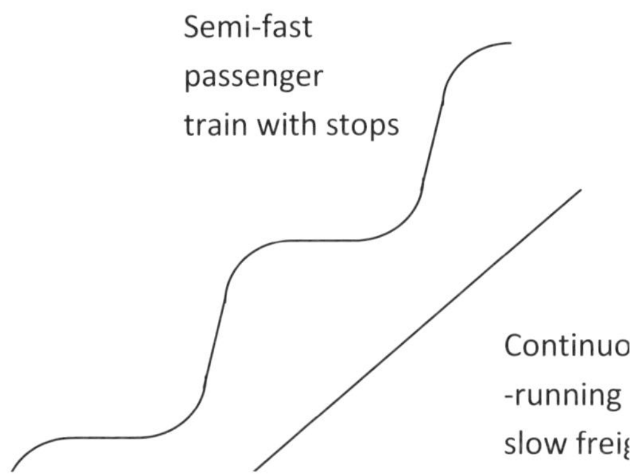

Figure 3.22. Expanded Train Graph of Freight and Semi-Fast Passenger Services

In train graphs one can differentiate between types of train: in Norway, passenger trains are shown as thick lines, freight trains as thin lines, and trains running only on demand, as broken lines. Figure 3.23 gives an example. Extra trains, running irregularly, are not always shown.

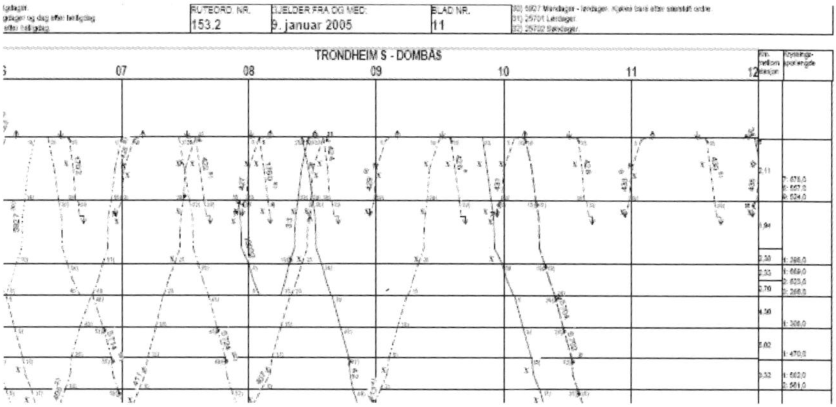

xample of train graph
everket

Figure 3.23 Example of train graph
Source: Jernbaneverket

One of the advantages of train graphs is that one can easily get a visual picture of train density – many lines close together mean a dense train service. Likewise white space indicates that there are no trains at these times and places; such periods may be suitable for works along the tracks.

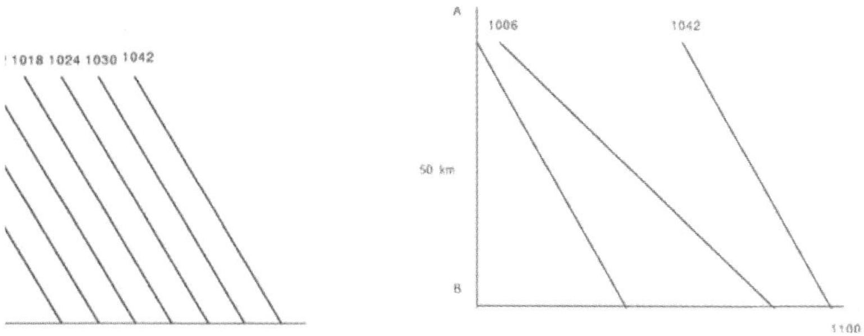

Figure 3.24 Difference in train speeds are shown by the line gradients in the train graph
Steeper lines represent faster trains

However, there are things that are poorly-represented on train graphs, and other things that are not shown at all. First, lines are normally drawn straight between timing points, whereas we have already seen that in Figure 3.22 that stopping trains should be shown as more of a wave shape. Secondly, train graphs do not directly show the ability of the network to run more trains, because the signalled headways are not normally shown – is it possible to run a second train three minutes after the first one, or not until five minutes afterwards?

Capacity Use Figures
Capacity use figures are helpful, at a summary level, for managing a network, because they give a simple impression of the proportion of capacity used. For an infrastructure operator, this is an ideal first step in identifying which parts of the network are under pressure, and are likely to require investment in expanded facilities, However, a simple "network is 75% full" rule (the point at which the UIC considers that a line is at effective capacity, given the requirement to leave room for trains to recover from delays) fails to take into account other vital elements of capacity, First, capacity is only useful at the times at which people and goods want to travel: spare passenger capacity at 03:00 is of limited value. Secondly, there are other methods of changing capacity, most notably using rolling stock (e.g. changing the length or seating configuration of trains). Lastly, as we shall see, different timetables use different amounts of capacity whilst still running the same number of trains.

3.7 Time Calculations

Running Times
The importance of using appropriate train running times cannot be over-estimated. It seems to be common all round the world that some times are either inaccurate, no longer accurate or inappropriate for newer types of rolling stock. These errors provide a background of minor delays which contribute to poor train service performance. In one case in Norway, route reconstruction on Østfoldbanen in 1929 led to the line being 400m longer than it had originally been, but it was not until 2012 that the running times were amended to reflect this!

The bases for calculating inter-station run times are the equations of motion which link distance, time, speed and acceleration, thus:

$v=u+at$ where s = distance
$s=ut+0.5at^2$ t = time
$s=0.5(u+v)*t$ u = initial speed

$v^2=u^2+2as$	v = final speed
$s=vt-0.5at^2$	a = acceleration

More accurate estimates are normally calculated by a computer program, sometimes held by the rolling stock manufacturer. These require more detailed data about:

- the line, including gradients, curves, maximum speeds, station calling pattern etc.
- the trains, including their power, maximum speed etc.

People often ask what are typical acceleration and braking rates for trains, but this depends a great deal on the type of train and its environment: metro railways operating in dry tunnels with ATO equipment may achieve acceleration rates of 1.1m/s^2 but driver-only operated EMUs in the open in wet weather would do well to achieve half of this, and heavy freight trains perhaps even less. Braking is similarly diverse, with lighter passenger trains achieving 1m/s^2 (1.3 m/s^2 in emergencies, rising to perhaps 2m/s^2 for trams), but freights again have considerably lower rates. Circumstances also affect what happens in practice: to reduce risk, braking rates would generally be less when approaching dead-end terminal platforms, whilst modern railways are increasingly encouraging their drivers to drive defensively in a wider range of situations. Signal spacing will also affect whether drivers need to brake at the maximum rate or not: if signal sections are longer, this may never be necessary.

However, acceleration is perhaps more complicated because of the way in which railway traction works: effort at low speeds is put into overcoming friction at maximum tractive effort, whereas that at higher speeds is limited by power output and can struggle to overcome aerodynamics. High-speed passenger trains often achieve 100 mph quite quickly, but can take miles to accelerate further to their cruising speeds of 150-200mph.

Timetable planners obviously have to take into account the maximum speed permitted, which may vary considerably along a line of route. However, gradients are significant in the operation of the railway (especially for freight), since the low coefficient of friction means that they have a more important role than for road transport. Different running times may be required in each direction, to reflect both the train's traction characteristics and line-speed limitations, which may prevent the train from making up time from faster running on downhill sections. As a first estimation, acceleration rates can be adjusted by the gradient percentage of the acceleration due to gravity (9.81ms^{-2}). For instance, a 1% upwards gradient would be expected to reduce acceleration by 0.0981ms^{-2}.

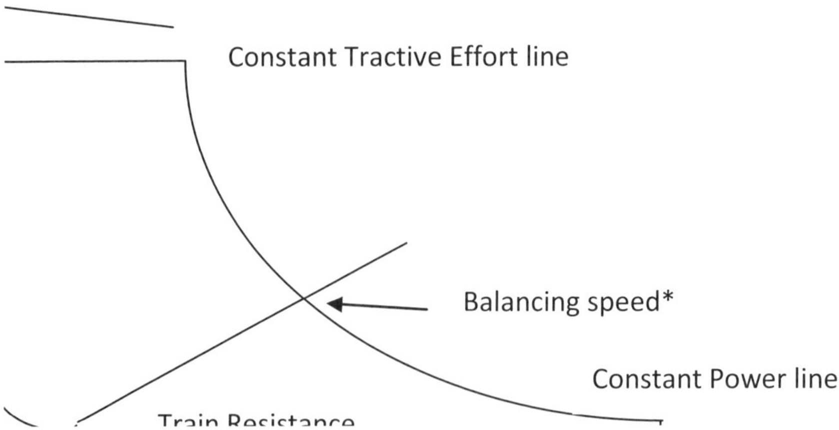

Figure 3.25 Traction Curve (source: Piers Connor, www.railway-technical.com)
* The balancing speed is the speed at which the tractive effort of the train equals the running resistance, so that the train neither accelerates nor decelerates

When the theoretical run time is calculated, various additions are made to generate a practical run time between stations. Slack time can be included in a number of ways. A common initial stage is to add a given percentage (e.g. 5%) to the times calculated from the manufacturer's specification. However, there are then various extra additions related to the infrastructure, which vary by country.

Three other elements of slack are known in Britain as circle, box and triangle time, to reflect how they were originally shown in the printed working timetable. Box time provides extra time along a route, in order to remedy the impacts of minor engineering-caused delays which might have accrued e.g. by temporary speed restrictions. Circle time is added as pathing time at junctions, where it is sensible to allow for occasional delays as trains may miss their booked path slightly. Triangle time was added 25 years ago when the railway adopted compensation charter commitments to provide refunds when trains were late at key stations; it is also often applied by inserting some extra time before major junctions, in order to improve advertised performance and to ensure connections are made more often than not. However, these extra time elements need to be reviewed on an ongoing basis. The faster and/or longer a train, the greater the impact of a given speed restriction; this means that the amount of recovery time should vary by train type – and, potentially, even just if trains are lengthened.

Some countries simply add a fixed proportion of extra time, in order to accommodate these time losses; in Norway, this basic addition is currently typically 4% of run time. Special infrastructure problems (e.g. larger infrastructure maintenance or construction works) may be dealt with by further additions. As a comparison a typical magnitude of time addition according to Pachl (2002) is 3-7% in Europe and 6-8% in North America. Some railways prefer to distribute additions evenly over the line, while others concentrate them near the terminal station. In Norway it has been common to have relatively generous timetables just before trains are approaching their final destination, or approaching Oslo Central. Whilst this may ensure better arrival at monitored stations, it may not maximise capacity: it is bad practice to add large lumps of extra time approaching termini or (especially) on single-track lines, since this can effectively 'lock up' the capacity at that location, and it will then not be possible to timetable another train at that time.

Good railway timetabling should match the insertion of these extra time elements to the places where they are most likely to be needed, and also to minimise the length of the extra time added at any one location. This is because, in order to maximise capacity, trains should run as closely as possible to their booked times. One might argue that the Swiss system, where the aim is for all trains to run within 15s of their booked slot, is an ideal target for infrastructure utilisation; this certainly cannot happen if 'lumps' of as much as 5 or even 10 minutes recovery time are inserted anywhere.

Although many railways have adapted schedules over the years to accommodate these allowances for problems with the infrastructure and interactions with other trains, some are now struggling with a newer phenomenon: defensive or professional driving. In order to reduce the likelihood of trains passing signals at danger, safety-conscious railways have been encouraging drivers to drive more cautiously, especially during periods of ice or leaves on the line. This has a knock-on (negative) impact on capacity and punctuality, a problem exacerbated by differences in behaviour between drivers. A further % addition may be required, in order to accommodate this latest problem.

At junctions where the diverging route has a much lower speed than continuing on the main line, signalling may be amended to introduce "approach control", where trains are brought down almost to a stand before being allowed to continue onto the branch. Although this clearly improves safety, it does add time in a way which may not previously have been taken account of in running time calculations.

Station Stop Times

Dwell times at stations need to be adapted to requirements, but these are dependent on a consideration of both fixed and variable elements, which are themselves both comprised of many factors; Harris et al (2014) characterised the factors affecting passenger flow as reflecting infrastructure, rolling stock and passenger flow variables, and these are summarised in Table 3.1. A key factor to understand is that many of the operational processes are effectively fixed: for instance, train doors typically take 3s to open but 5s to close, however many passenger movements there are (if there are any at all). In addition, directives from the EU (2014) and other authorities often require 'door beepers' or 'hustle alarms' to give an audible warning for several seconds before the door closure process begins, especially for the benefit of the mobility-impaired. This means that the minimum possible time for a station stop is typically around 20s, if all processes are followed properly. Railways need to think carefully about their processes and the impact of the timetable on background factors – for instance, less-frequent services, or timetables with gaps in the service, will lead to higher numbers of passenger movements on following trains. On metro-type railways, this leads to further delays and service instability, which should serve to remind us that such railways effectively need to function as a pipeline.

Methods of train despatch vary widely, and include the use of batons, flags, platform-based equipment (see Figure 3.26) and even mobile phones

Figure 3.26 Despatch Displays on the Munich S-Bahn, Germany (a) White 'T' (despatcher satisfied that platform is clear, so doors should be closed; (b) Green Circle (despatched satisfied that train can depart safely)

Fixed Elements	*Factors Affecting Passenger Flow Rates*		
	Infrastructure	*Rolling Stock*	*Passenger Flow*
Door release/ opening	Platform width	Door width	Number of boarders and alighters
Despatch*	Position of access & egress points	Standback width	Ratio of boarders to alighters
Hustle alarm	Platform: train gap	Seating density	Proportion with luggage
Door close	Information systems or markings to spread passengers out	Total door width/ car area	Proportion with mobility impairments
Traction start		Width of aisle between vestibule and saloon	
Train crew changes*			

Table 3.1 Elements of Station Stop Time
* not fixed, but not dependent upon passenger flow either

(Figure 3.27). Adequate time needs to be allowed for this, and this may not be obvious: for instance, work undertaken for NSB showed that the average time taken just to get a phone connection (before confirmation of any message) was 9s. Platform staff (where present) may also participate in despatch, which can help safety but introduces another element (and potential cause of delay) into the process, as staff have to communicate with each other; lights or other indicators may be provided to the driver. This may be in a two-stage process, with a 'ready to depart' type instruction (i.e. train and driver present, all passengers on board) separate from a 'right away' (i.e. all doors securely shut) signal.

Despatch (i.e. the time between the last passenger movement and the beginning of the door closure procedure) typically takes 10 seconds, not least

Figure 3.27 Train Despatch by Mobile Phone, Norway

because traincrew need to be sure that the platform:train interface is indeed safe (which can be difficult to assess, if the platform is crowded). Erring on the side of safety typically means waiting a few more seconds. However, in order to improve safety further, many railways have also recently imposed 'double-close' regulations that all passenger doors should be confirmed as closed, before the door directly controlled by a conductor or guard is closed; this effectively adds an entire door closure process (typically of about 8s) to every station stop time. In some cases, physical interaction between staff is required, for instance if physical tokens[7] have to be exchanged between signal staff and traincrew (see Figure 3.28).

The variable part of station stop time is determined by the flow of passengers at the busiest, or critical door. Although 1 second per passenger movement is a good starting basis for estimating the passenger flow time, train planners can

[7] Physical items providing authority to proceed on a single-line section, interlocked between adjacent signal boxes to ensure that only one can be issued at once

influence this, even for a given number of alighters and boarders. For instance, providing a longer train is likely to spread the passenger demand between more doors, thereby reducing the maximum expected duration of passenger flow. However, passengers may have to be encouraged to use all the doors, by providing cover from the weather along the whole length of the platform, desirable facilities (e.g. seats, coffee shops) away from the point of entry onto the platform, notices or announcements to move along the platform.

Figure 3.28 Token Exchange, St Bees, Britain

Broadly-speaking, the greater the number of passengers, the quicker the passenger flow, but this reduces when volumes of boarders and alighters are similar. Trains should have doors at least 1.3m wide, but standbacks behind the doors are also helpful, as are a lack of constrictions within the train e.g. to access the passenger compartment. The number and location of platform entrances and exits, together with the gap between the platform and train, are also important, but Platform Screen Doors or Platform Edge Doors (whilst having various safety and environmental benefits) reduce boarding and alighting rates. There is a wealth of analysis on this subject in the literature (e.g. Daamen & Hooghendoorn, 2004; Harris & Anderson, 2006; Harris et al, 2014), but a summary of key values is set out in Table 3.2 below.

In addition to the planned elements of station stop, there may be unplanned delays. Harris (2015) compared the extent of these in a number of European countries, which demonstrated the impact of people (staff and passengers) in providing a range of timings. Delays commonly can average 15s per departure – but the real problem is the variability between successive trains (and hence loss of line capacity) which this can lead to.

Element	*Typical Duration (secs)*	*Notes*
Door open	3-5	Doors may require release before opening
Passenger alighting	5-20	Up to 1 minute for inter-city
Passenger boarding	5-20	Up to 1 minute for inter-city
Despatch	5-15	May need to be repeated for conductor's door
Door close	5	May need to be repeated if passengers or their luggage are in the way
Driver delay	3-10	Affected by any change in position required of the driver e.g. to see mirror
Total	26-75	

Table 3.2 Table of Typical Station Stop Time Elements
Source: RCL/RTSC database

Ideally, the values used in the timetable should reflect what actually happens – although should not include sufficient time for 100% of eventualities, otherwise unnecessary time will be provided. There is therefore a management decision which needs to be made, as to the proportion of station stops which will be possible within the allotted time. Even allowing for 2 standard deviations (95%) is probably excessive; an allowance of 90% might reasonably be recommended. Figure 3.29 shows an example from Kolbotn station in Norway, which shows the actual distribution of station stop durations, and hence what might potentially be an appropriate planned station stop time.

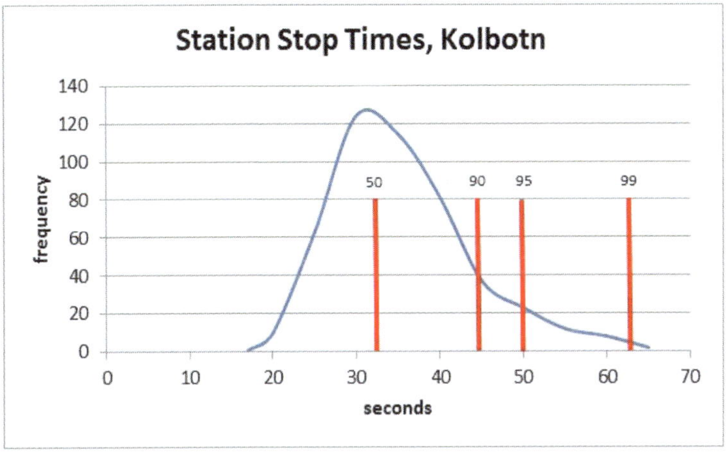

Figure 3.29 Distribution of Station Stop Times, Kolbotn, Norway
Figures above red bars show cumulative distribution values (in %)

Turnround Times

When trains arrive at the end of their journey (or at a terminus station where they must reverse), normal station stop time rules do not really apply. The turnround or layover time allowed in timetables here has a number of functions. Passengers need to alight, and others to board, but (except where there are very large numbers of people all with luggage) this rarely takes more than a couple of minutes for each. Traincrew may have to shut down the engines from one cab, and then start them up at the other end. In some countries, it is an operating requirement that a brake test be undertaken before departure, which adds typically 30s. More onerous in some cases is the time that IT systems need to re-boot the train (perhaps also downloading train running and passenger booking information). If the same traincrew take the train out as arrived with it, time needs to be allowed for them to get from one end of the train to the other; a typical allowance for this in Britain is 4 minutes, but this might be extended if (for instance) a cab is off the end of the platform or, indeed, if the platform is so congested with passengers that the driver's movement is inhibited. Catering trolleys may need to be unloaded and loaded again, whilst cleaning may also be undertaken. However, it is a sign of the times that an increasing amount of train cleaning (especially litter-picking) is now undertaken whilst the train is in motion, as the relative cost of trainsets is far higher than that of lowly-paid cleaning staff. Note that (except for long-distance and luxury train services) full cleaning and toilet water replenishment are not usually undertaken at the end of every journey, but more normally every working day or two, at the end of traffic.

But, whilst many of these tasks take only several (five?) minutes and can be undertaken simultaneously, a key tool for the timetable planner is the amount of extra time that should be added to turnrounds, in order to make them more robust. With the exception of short trains on short branch lines, very few railways plan on turnround times of only 5 minutes – even most metros assume 7 or 8. However, the duration of layovers should bear some relation to the length of the incoming journey: greater amounts of time are needed, if longer-distance services are to be operated punctually. For instance, on Britain's East Coast routes, services arriving at London King's Cross from Yorkshire (Leeds etc., 300kms away) are normally given a minimum of 30 minutes before forming their next departure, whereas those from Newcastle/Edinburgh (400-600kms) are given 45 minutes, and those from further afield at least one hour. Similarly, Deutsche Bahn uses a fairly standard 45 minutes as a minimum for IC and ICE services.

These figures clearly reflect trade-offs between the (cost of the) number of vehicles required for service, and the level of train service performance the operator is trying to achieve. Long-distance operators, with large quantities of high-yield passengers, are likely to want longer turnrounds, because the commercial consequences of lateness are much higher; regional operators are more likely to endure lower turnrounds, because minimising service operating costs is likely to be more important.

However, recognising that even these values may not be enough, train operators may have rules for turning trains round more quickly during times of disruption. They may, for instance, agree not to add seat reservations, clean the train or to re-fill it with water, if they deem it more important to get the train moving again.

Simulation

Many rail companies now use computer traffic simulation. First, an infrastructure model is built in the program (requiring detailed data about line speeds, points, track sections and signalling), before adding the timetable to be simulated. Information about rolling stock (e.g. braking rates) is also needed. Usually, assumptions are also made about delays and other random variables in train service, for instance station dwell time variations. A large number of simulations should then be run, testing the impact of these random variables on a particular combination of timetable and infrastructure.

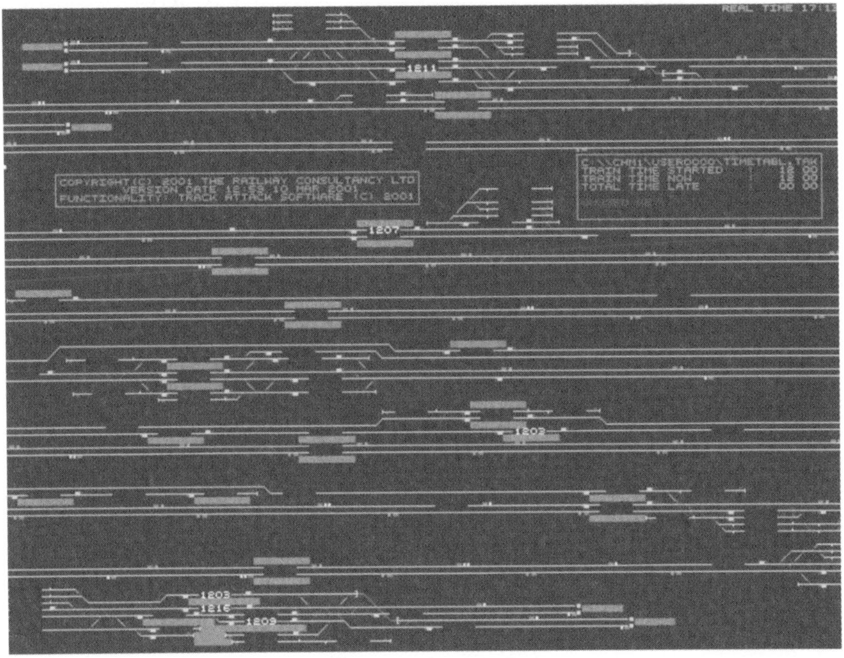

Figure 3.30 Typical Screen Shot of Train Service Simulation

Route runs successively from left to right; all tracks, signals, pointwork, platforms, trains & booked departure times shown. Trains are often coloured differently if running late

There are several simulation programs available in the market. Relatively few simulations, however, are able to consider the impact of differing passenger flows on the train service, and the LUL TSM (Weston & McKenna, 1990) is a rare exception.

3.8 Summary

The train planning task is not limited to the insertion of trains into a timetable. Instead, it may need to start many years before, in connection with land-use planning of areas around the railway. It needs to take into account a range of factors, including providing sufficient transport capacity at appropriate speeds, marketability of the service, and the laws of physics and those relating to health and safety of the workforce. Inevitably, trade-offs are needed between such variables as operating cost, seating provision, reliability, service frequency and train length; we discuss energy separately in chapter 10.

A wealth of information is needed to undertake this task properly, and it is our experience that poor data is a key contributory factor to poor timetables. In particular, although it is relatively easy to provide accurate running time information from simulations of the relevant rolling stock, many railways have paid insufficient attention to the time required for the various tasks undertaken during station stops. Furthermore, the absolute minimum technical times for turnrounds really should not be used in practice, otherwise inbound delays will inevitably create outbound delays.

4 Capacity Planning

4.1 Railway Capacity

"Capacity" is a word often used in the railway industry, but care must be taken as to exactly what it means. First, capacity may be seen to be related to the overall transport system, which means a wider perspective than just the number of trains. White (2009) noted that railway system capacity is actually a function of

- Number of passengers per carriage
- Train length, i.e. number of carriages per train
- Number of departures per time unit

...and might be measured in passengers per hour per direction (pphpd).

In a similar way, freight railway capacity is a function of

- Load capacity for each wagon
- Train length, i.e. number of wagons per train
- Number of departures per time unit (in periods of high demand in particular)

However, "capacity" is generally used to refer to line capacity i.e. the number of trains that can run on a line in a period of time, and given as a number of trains per hour. Even here, one can distinguish between various capacity concepts, which themselves vary, depending upon the length of line considered (see Table 4.1).

Capacity on a double track line is easier to calculate and visualize than capacity on a single track line. The theoretical maximum capacity C (number of trains which can be run) on a double track line during a time-period P is

$$C = P / T$$

where T is the minimum headway (in minutes) of the slowest train (based on Skartsæterhagen, 1998).

Scott's formula gives us the total capacity of a railway line per day, as:

$$C = \frac{(24 - w) \times 60}{T + t}$$

where w = "white period"
T = time taken for the slowest train to cover the track section of interest
t = time taken for signalling systems to set and reset before and after the train

Concept	*Explanation*	*Typical Value on mainline railway (tph)*
Theoretical maximum (signalled) capacity	The theoretical capacity, given an identical train movement profile for all trains	40
Theoretical minimum (signalled) capacity	The theoretical capacity of the constraining longest signal section	36
Recommended maximum capacity	UIC suggestion, making allowance for recovery from pertubations	24-30
Theoretical capacity	Theoretical capacity, taking into account planning margins	24
Practical capacity	Capacity that can be utilized in practice when the actual timetable is considered, including the impact of differential train speeds, junctions, stations etc.	10

Table 4.1 Concepts used to study railway track capacity

There are two main reasons why it is important to understand the fuller version of this formula. First, the railway may not be available for the entire period of interest: infrastructure authorities normally have some time of day (normally at night) when lines are closed for inspection and maintenance – this is the white period, w. Secondly, there is a small (but not zero) time t between each train movement which is taken up by systems being re-set; in old-fashioned signalboxes, this could be many seconds, whilst various levers were pulled manually, but the value is not zero even in electronically-controlled signalboxes, because of safety checks undertaken between the computers involved.

Note that a key implication of Scott's formula is that the capacity of a line will correspond to the *lowest* value of the capacity of any of its sections. There are various reasons why signals may not be spaced to enable an even time division of a line – for instance, signals must be sighted where they can be seen clearly (so not immediately after an overbridge), whilst the inclusion within a signal section of a station will increase the time spent in that section for trains calling at the station. This means that trains closely following the previous one may be subject to delays just before the critical signal section.

As noted above, the maximum number of trains per hour is determined by the minimum time interval necessary between trains. This is called the timetabled headway, and is influenced by:

- The signalled headway derived from the braking distances of the critical train (that taking the longest distance to brake), the type and spacing of signals etc.
- Variations in run times between trains
- Station dwell times
- Time buffer between trains to avoid knock-on delay effects
- Meeting traffic on single track lines

Capacity is usually quoted per hour, so that T = 60 minutes. If the headway is 3 minutes, the maximum capacity is 60 / 3 = 20 trains per hour, all trains have the same speed profile, and without any slack in the timetable, see Figure 4.1.

However, all the measures of capacity noted above are dependent upon one of the key characteristics of railways: the low coefficient of friction (about 11% of that of road vehicles) and the resulting long braking distances. Trains travelling at 200kph would typically require a distance of 2km in which to stop safely, and that is rather greater than a train driver might reasonably be able to see. We therefore need to give train drivers a better indication of their ability to proceed than merely a stop/go signal. Multiple-aspect signalling systems have been developed precisely to enable this to happen. They also enable either higher-speed operation and/or an increase in train frequency.

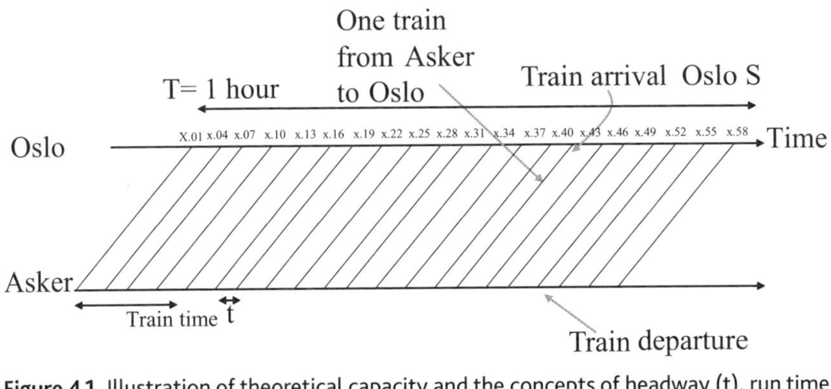

Figure 4.1 Illustration of theoretical capacity and the concepts of headway (t), run time and capacity.

Four-aspect signalling systems are common, in which there are two cautionary types of signal, reflecting respectively "stop at the next signal" and "stop at the next signal but one". Whatever the specific combinations of lights used in different countries to signify this, these provide train drivers with guidance on reducing their speed, and help the train service to be managed: if one train is running slowly, subsequent ones are automatically controlled to run slowly behind it. Note that, especially for suburban services, the yellow signals may not actually have much impact on train speed, if the service is due to stop at a station within the next block or two anyway.

However, the time taken for a train to travel a given distance obviously falls as train speed increases – but the associated braking distance rises roughly with the square of the speed. The distance separation of trains therefore also has to increase as trains run at higher speeds, which means that headways have to increase and capacity fall. This means that there is an optimum speed for operation at a minimum headway.

However, it is important to understand the elements which make up this capacity. Trains are energy-efficient because of the low coefficient of friction of a metal wheel on a metal rail (about 11% of the corresponding value for road traffic). Unfortunately, this makes trains relatively difficult to brake. A high-speed train travelling at 200kph would normally expect to brake over a 2km distance, although might achieve this in 1.5km in emergency mode. Such distances are far beyond what a train driver could reasonably see, so most railways (as opposed to urban tramways) cannot be operated on a 'drive on sight' principle. Indeed, the faster trains go, the more information needs to be given to drivers, to enable them to stop in time.

Because trains have to be able to stop between the signal which shows double yellow and that which shows red, this also enables us to derive an alternative definition of train headway in a 4-aspect environment:

$$H = (1.5 * D) + S + O + L$$

where D = the braking distance of the train
S = the sighting distance (the distance before the signal at which the driver reacts, which might be 10s before passing it)
O = the overlap (safety margin beyond the signal, typically 200m)
L = train length

[Note that the factor by which D is multiplied necessarily varies according to the number of signal aspects]

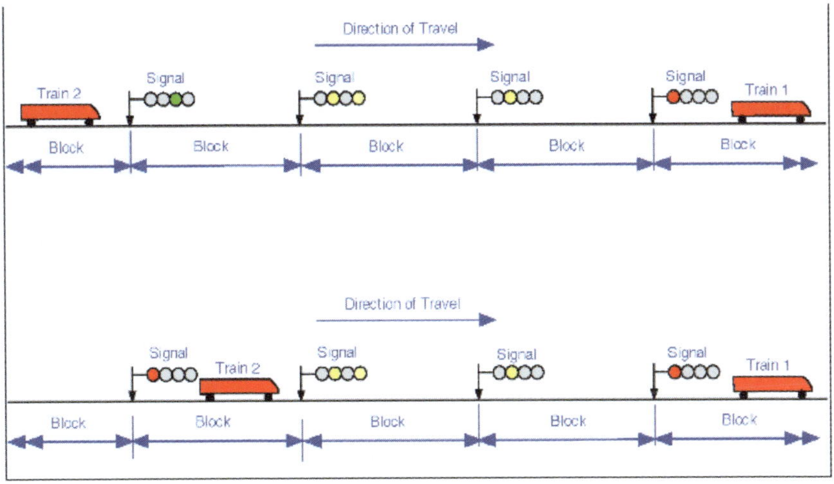

Figure 4.2 Train Braking in a 4-Aspect Signalling Regime
Source: Connor, P at http://www.railway-technical.com/sigtxt1.shtml

In practice, the planning headway will be 30-60s above the signalling headway, in order to accommodate the various allowances discussed in the preceding section. The planning headway will also have to take into account any variations along the line – for instance, one section may be slightly longer, in order to accommodate a junction or tunnel. Capacity can also be reduced by safety considerations e.g. speed may be reduced at level crossings with a high risk profile.

Even when lines are signalled to allow an even spacing of trains, it is important to realise that the duration for which a section of track may not be used by another train is rather greater than the time spent by one train in it (see Figure 4.3). This is because a route cannot be set into a track section either just before a train is due to enter it (because signals have already been cleared) or immediately after it (because the rear of the train will not have cleared the overlap into the next signal section).

Although the front of the train (as the line depicted in the train graph) is only occupying the track section C-D for a short period of time, the track is effectively occupied ("blocked") for a longer period, including sighting time before (so that the train is not impeded before entry) and clearance time afterwards (for the back of the train to clear the signal overlap). Trains can only run unimpeded if they are (E-A) apart.

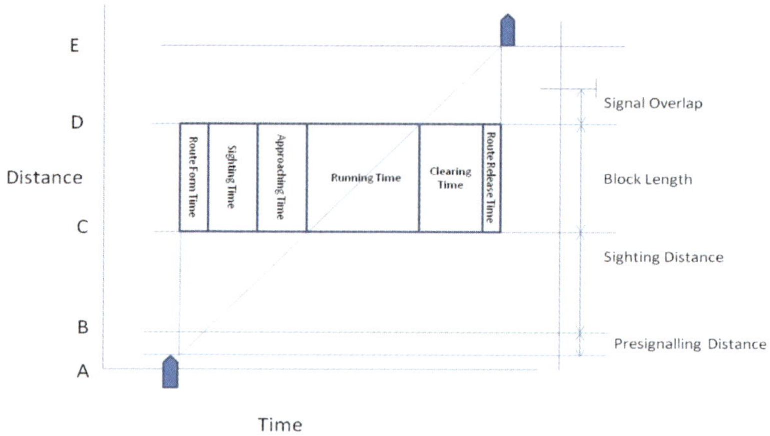

Figure 4.3 Capacity Implications of Train Moving through Section C-D

These principles continue to apply as a train passes through different track sections; these are freed for use by subsequent trains, but other sections ahead are, in turn, blocked to ensure that the braking distance for operation at full speed remains available. This enables us to draw blocking time diagrams, showing the occupancy of a line rather more comprehensively than is merely shown by a simple train graph (see Figure 4.4).

Theoretical capacity also depends on the timetable: the differences in run times reduce the theoretical capacity compared to the ideal one (see Figure 4.5).

Note that on double track it is mainly *variations* in speed that lose capacity, although speed itself does have an impact on capacity because of the increasing braking distance of trains travelling at higher speeds. One might therefore achieve the same capacity on a double track line for slow as well as very fast trains, when they all run at the same speed and have the same stopping pattern (see Figure 4.5). On the other hand, mixed traffic operations reduce capacity considerably (although note that it may still be possible to run trains part of the way between A and B, so perhaps Figure 4.6 does not actually show 100% capacity utilisation).

It can therefore be helpful to develop the concept of a 'standard' path on a particular piece of line, when trying to understand its capacity in terms of the number of slots available per hour. For instance, a line with a mixed service of 8 trains per hour might be analysed thus:

- 4 fast trains @ 1 standard path each = 4 standard paths

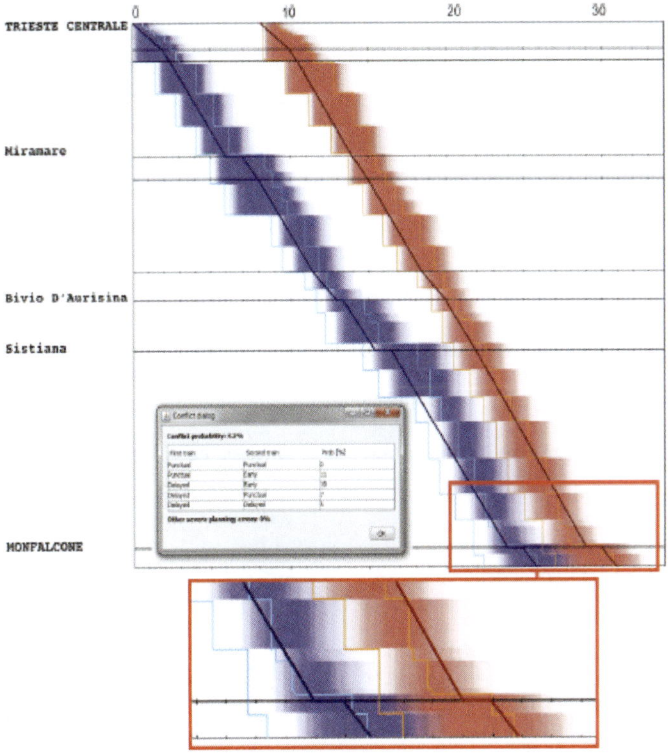

Figure 4.4 Staircases of Blocking Times
Reprinted from Figure 15 of Jnl. of Rail Transport Planning & Management vol. 1 no. 1 (2011) "A Method for Improving Stochastic Blocking Times", Medeossi, G, Longo, G & de Fabris, S, with permission from Elsevier, ref. 3739510717240.

- 2 stopping trains @ 5 standard paths each = 10 standard paths
- 2 semi-fast trains@ 3 standard paths each = 6 standard paths

So the total number of standard paths used would be 20 i.e. the 8 trains have used up most of the line's capacity.

In order to minimise the capacity loss on mixed-traffic lines, a concept known as 'flighting' is often used. Unfortunately, this phrase has two slightly-different meanings. In one, it is used to refer to the situation where trains with similar characteristics are planned to operate consecutively; this is not often helpful for passengers (who want their departures evenly-spaced) but might reasonably be used for a pair of freight trains, or for pair of passenger

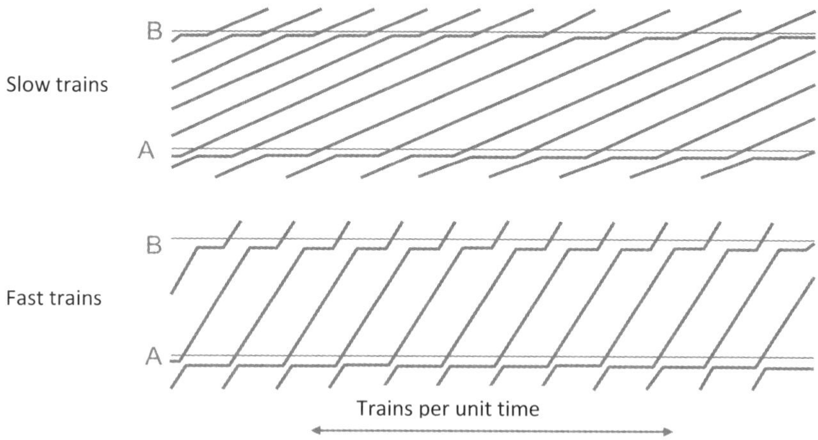

Figure 4.5 Capacity is highest when all trains run at the same speed

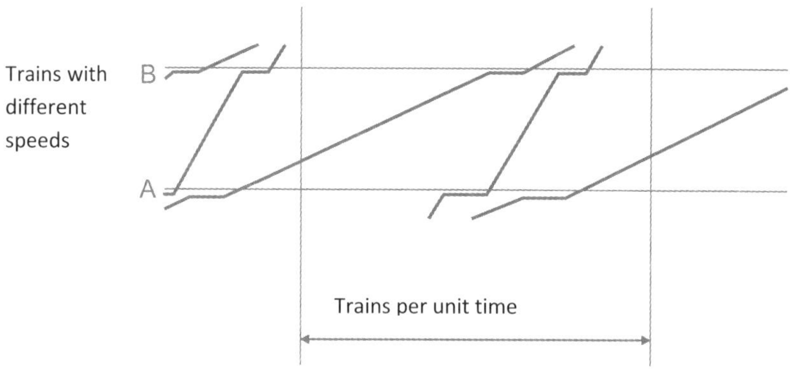

Figure 4.6 Reduction in Capacity when fast trains and slow trains run on the same line

trains sharing a section of route. The term 'flighting' is also used to describe the grouping of trains with a fast train followed by a semi-fast and then a slow service. In both usages, however, flighting achieves an increase in line capacity by minimising the 'white space' time on the train graph. Both examples can be seen in Figure 4.7, a historic train graph from pre-HS2 days in Britain. Consecutive Eurostar services to Paris and Brussels can be seen to be followed by trains of decreasing speed.

In order to quantify the capacity utilisation of a railway with trains of different types, a technique known as "compression" is used. This squeezes together all the trains that are run within an hour (reducing all the spaces on the train

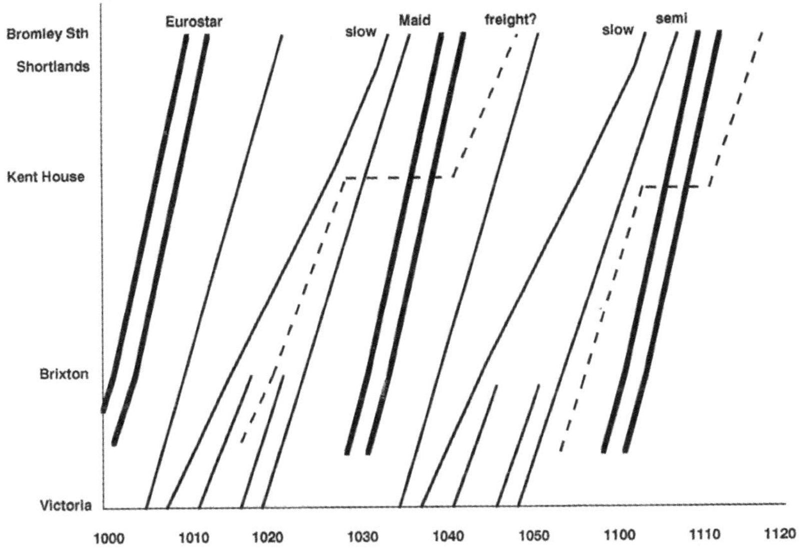

Figure 4.7 Train Graph for the Victoria – Bromley South route, London showing the flighting of services. The dashed lines represented possible freight paths, which were rejected due to a lack of line capacity

graph to the minimum possible allowed, whilst retaining the order of trains), and then calculates the total amount of time used as a proportion of an hour. This needs to take into account both the margins at the beginning of the route and the end. In Figure 4.7, there is almost no remaining space except a couple of minutes between 10:03 and 10:05 at Brixton, after the two Eurostars. 58 minutes used out of a total of 60 would lead to a capacity utilisation figure of 96%, which is very high.

The International Union of Railways (UIC) recommends a peak hour capacity of 75-85% and a day capacity of 60-75 % of theoretical capacity. National railways typically follow this type of rule: in principle, Jernbaneverket uses a practical capacity of 80% of theoretical capacity during peak hours, and 60% at other times of the day. The situation shown in Figure 3.26 is therefore untenable, and the request for the freight paths (shown dashed) was therefore refused. Lindahl (2002) explains that, at a capacity utilization level of 40 to 60% there is a balance between the number of trains and the ability to recover. At capacity utilization levels between 60 and 80% there will be problems with recovering from delays. Capacity utilization of more than 80% indicates a lack of capacity, although it may be necessary, simply to carry the load in busy areas.

Modern computerised signalling systems offer some improvements to the capacity of lines, typically by shortening the length of the signalling blocks. What moving block technology does is effectively to reduce the length of the signalling blocks even further, especially where trains are moving slowly. Reducing the length of line blocked for a particular train movement therefore enables an increase in capacity.

The new European Train Control System (ETCS) has three system levels, with quite different characteristics. Level 1 merely adds automatic train protection to conventional block signalling. Level 2 still relies on trackside train detection of some sort (either by track circuits or axle counters) but uses GSM-R radio to transmit the instructions to the train. Although this effectively retains fixed blocks, it potentially enables more of them within a given distance. ETCS level 3 is effectively a real moving block system. It enables a reduction in infrastructure costs (and in the safety risks associated with its maintenance), but at the expense of more complicated electronics in rolling stock.

The capacity of a railway not only depends upon plain line but also on capacity at stations. At stations conflicting train paths are often an important capacity limitation, as are the number of platform tracks and conflicts with other train movements. It should be noted that moving block technology will not solve all the capacity problems of railways, for instance those which are limited by platform reoccupation (Barter, 2008).

Capacity on a single track line depends on where it is possible for trains to meet, and how they can pass. There are potential safety issues with this, which are discussed in the section below on single track.

In analysis of single track lines, the question is often how to increase capacity, or how to improve punctuality. According to Skartsæterhagen (1998), there are three types of activities to be made to increase capacity on a single track line:

- More passing loops
- Improved design of existing passing loops
- Increased speed

More on railway capacity is to be found, among others, in Skartsæterhagen (1998) and Pachl (2008). Handstanger ((2009) and Lindfeldt (2007) have studied capacity on single track railways, which is of particular importance to the situation in Norway.

A further area which is less well-understood is that of the loss of capacity at junctions, to which the UIC method did not extend. One simple method of addressing this issue is to assume that each conflicting train movement loses a further headway; although in theory it may be possible to timetable simultaneous parallel train movements, there is often something of a loss in performance, as knock-on delays can become significant.

However, there is a long-established method of examining capacity at stations, and that is through the platform occupation graph (see Figure 4.8). This shows the time-periods during which a platform is occupied as horizontal bars, although the white periods in-between cannot entirely be filled, since one needs to take into account the run-out/run-in time between the platform and the signals protecting it. Trains of different operators can (as here) be shown in different colours, whilst one can also demonstrate circumstances where two trains can be in the same platform at the same time (although, at a terminus, the train which arrives later has to leave first).

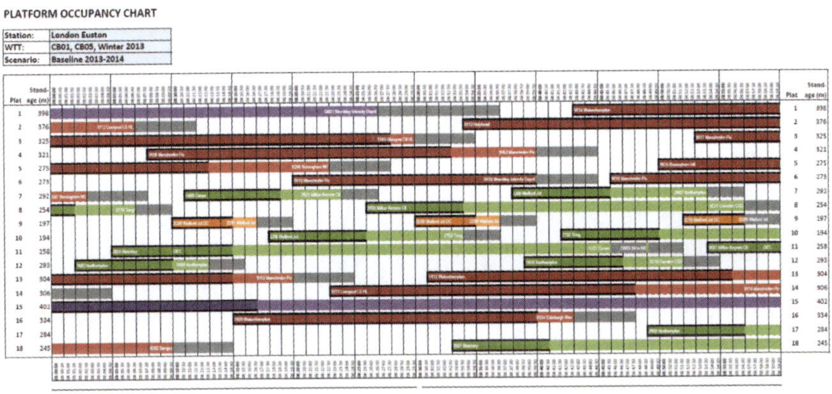

Figure 4.8 A.M. Peak Platform Occupation Graph for London Euston
Source: Parsons Brinckerhoff, 2014

4.2 Track Layouts

Although the process of timetabling generally comes after the provision of infrastructure, in the best-run railways the two are considered together.

Double Track

This is the standard arrangement, against which the discussion of capacity in the previous section has taken place. However, one possible modification of it is the use of bi-directional signalling, in order to allow trains to run in either direction on either track. Opportunities for doing so can be provided by crossovers every few kms along the track, crossovers which may be needed for engineering trains anyway. Bi-directional running is used in various countries in Europe, and its application in Britain sometimes suggested, so it merits explanation in greater detail.

Capacity can still be calculated using Scott's formula or other approaches as noted above. However, the time used up by a train running in the 'wrong' direction is very substantially more than that running in the conventional direction. For instance, if a line has sections A – B – C – D - E, each of which takes 1 minute to traverse, the line capacity in the prime direction, Figure 4.2 shows us that it will be possible to run trains under green signals at line speed if one train is on section D – E and the following one on A – B, 3 minutes behind. In the other direction, though, as soon as a train leaves E for A, no trains can leave A in the prime direction. Neither can they do so until that train arrives at A (and the appropriate signalling and safety processes have been worked through, and planning margins applied). In order for the next train in the 'prime' direction not to be checked by the contra-direction train, it will need to be a further three track sections away. That immediately at least halves the effective capacity, as well as introducing the range of conflicts between trains in opposing directions which are discussed below in the section about single lines.

So, although bi-directional working is certainly useful in emergencies, by allowing trains to bypass an obstruction (such as a failed train) without long-winded and potentially less-safe manual processes of train authorisation, it can be difficult to arrange in practice, especially as train frequencies rise to the levels typically seen in Britain. Furthermore, there are of course greater costs in installing and maintaining the greater complexity of signalling equipment, whilst human factors issues related to the sighting of signals by drivers also need to be taken into account.

Single Track

Single-track sections provide a significant headache for timetable planners because, by definition, trains can only pass or overtake on them where passing loops are provided. With trains running in opposing directions, the mis-location of a passing loop can easily require one train to wait several minutes unnecessarily for another. As single track is common on more lightly-used lines, it is also no surprise that passing loops may be very distant from each other: although Norway's main lines have been constructed with loops at every 5-10 kms, some rural lines in Britain have loops only every 50kms, whilst those in larger more sparsely-populated countries (e.g. Australia) may be even further apart. The entire timetable may therefore be determined by the passing times of trains at key loops, and planners may have to work back from this. Importantly, when planning infrastructure, loops should be located at equivalent time intervals from each other, if regular train services are to be provided.

We have already seen that allowances need to be established for conflicting train movements, one key type of which is passing opposing trains on single-track lines. This is acknowledged to be a risk in terms of maintaining high levels of punctuality, as it can transfer delays from one direction to the other, as well as to following trains. The timetabling process needs to be alert to the potential, and to include appropriate margins, so that minor delays do not cause secondary delays. This process is made more difficult by the (not unreasonable) safety rule that simultaneous arrivals ("samtidig innkjør")of trains in both ends of many loops not be permitted, unless appropriate safety equipment/facilities (e.g. trap points) is provided to prevent an over-run; instead, one train must often arrive and come to a stand before the other one is allowed to enter. This normally leads to a signal locking delay of 2-3 minutes, depending upon the length of the loop (Jernbaneverket, 2011).

A good timetable will include margins for crossing so that the train graph appears as in Figure 4.9. However, there may be a temptation for timetable planners to attempt the train movement depicted in different ways, including the examples shown in Figures 4.10a and b.

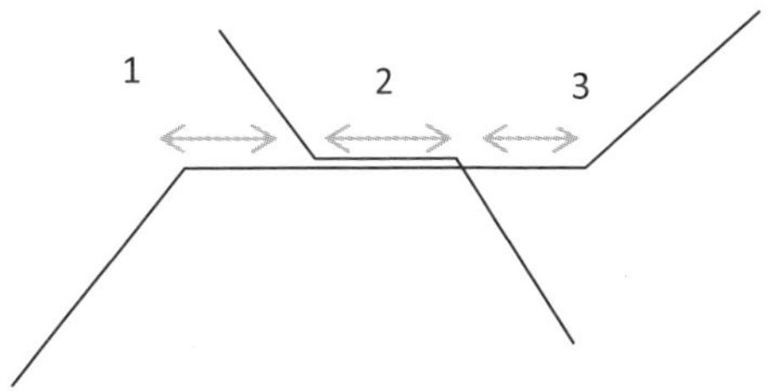

Figure 4.9 Graph of Ideal Train Crossing
Margin 1 is time between successive arrivals
Margin 2 is time between the arrival of the second train and the departure of the first
Margin 3 is time between successive departures

In Figure 4.10a, the crossing movement has been compressed, perhaps because of line capacity issues. Whilst the simultaneous departures may not be too

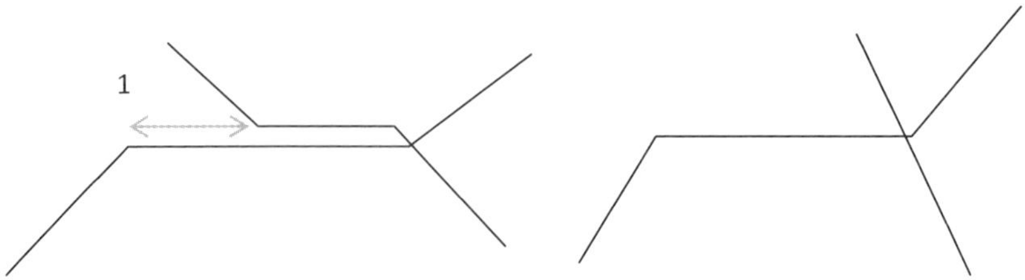

Figure 4.10 Graph of Sub-optimal Train Crossings
(a) Both trains stopping (b) with one Non-Stop Train
Margin 1 is time between successive arrivals

much of a problem, margin 1 has been reduced to a point where it may be near, at (or hopefully not beyond) the minimum required to satisfy the 'no simultaneous arrivals' rule. Of course, if the first train is late arriving, the second will be stopped outside the loop and, having had to stop and restart, will arrive late into the loop as well. Depending upon the length of time needed (for passenger alighting and boarding, for instance), this could also prejudice its on-time departure.

However, there may also be examples as depicted in Figure 4.10b. Here, one train is made to stop to enable a non-stop train to pass through, with simultaneous departures expected. This, however, may physically be impossible, depending upon the exact nature of the site, as shown in Figures 4.11 (a) and (b).

In case (a), if train A is booked to leave at the same time as an opposing freight train passes the station, the rear of the freight train is likely to have passed the point of conflict. Even if this has not yet occurred at the time of departure from the station, it is likely to have occurred when train A gets there. However, in case (b), train A is unlikely to be able to leave, since not only may the rear of the freight train still be over the conflicting pointwork, but there is then a small route-setting time for the signalling before a new route can be set for train A. Even if the freight train is apparently on time to the second, it may cause a delay. This leads to an inherently-unstable railway, and is not good practice.

Good practice is to insert extra time at the locations at which trains are booked to pass, in order to minimise the impact of trivial delays in one direction affecting trains in the other direction. Although these may not be necessary when services run perfectly, they are essential to maintain some form of adherence to the timetable when small delays have otherwise crept in. (When large delays exist, line controllers need to do the best they can, as allowing for this in the timetable is not appropriate).

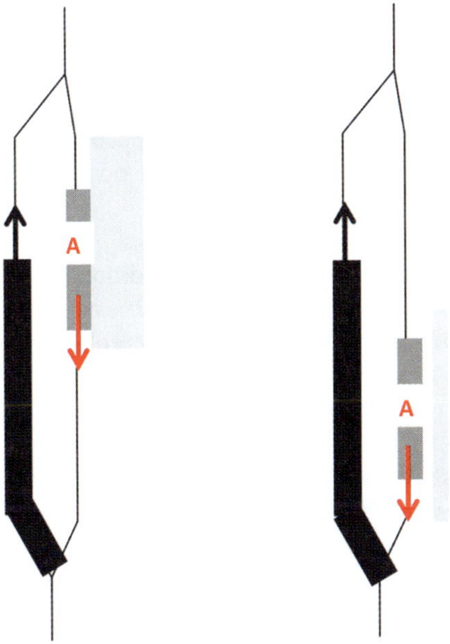

Figure 4.11 Diagrams of Track/Platform Layouts at Crossing Loops
(a) with platform near point of entry; (b) with platform near point of exit

Examination of the Network Rail Scotland Rules of the Plan (their detailed planning guidelines) for the Highland main line shows that they require a margin of up to one minute to be applied to a train departure following an opposing train passing movement (e.g. at Dalwhinnie). However, there are also rather more generous passing allowances (for instance, at Kincraig, a Northbound freight arrives at 08:29 for the London-bound HST to pass at 08:36 whilst the freight then leaves at 08:37).

We hypothesise that the inadequacy of crossing margins is one reason why the ratio of secondary delay: primary delay is relatively high on the Norwegian railway system. Planning processes should design a timetable which does not generate secondary delays from small primary delays, but the lack of crossing margins as shown in Figure 4.9 above will generate knock-on delays from primary delays of as little as 30 seconds (which was recorded in practice at Strandlykka).

Passing Loops

A key timetabling issue for many railways with single-track sections is where trains pass. Infrastructure can become very timetable-dependent, which is not ideal, as sometimes timetables have to be amended for other reasons. Where trains run at regular intervals, passing loops should also be at regular intervals – but as measured in the run-time between them, not the distance. For instance, if trains average 100kph and run every hour, passing loops are likely to be needed at about every 50kms – but not exactly so, if line speeds vary. What is more important is that trains will need to pass one in the opposing direction every 30 minutes.

As train service frequencies rise, investments may be made in additional passing loops, but this can cause problems. A loop may be desirable at a station, but this may split the line into sections which prevent a regular (e.g. half-hourly) service operating, and so services may be at uneven intervals (e.g. 20 and 40 minutes).

At the margin, there are various tricks for enabling trains to pass more smoothly at passing loops, especially when one takes into account the way in which trains are actually operated. Where trains are expected to stop (for instance in a passing loop), they will of course slow down. However, the second train approaching may be approaching the loop when the line is already clear not only in the loop but out through the other side. It may therefore be possible to run through the loop at speed, saving the time otherwise required to stop. This difference in use of a loop can also be used to enable a train service to operate regularly where loops are not quite properly-spaced.

Passing loops are also needed on double-track lines, in order for trains to overtake others going in the same direction. For timetablers, the balance here is between the second train catching up the first, as it enters the loop (causing knock-on delays to operation), or the first train being put in the loop so early that it renders the train path commercially-undesirable. In reality, trains approaching loops are constrained by the need to stop completely at the far end, if not to negotiate low-speed pointwork leaving the mainline, so they may use up much time (and hence capacity) whilst being looped. Moreover, freight trains accelerate only slowly so, for the best timetabling policy for robust operation may be for them to continue unchecked at their maximum speed.

Of course, there are specific circumstances in which being stationary is useful – stopping at stations being the main one. Passing loops may therefore be of more use for fast passenger trains to overtake slow passenger trains, rather than freight trains. However, there is a catch: the time taken for most trains to decelerate towards, stop at and then accelerate from a station stop is of

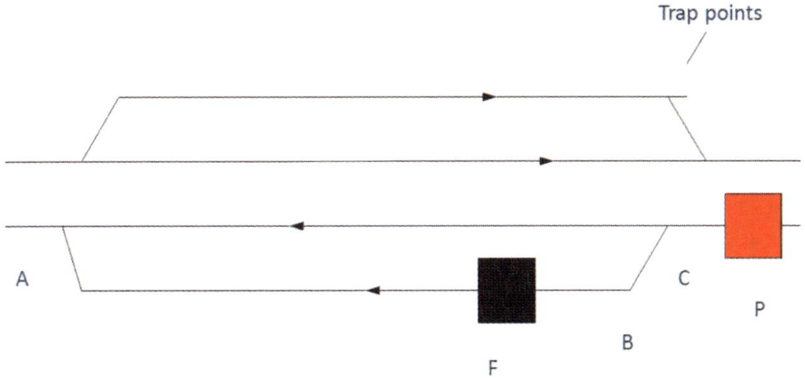

Figure 4.12 Passing Loops on Double-Track Main Line

the order of 3 minutes[1], which is unfortunately a typical headway on modern railways. This means that a slow train having stopped, and a following (non-stop) fast train would present themselves at the far end of the loop (point A in Figure 4.12) at the same time. Ideally, passing loops should be longer if trains are to overtake unchecked, either by including two local stations or being sufficiently long (5km+) that the speed differential is sufficient to provide the time separation needed (6 minutes i.e. 3 minutes before to 3 minutes after).

Multiple Track

The key advantage of multiple track is a substantial increase in capacity, as trains of similar operating characteristics can be run on the same track. This can enable *each* of the (e.g. Northbound) tracks of a multiple-track line to carry more trains than one track trying to support a mixed service (see Figure 4.6). However, a safety factor does constrain this slightly, as follows. To avoid drivers mis-reading signals, it is normal practice to co-locate signals on both tracks on the same gantry ("parallel positioning"). If (as is usual) one line is intended for trains with a slower speed than the other, signal spacing and hence headways are extended on the slow line.

Even the way in which multiple-track routes are arranged can have direct consequences on timetabling and the wider operation of the railway. The two main layouts are by direction or speed, which have the format shown in Figure 4.13 and whose advantages and disadvantages are summarised in Table 4.2.

[1] This figure obviously varies by speed, being only c.2 minutes at low speeds but more like 7 minutes for high-speed (200kph) operation.

Where trains cross from one line to another when tracks are paired by speed, it would be good practice to add an extra allowance for pathing, in case late-running of an opposing train created a conflict.

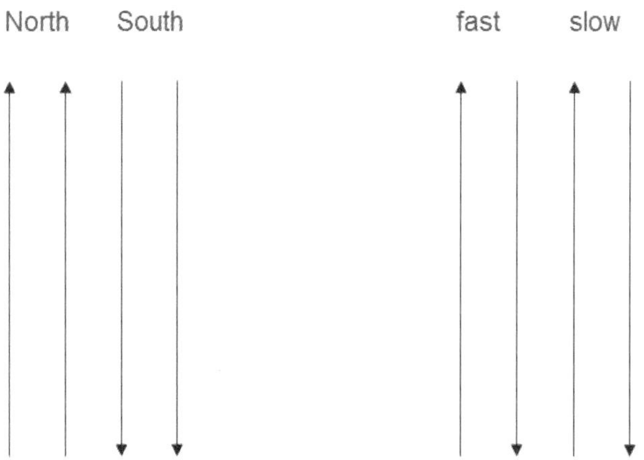

Figure 4.13 Alternative Ways of Pairing Four Tracks

Arranged by speed	*Arranged by direction*
Ability to continue to run a train service in both directions (e.g. during maintenance works) given any two adjacent tracks	Ability for passengers to a given destination to use services from either side of an island platform
Ability to segregate passenger flows & facilities, and train services at termini	Ability to overtake without causing conflicts to trains in the opposing direction
Ability to provide fewer conflicts at junctions (at least with routes approaching on the 'slow' side of the alignment)	
Ability to ensure that lines designed for higher speed can be straighter, with any deviations for platforms limited to the slow lines	

Table 4.2 Relative Advantages of Arranging 4-track Lines in Different Ways

Junctions
The way in which tracks are joined together also has an impact on the total capacity of the railway. Junction types permitting simultaneous train movements are to be preferred operationally, although one must also take into account capital cost and maintenance requirements. The standard double junction (see Figure 4.14) contains elements of rail subject to heavy and conflicting forces, which require frequent (e.g. weekly inspection). Although it might appear that capacity can be maximised through careful timetable planning, trying to organise that trains both on and off the diverging route cross at the junction does put a constraint on timetable planning, probably equivalent to the loss of a few minutes' worth per hour. In practice, the situation may be somewhat worse, as trains do not always run to time, so some knock-on delays are likely. However, there have been notable examples of timetables being rewritten around the needs of key double junctions e.g. the British SWT timetable recast of 2004 revolved around ensuring that Portsmouth line trains were booked to cross the flat junction at Woking simultaneously.

Single-lead junctions are considerably cheaper to construct (indeed, it can be possible to construct them entirely within a factory environment), but the loss of flexibility and capacity is greater – and increases, the longer the section of reversible line. However, with modern safety systems, the head-on collisions that occurred at such junctions in the past should no longer occur.

Much the highest capacity is achieved with grade-separated junctions, where the diverging line passes under (in a burrowing junction) or over (as a flying junction) the main line. Almost no capacity is lost here, but the construction costs are significant: Network Rail recently constructed one of these at Hitchin, at a cost of approx. £40m (excluding the costs of 1km of new line).

In areas with several junctions close together, it is good practice to ensure that there is a complete track section between the junctions, even if the connection could be made with slightly-less track. This enables a train to be held entirely within it, so that an inability to access a new route does not lead to the train blocking-back onto its previous one. A recent example of this in Britain is the "Bacon Factory curve" in Ipswich, which links the Felixstowe branch to the main line between London and Norwich; the curve is long enough to accommodate a full-length container train.

Termini
The layout of the infrastructure at termini can provide assistance or restrictions as to the ease of desired train movements. In the simplest designs, a single track simply comes to an end – this may be cheap, but it means that every train

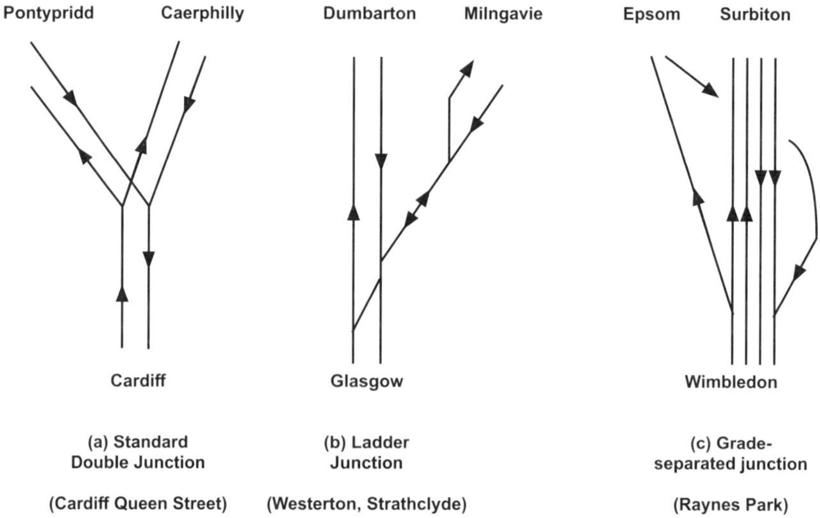

Figure 4.14 Types of Junction Layout

which arrives must already have some method of driving from the rear of the train (e.g. another locomotive or driving cab), because driving trains from the rear cab in passenger service is normally forbidden under safety rules.

Indeed, this raises the more general issue that, when trains arrive at the end of their journey, time has to be sufficient to enable them to be made available to

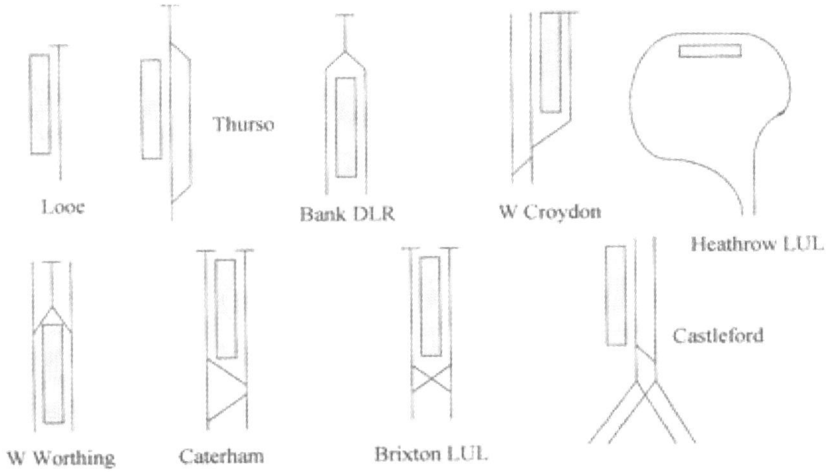

Figure 4.15 Different Types of Rail Terminus Layout in Britain

operate in the reverse direction. The necessary time for turning depends on train type and infrastructure at the turning site. A change of driving direction will require various procedures to be undertaken, ranging from closing down one cab and accessing the other, to safety checks, such as testing the brakes.

With locomotive-hauled services, this can be a minor problem, as either the locomotive which arrived with the train has to be uncoupled, run round it, and recoupled at what was the rear (which is done at Thurso (see Figure 4.15) for "land cruise" excursion trains), or another locomotive has to be provided. The strategy adopted has a direct impact on the track layouts required because, if another locomotive has to be provided, it needs to be parked somewhere beforehand. The short sidings for locomotives just outside termini that were required in steam days have generally disappeared, as a knock-on benefit of multiple-unit train operation.

Side-reversing sidings (such as at West Croydon) are common but should be avoided, as they lead to conflicts – for instance, in that example, arriving trains have to cross opposing services, and may therefore delay following ones. The centre-reversing arrangement of West Worthing avoids all these conflicts, and traincrew can reverse the train at their leisure – although there can be something of a delay if the train has to be checked by staff to be empty before entering the siding. Where centre reversing occurs in a platform track, it is preferable if this provides departing passengers with trains on opposing sides of the same platform, such as with the new platform 5 at Crystal Palace, London (see Figure 4.16b).

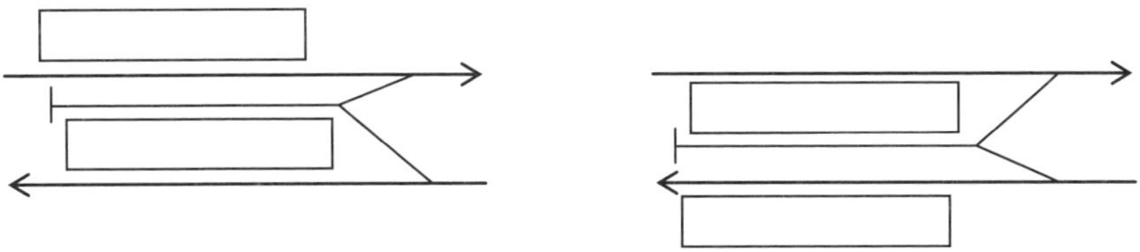

Figure 4.16 Alternative Arrangements for Centre Reversing Tracks
(a) arrival platforms shared; (b) departure platforms shared

A pair of crossovers (such as at Caterham) is normal at the end of a double-track line, although the higher-maintenance option of a scissors crossover has been used at Brixton, where the line is in tunnel and where the higher costs of construction outweighed this.

Other more unusual layouts include loops (although these are quite common in tram systems), awkward movements in remnant layouts (although at Castleford this enables all trains to use a platform adjacent to, and accessed by a ramp from, local shopping facilities) and other locations where access from a single platform face is required (e.g. Cronulla, NSW, Australia – see Figure 4.17).

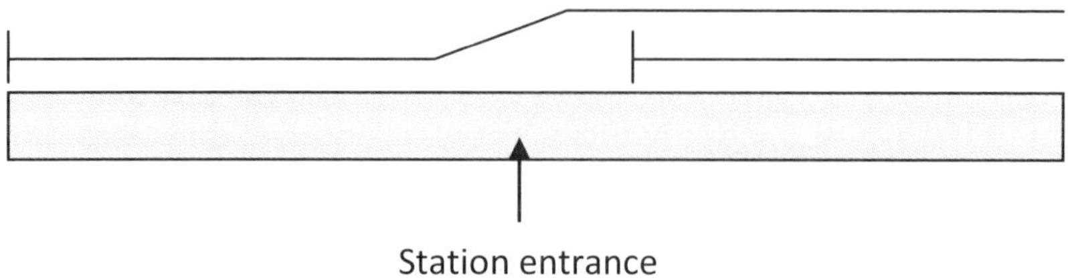

Figure 4.17 Multiple Tracks Accessed from the Same Platform (Cronulla)

The manner in which platforms are used within a timetable also affects line capacity, since only some train movements in the station throat are conflicting. In countries with left-hand running (such as Britain), platform occupation should ideally be in sequence, starting with the platform furthest on the right (for the arriving train); this means that subsequent trains can enter their platforms without conflict with the first arrival, which can then depart without conflicting with yet later arrivals. When all the platforms have been used in turn, just one major conflicting movement is then created as the first train of the next batch has to cross all other lines to reach its platform. Of course, on systems with right-hand running, the sequence of platform usage needs to be reversed.

Constraints with the station throat, however, can actually be the critical constraint in some track layouts – for instance, if there are relatively many platforms. Grade-separation of approach tracks can be valuable here, potentially splitting one large fan of tracks into two smaller ones, but the cost of undertaking grade-separation in inner urban areas may be prohibitive.

The complexity of track layouts such as those shown in Figure 4.18 is a direct balance between the needs of operators and maintenance staff: Llandudno Town is entirely dependent upon the functioning of two individual but separate turnouts, which is relatively-risky in operational terms (even an asset failure rate of only 0.1% for both of the critical points could leave the station without service for 16 hours per year). This may be satisfactory at a quiet terminus, but approaching London Waterloo (Britain's busiest station, with c. 100mppa and train services of up to 70tph in each direction at peak times), the operating and commercial consequences of failure are unacceptable. Instead, it is worthwhile spending considerable money on the maintenance of very complicated pointwork, which minimises the impact of any failure and maximises the chance of finding another route or platform almost immediately.

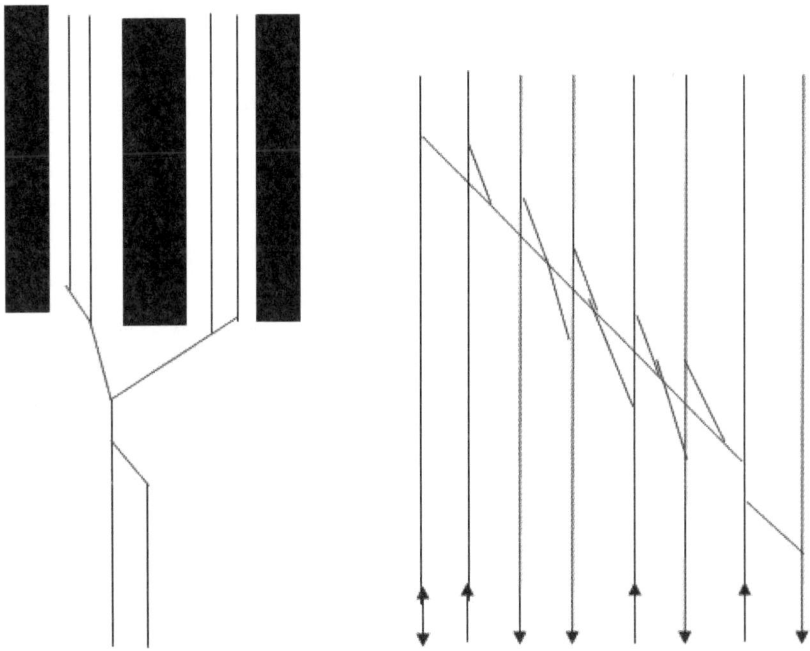

Figure 4.18 Extreme Examples of layouts with (a) No Flexibility (Llandudno Town) and (b) Great Flexibility (London Waterloo)

The distance and speed of pointwork also has direct impacts upon the timetable, whether at termini or at stations en route. Modern trains accelerate and brake more quickly than earlier ones, so can easily be travelling at 50tph at the platform ends. Pointwork with lower speeds can therefore be a constraint, not only for stopping trains, but for non-stopping ones, which may catch up those slowing for the stop. At termini, sufficient time must be allowed for trains not only in the platform, but also for them to run between the platform and the conflict point, which would normally be several hundred metres away - but could be rather further.

As an example, the local service between Gospel Oak and Barking in North London runs between a single platform at each end (although both stations have more complicated layouts with platforms on other lines), but that at Barking is reached by 1km of single line. As well as the time needed in the platform at Barking, a further six minutes is needed for the train to travel each way along this single track, plus a margin of extra time to ensure robust performance. With trains running every 15 minutes, this gives little flexibility in running times, should timetablers wish to amend these, in order to avoid conflicts with other train services elsewhere on the line. Trains cannot arrive at Barking much earlier (because the previous train would not have left) nor much later (because this would leave insufficient turnround time at the terminus).

4.3 Summary

The capacity of a railway line can be defined in a range of different ways, from the technical headway calculated by a signalling engineer to the operational headway used on a day-to-day basis, which includes an appropriate proportion of slack. The capacity of a railway system, however, can be quite different from this, as it will need to take into account the capacity of the other elements of the railway e.g. rolling stock, stations etc.

Variations in train performance lose capacity, which is therefore directly impacted by the details of the timetable. An increased number of tracks therefore enables a greater increase in capacity, as trains can be grouped together to minimise the 'white space' between them. Junctions, passing loops and termini all have detailed impacts on line capacity, which need to be considered during the infrastructure planning stage as well as during timetabling. Ideally, bottlenecks should be avoided, and the railway should be planned to operate trains simultaneously, more like a pipeline.

5 Personnel Planning

5.1 Introduction

Personnel planning is about allocating the staff resources for the trains to be run. It is important to all transport companies because staff are a major element of total costs (perhaps around 2/3 in the railway); even on high-speed lines where the need efficiently to use the capital value of the trainsets completely overwhelms many other costs, staff costs remain an issue for the planner. Personnel planners must take into account a series of conceptual constraints e.g. safety, staff depot locations and the competence/training levels of individual members of staff. However, personnel planning is further constrained by a number of framework conditions, including national legislation about the work environment and holiday regulations, and central collective agreements and company specific agreements with trade unions.

Most countries have legislation about health and safety at work, which covers both equipment and the working hours of staff, which tend to be more onerous for those in safety-critical environments, such as the railways. These may regulate the maximum amount of time between breaks, and the minimum amount of time between shifts, but most railways also have a safety competence system which requires staff to be trained for particular tasks on particular types of equipment and rolling stock. However, the rules about working hours are perhaps the most important ones for personnel planning.

The agreements with the unions for train drivers (NLF in Norway) and other specific railway workers (NJF in Norway) are also very important. The agreements include various forms of wage supplements affecting the costs of the plan. There are also protocols and notes from meetings between company and unions of importance for personnel planning. In addition to current laws, rules and agreements, today's driving patterns and depot structure etc. also effectively make more framework conditions.

Different railway companies will also have different views about the need for different types of shift e.g. short ones to cover peak periods, long ones to maximise the number of days off for staff, and split shifts. Split shifts require a member of staff to work for several hours, before having a non-trivial break and then working several more hours. They may enable staff to work productively in both commuting peaks, but effectively do not give them complete freedom of the time off in between – unless staff live very close to the depot. The time during the break (which may be as long as 4 hours) may be paid at full pay, half pay, or not at all, depending upon the agreements negotiated with staff.

The number of constraints associated with the railway has led to various attempts to computerise this process; as long ago as 1994,Wren et al. showed that planning of train drivers is more complicated than planning of bus drivers.

5.2 The Personnel Planning Process

There are two key elements of the personnel plan:

(i) Development of shifts which cover the operation of all the trains in the timetable, and provide sufficient time for training etc.;
(ii) Development of a roster of shifts, which enables sufficient holidays, rest days and time off to be organised between those shifts.

The first of these is a non-trivial problem if the duration of the journey means that a change of crew will be required en route, because the number of options can rise very quickly. As a result, specific locations (obviously including those places where traincrew are based, so start and end their duties) are normally identified as appropriate places to change crews. But there are other reasons to minimise the number of options. First, this means that complexity is reduced, which may be critical when the service is disrupted. Secondly, a proportionately-lower number of spare crew will be needed if there are fewer potential places to manage (Harris, 1988).

NS Reizigers in the Netherlands use three main criteria for evaluation of a personnel plan. These are:

- Feasibility: This states if the plan is likely to work in practice, i.e. how robust it is to delays and other unforeseeable incidents like absence due to illness.
- Efficiency: (as measured, for example, by the percentage of productive time in duties). Productive time is the time used for train driving, taking rolling stock in and out of depots and supervising it in stations etc. Non-productive time is time to move between duties/tasks, paid and unpaid breaks, movements by train between tasks/duties and turn-up time/time to leave. It may be difficult to average more than 50% real efficiency (driving trains in revenue service) across an entire roster.
- Acceptance: This is a qualitative goal referring to the probability of the plan to be accepted by the drivers.

Figure 5.1 A New Driver is Brought to the Train in Mannheim, to take it out of Service

During planning available resources are distributed across:

- Trips (i.e. duties with active trips)
- Days off (i.e. extra days off, days off during the week and days off in roster)
- Framework duties (i.e. not allocated to a specific task)

Resources for staffing trains are laid down in duties and rosters, and based on train production volumes. Personnel planning at a tactical level is in Norway done yearly, with half-yearly adjustments at timetable change periods. The planning starts with developing duties for train crew. This process is according to a defined procedure which will require union involvement at some stage. Duties are then combined into rosters, which are work plans for a given number of weeks, mostly four. The permanent roster sets out a combination of duties which satisfy legal requirements. Thereafter duties are adjusted and adapted for holidays, training, periods of track construction work, and other deviations from the original plan, to produce a weekly roster; this may also attempt to spread morning, afternoon and night work more evenly between drivers.

A key task is to calculate the "establishment" i.e. the number of staff required to cover the workload. This is a function of the number of diagrams to be worked every week, divided by the number of duties per week in a particular roster. Depending upon local conditions, Sundays may be either included in, or excluded from, the "normal" working week. Changes to the type of duty may also affect the workload; as this book went to press, London Underground staff were in dispute with management about the number of extra staff and/or money needed to cover duties after the proposed introduction of 24-hour running at the weekends.

Spare duties (or "Cover Turns") will also be required to cover both for known shortfalls (e.g. holidays) and unknown ones (e.g. on-the-day sickness). Annual leave may have to be rationed by month, if the railway is not to run out of drivers during the school Summer holidays. The increasing multi-racial and multi-cultural nature of staff should help here, as different staff may wish to have time off around festivals for a range of religions, which helps to spread out leave requests around the year.

As is common also in other countries (Jorna et al. 2005), when duties and rosters have been compiled, the final work plan then needs to be notified to personnel at least 14 days in advance, although employers and unions may sometimes agree on a shorter notice period. The process is shown in Figure 5.2.

Staff often have some input into the process. For example, drivers (particularly the more senior ones, or trade union representatives) may (in some circumstances) be able to request specific turns in specific weeks. It is also relatively common for staff to swop shifts, or entire weeks of shifts, between themselves, in order to fit in domestic commitments (e.g. childcare or the working hours of spouses). However, any such swops need to be agreed with the roster clerk, and must satisfy safety requirements such as time off between shifts.

If they cannot be accommodated by staff booked to be spare, all changes after a personnel plan is fixed are likely to require overtime pay. In Norway, this is based on the Working Environment Act, saying that you shall know the work plans at least two weeks in advance, if not otherwise agreed. Short term duty changes are made to cover for unmanned duties because of absence, holidays or other tasks. Then plans are carried through, and documentation of work done is sent over for payment calculations.

Traincrew duties normally show the times for train operation in service, times for taking rolling stock in and out of depots and other tasks planned to be done; it is a list of tasks to be done by one person during one duty. The other type of duty is a frame duty, reserve or cover turn, in which it is only decided within which given times you have to work. Planning work duties are often

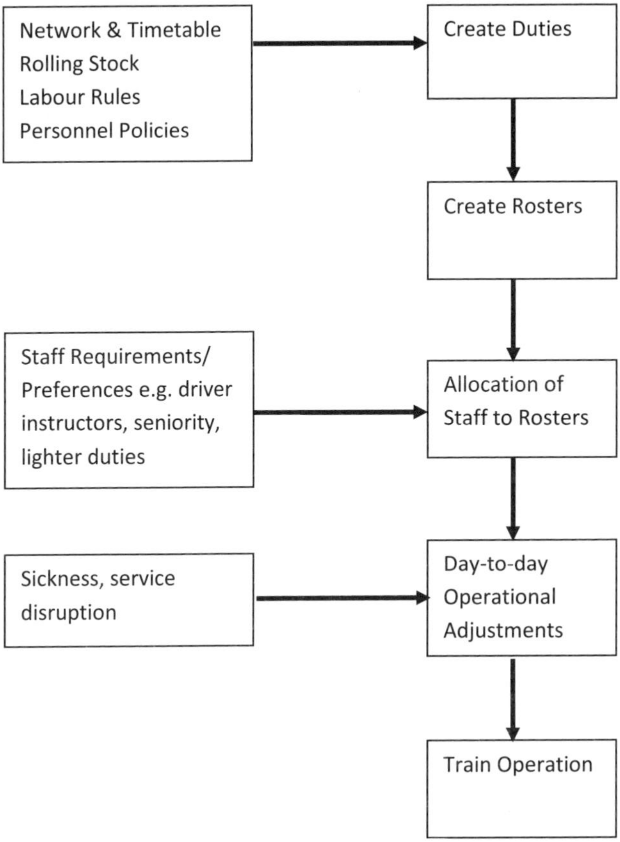

Figure 5.2 Principles of Personnel Planning

developed using a line diagram ("strekliste"). A line diagram is a graphical representation of duties (Figure 5.3), all of which have a defined starting and ending time. Duties are made according to the Working Environment Act and agreements between employers and unions. For instance, there are likely to be agreed durations for the time required to start up and check a train before taking it out of the depot in the morning, or for closing down one cab, walking to the other end of the train, and starting up the train from the other cab, when trains have to reverse.

A roster is a combination of duties (Figure 5.4). The roster is often made locally, with strong personnel involvement. The roster is a work plan showing which duties should be done on any specific day. A roster is normally for a number

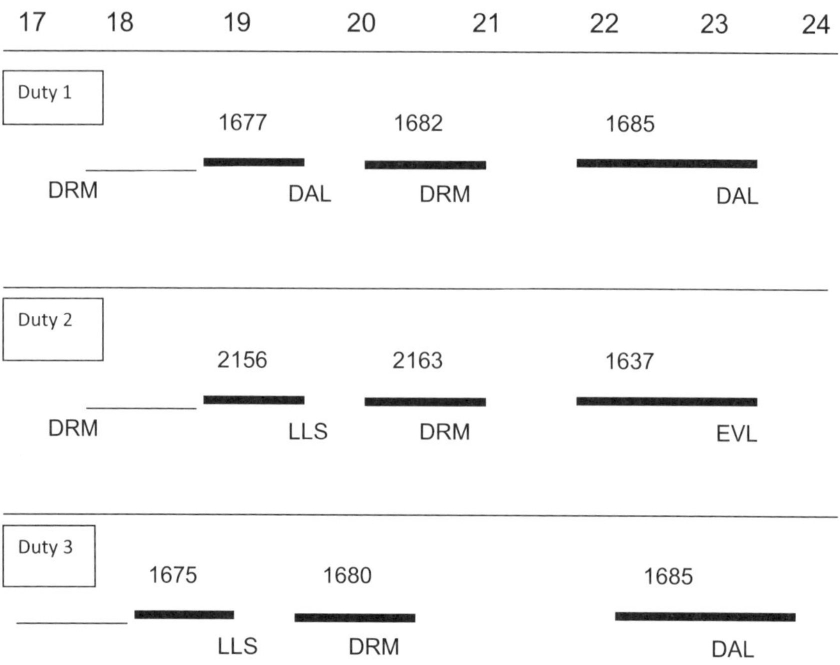

Figure 5.3 Example of a Crew Line Diagram ("strekliste")

of weeks, often two to four weeks, which might include two weeks of morning duties and two weeks of duties later in the day. The work plan also shows days off and times for the start and end of duties. Rosters need to be set up to ensure that the average number of duty hours per week fits the agreement with the unions, although there will be some variation between weeks: an average of 37.5 duty hours a week might include as much as a maximum of 48 hours for a single week.

A greater understanding of human factors is now pervading the construction of rosters. For instance, international research has shown it to be less strenuous to have the longer shifts at the beginning of a series of duties. The risk for exhaustion increases with long shifts in the end of a work period (Ashton and Fowler, 2005). Care must also be taken when requesting staff to work overtime, in order to ensure that they still have the required number of days/hours off between shifts. It is also known that repeating the same duties day in, day out can lead to boredom (which has an associated safety risk); on the other hand, large changes in the start time of shifts for successive days lead to disrupted sleep patterns, which also has safety implications.

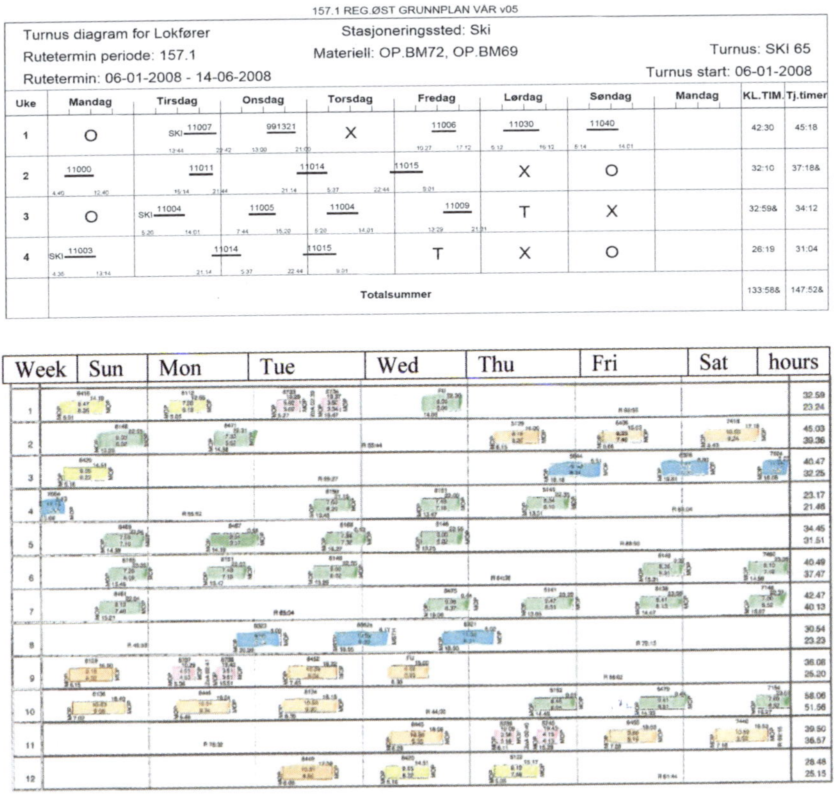

Figure 5.4 Examples of Rosters
Note that the days shown in pink are split shifts

5.3 Depot Sizing and Spare Cover

Traincrew employees are usually allocated to a specific depot (in Norwegian, "tjenestested/stasjoneringssted"). The depot is a fixed point for the personnel. A duty starts and ends in the depot, unless an overnight stay outside the depot is planned (which is not normally appreciated either by staff or management). The depot pattern ("stasjoneringsmønster"), i.e. how many staff are allocated to each depot, is therefore an important constraint for personnel planning.

At a strategic level, the concept of depot pattern has several impacts. It includes where personnel are based, how many are based in the different depots, and how permanent these conditions are over time. Over a longer time-period, depot patterns may be adjusted, for example by recruitments, and how vacancies are filled.

For some freight companies, where traffic flows are relatively infrequent, remote signing-on may occur. This enables a driver to ring into a control centre to confirm his/her availability for work, but that may then be followed by them having to drive to a particular depot or set of sidings to pick up or take over a train. Clearly, safety protocols need to be put in place, as the historic face-to-face check of staff by the depot clerk to ascertain fitness-to-drive does not directly occur in this method of operation.

As noted above, a given train service needs a certain amount of duty hours linked together into duties and then combined into rosters. However well rosters are constructed, it is unusual to be able to use individual drivers for more than about 2/3 of their duty time, once the need for safety briefings, meal breaks etc. is taken into account. Even within that, not all the time is really productive – for instance, a driver may be at a station at the end of the line, waiting for the appropriate return departure time.

Nevertheless, in order to ensure an adequate staffing of all trains, train operating companies need a reserve in addition to the demand that is directly implied by the train service. The reserve needs to cover for various forms of deviations in train production, and for absence as sick leave, holidays, courses and safety tests. To ensure staffing of trains in the short-term perspective, there is a need for a reserve to cover for upcoming deviations, for example sick leave. To ensure staffing in the longer-term perspective, there are other needs e.g. to send personnel to training courses to uphold formal certificates, to have instructors for various types of training, and for doing other tasks where there is a need for experience from train crew. On the other hand, if there is no absence, and all rosters go as planned, there is no need for reserves, and traincrew thus allocated will land up sitting around at the depot, which again is appreciated neither by staff nor management.

The size of the reserve size is based on experience. In principle, the reserve is an addition on top of the calculated production volume. In practice, reserve is the difference between the available resources and planned duty hours. The reserve may then be over or under the desired quantity, especially on a day-to-day basis, and will vary between depots. The reserve also includes a buffer because of variations in sick leave, personnel quitting or moving to other positions within the company, and the volume of courses/ training. Many depots run without a proper buffer, assuming that staff on overtime will make up any shortfall; this is OK in theory, but gives a problem if the staff do not wish to do so.

The reserve may be expressed as a reserve percentage, but it is important to understand that the reserve percentage should be calculated as a reserve divided by the total personnel resources: a reserve of 15-20% might be reasonable. This means that the total amount of time actually spent driving within an entire roster may be about half the total time available (2/3 less 15-20%).

Available personnel resources are reduced during weekends. Overall, there is also of course a reduction in train service at week-ends, but not for all types of service; for instance, there are likely to be more engineering trains to operate. In total this means that week-end train production is a resource challenge.

There are also likely to be changes in personnel requirements at different times of year. On commuter lines, demand will be lower in the Summer months and, in some countries (including Norway), there is a reduced train service during the Summer; however, the train service reduction may be less than the reduction in available resources during the Summer period. The period of reduced train service is also shorter than the personnel holiday period. On some lines (for instance, in the British South West) the train service, and number of passengers, also increases during Summer, precisely at the time at which staff want to take holiday. Restrictions therefore have to be put in place, in order to ensure that sufficient staff are available – but the staff also need to be provided with their annual leave entitlement. Thus a major event in the Summer (such as the 2012 London Olympics) disturbed traincrew rosters for the entire year, as holidays were either brought forward or delayed.

Ideally, of course, staff availability is scaled up and down exactly with traffic requirements, although specific problems may occur e.g. on Summer Saturdays, which is a peak day for holiday rail travel by passengers, and also for holiday travel by members of staff. Figure 5.5 illustrates a possible summer holiday situation with reduced production. The question is whether total train service decreases so much during Summer that it can be covered by reserves. The grey area here, where demand surpasses the number of available staff, represents the problematic area, which may need to be covered by overtime, if service cancellations are not to occur.

The Summer production volume may be changed stepwise, so that you go from full production to the reduced summer production via an intermediate production level. Figure 5.6 shows a Summer holiday train service production with a stepwise down- and up scaling of production volume during summer. Here the grey area illustrates a situation where the demand for personnel exceeds the number of available resources. One response to this might be

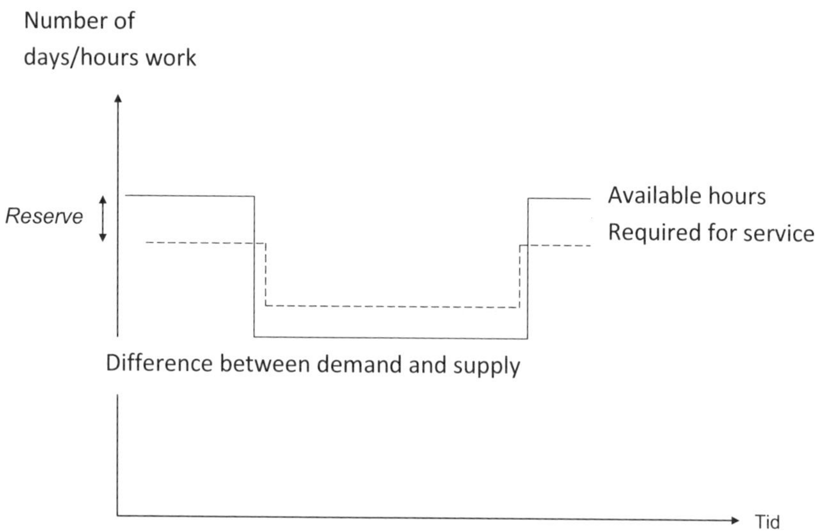

Figure 5.5 Principles for Holiday Personnel Situation

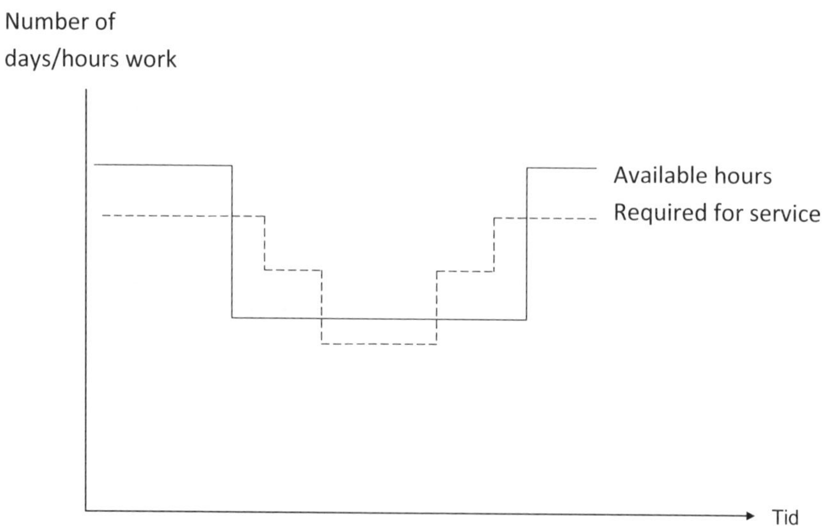

Figure 5.6 Stepwise down- and up scaling of summer train service

to reduce the size of the reserve needed to cover for sick leave and other absences, although this would make the resource situation more vulnerable to service disturbance or sickness.

From the employer's point of view, it is desirable to have a holiday system that generates as little demand for overtime as possible. This means that the grey areas in Figure 5.5 and Figure 5.6 should be minimized, but this is only possible after a consideration of demand, the number of employees and the holiday law regulations.

The reserve, illustrated in Figure 5.7 as the difference between available hours and production demand, can be divided into one part that can be planned, and one part that cannot. Activities that can be planned include personnel on courses, used as instructors etc. Sick leave and other things where the demand appears later than 14 days ahead, cannot be planned.

It is common not to have planned absence in periods of extensive holidays, such as those at New Year or around religious festivals. Yet you need a reserve to cover for absence that cannot be planned.

Real shortages in traincrew have been added to the generic sketch of Figure 5.6, and are marked in Figure 5.7 with a vertical arrow. The shortage is partly due to demand for more personnel than available for driving planned trains (grey area in Figure 5.7), but also to have a certain reserve also during holiday

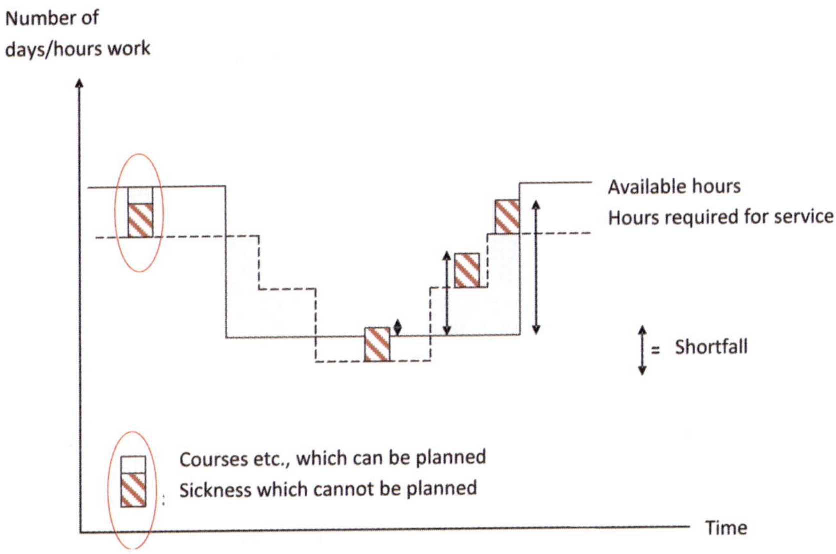

Figure 5.7 Illustration of Shortage with stepwise down- and up scaling of Production Volume during Summer

period (the slanted red lines). The real shortage is therefore equal to the apparent surplus or shortage and the need for a minimum level of reserve. Here it is assumed that you only need reserve to cover for sick leaves and other non-planned leaves during the holiday period.

Because train drivers and conductors have different job functions, the requirements for the role are different – and so often are the restrictions imposed for safety reasons. For instance, most countries have regulations determining the maximum length of a shift, the minimum time between shifts, and the maximum time before a break is required. However, these regulations may differ between different traincrew roles, which then means that the planner has to ensure that different (potentially conflicting) requirements are met. In order to save costs, it can appear advantageous to use the different rules associated with different jobs, but this can lead to disarray during service perturbation, as a train may have a driver available, but no guard, or vice versa. "Full crew working" (in which driver and conductor spend the entire shift working together) is to be recommended, if high levels of performance are required. On the other hand, staff who are technically not essential (such as catering and cleaning staff) may reasonably be used to their maximum extent (which is likely to be greater, because of the non safety-critical nature of their job).

As with rolling stock planning, some railways are inherently more efficient than others. Britain's East Coast main line serves Newcastle (3 hours from London), providing ideal working days for traincrew: sign on, 3 hours in one direction, meal break, 3 hours return, and go home. Catering crew tend to work longer days, undertaking the whole London – Edinburgh journey (4.5 hours) and return. On the other hand, the journey between London and Manchester, on the West Coast route, takes only 2 hours 10 minutes, giving insufficient time for two round trips per shift but not enough work per shift if only one round trip is completed. Inter-working staff with the London – Birmingham route (1 hour 30 minutes) increases staff efficiency but potentially at the expense of greater knock-on delays when there are problems.

For freight operation, it may be possible to organise local trip working within the normal shift lengths of staff, with meal breaks undertaken whilst local operatives are loading or unloading the train. However, for long-distance freight as with the inter-city passenger examples given above, yards may not be at useful (e.g. 3-hour) time separations. It may therefore be necessary for the train to stop specially for crew changes, either at passenger stations, yards/sidings at which no traffic is to be picked up/set down, or even at intermediate signals on running lines. There is thus something of an iterative process between the exact speed/timings of freight trains, and where they will need to stop for crew purposes. In more remote areas, where such changes are not practical, off-duty staff may travel either in the rear cab or in a passenger carriage within the train, with staff changing over at a specific clock time whilst the train is still moving.

Figure 5.8 GBRf Traincrew Change at Broxbourne, England on an Engineers' Train

5.4 Training and Authorisation

To ensure the high standards of safety required by operating heavy and/ or fast-moving trains carrying potentially a couple of thousand passengers, railways are required to provide a rigorous system of driver training. It typically takes 9-12 months to take someone "off the street" before they can become a fully-fledged train driver. During this period, a huge amount of knowledge and skills have to be imparted, in order to develop a member of staff who is going to concentrate every day and deal appropriately with any issues that may arise. Basic safety and operating procedures can take several months to master, after which potential drivers turn their attention to the specific work they are likely to undertake.

Most countries have a system of certification for safety-critical staff including traincrew. Staff need to prove they have a level of competence before they are permitted to operate trains, and this reflects the cost and time involved in their training. The authorization to work is given by a railway organization (often a train operating company), and includes (among other things) which types of rolling stock the driver can drive, and on what lines. This provides another area of complexity for the operational planner, since the apparently-obvious solution of replacing a train of type X with one of type Y may require several days' "conversion" training of several hundred traincrew, so that they can all be familiarised with the operational and minor maintenance details of a different train type.

Figure 5.9 Need for Traincrew Familiarity with Rolling Stock: Train Driver Checking Fault on HST, Swindon, Britain

The authorisation to work on particular lines is particularly important in countries such as Britain where 'route knowledge' is needed by the driver because full information on line speeds, where to brake etc. is not provided by the signalling system. This is particularly onerous where the network to be driven is complex (see Figure 5.11) and/or for freight operations, where many services may be relatively infrequent, cover long distances and be more subject to diversions when running overnight and at weekends. Equivalent arrangements are made for guards/ conductors, with TOCs maintaining a register over who is certified for service on which types of rolling stock and on what lines.

Mastering knowledge of particular routes was traditionally undertaken by accompanying experienced drivers on trains on the route, but that rarely allowed practice in emergency situations. Most railways now use simulation in driver training centres (as per Figure 5.10) to deal both with general issues such as train breakdown or a tree on the line, and line-specific ones such as particular gradients or changes in line speed[1]. Planners involved with a new line need to remember that their work must be completed sufficiently before the commencement of service that time for driver training remains.

Figure 5.10 Train Simulator used for Driver Training

Where networks are extensive, the time taken for driver "route learning" can be considerable e.g. 6 weeks. This is quite a cost for the TOC to bear, when the driver is already competent in the safety, maintenance and general operations aspects of the job. Until the driver has passed his/her route knowledge for a route, (s)he is unable to drive on it – except usually at minimal speed (e.g. <30kph) in emergencies. One solution to this problem is to divide traincrew into "links", with junior staff only knowledgeable about key routes and/or

[1] Note that, whilst such issues may be marked along the lineside, any markers show where the changes are, and not where drivers need to adjust to them e.g. by braking

those near the depot, and senior staff available to work more widely across the network. This enables staff to get through the initial training programme more quickly, and also provides for career progression. Driver supervision will only occur from the more senior drivers, who will also be drawn upon for promotion into management.

In some systems, there may also be a separate (lower/cheaper) grade of drivers for shunting. These drivers may also be on restricted duties due to their (ill) health, or as a result of some misdemeanour.

Traditionally (for instance on nationalised railways), it was not uncommon for drivers to be organised geographically, working any train in their area (inter-city or local passenger, or freight) as required. This limited the training requirement for route knowledge, but maximised it for traction knowledge. More recently, moves towards a more commercial railway have generally split drivers between passenger and freight, which has the reverse effect; some freight train drivers need to have enormous route knowledge (especially since they are more likely to drive engineering trains, into and out of sidings, and at night and at weekends, when 'normal' routes may be unavailable). Worse, some of these routes may be used only occasionally, so it can be easy to lose route knowledge.

Personnel competence on various types of rolling stock and lines are therefore important constraints in planning. Developing and maintaining competence determines training requirements, not least because route or train type knowledge would normally be considered as expired if it had not been used for a year. This can happen if lines are closed for maintenance for even quite short periods (e.g. one week), as particular drivers may miss their opportunity to refresh their knowledge on a service train which may run infrequently, and on which they have not recently been rostered. So not only does the HR function need to ensure that drivers are suitably (re)certified, but it also affects other parts of the personnel plan (because you need find senior drivers to help with training, and a reserve of other staff to cover for those on courses) and potentially engineering works planning (which is outside the scope of this book)).

The extent of staff is partly a management decision: a railway will be more robust if its staff can cope with a greater degree of out-of-order running (including on diversionary routes, or into and out of siding complexes), but that costs more in training. Traincrew planners therefore need to remember which depots staff are based at, because each depot is likely to have a default set of routes over which its staff are trained. Trade unions can become wary of

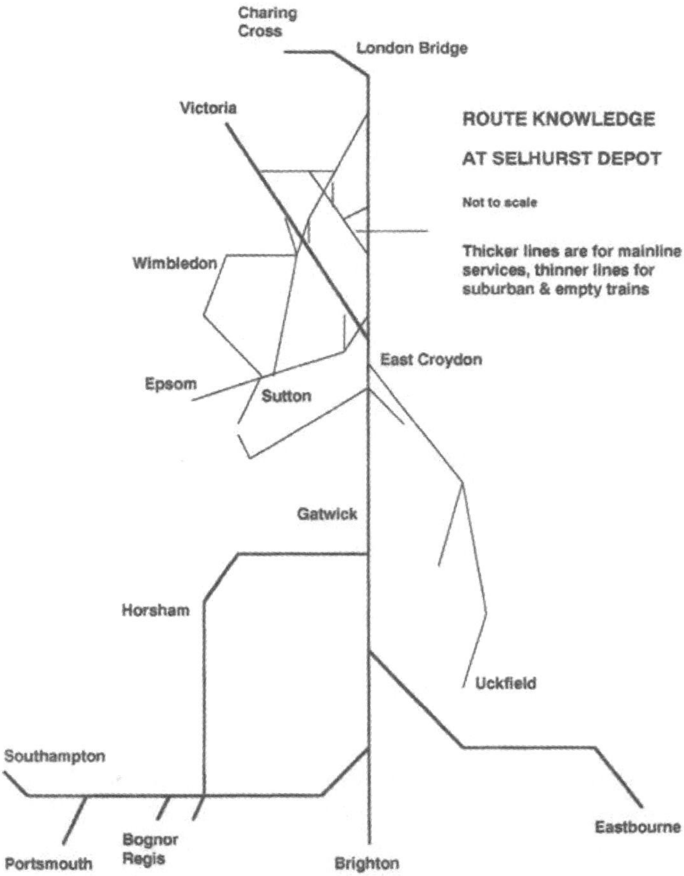

Figure 5.11 Route Network for Drivers at Southern's Selhurst Depot, London

work being transferred between depots, so maintaining a balance of work is important.

However, there are other trade-offs. If staff are unduly limited in their route knowledge, jobs can lose interest, with potentially-significant consequences: boredom with a task can be the beginning of difficulties in recruiting to that position, or even a descent into unsafe working practices. This can be a particular problem in metro railways, where much or all of a route may be underground (therefore with very little visual stimulation). On the other hand, just occasionally solutions arise which resolve staff issues as well as providing improvements for passengers. Traditionally, sleeper trains have required the attendants to travel with the train overnight, and then rest during the day in a hostel hundreds of miles from home; this is not entirely popular with staff, leads to difficulties in recruitment, and costs the railway money. However, there may be solutions. For instance, the duration of the sleep available to passengers on the Paddington – Penzance sleeper in Britain is rather short, as the route is only 300 miles long (unlike on conventional trains, minimising generalised cost on sleeper trains can involve maximising the amount of useful sleeping time). It would therefore be possible to plan the two overnight trains (one in each direction) to meet for an hour mid-way along the route at c. 02:00, during which time the staff might transfer from one train to the other, enabling them to return home every day, and saving the operator hotel costs.

5.5 Number of Staff Required

A key cost determinant of railway costs is the number of staff required, of which traincrew are a major part. Minimising this is therefore important, especially on lines with relatively low income. On-train conductors may be common in rural areas, where no stations are staffed, but a different situation can arise in urban situations, where all stations may have ticket-issuing facilities and ticket gates; here, it may be possible for the train to be operated by one person.

The use of driver-only operation (DOO), however, is not just about trying to save money. Staff need to be provided for customer care and revenue protection duties, so whether these are undertaken by train-based or station-based staff should depend upon the relative train service frequency and how much time passengers spend on that leg of their journey. With 24 trains per hour and 10-minute journey times, metros normally find it more efficient to protect revenue at stations, for instance through ticket gatelines, which may be staffed, or compulsory ticket validation at stations, and a control/fine system for in-train ticket controls. InterCity operations are usually less frequent, and passengers may spend several hours on the train, during which time there is plenty of time for ticket inspection and a higher level of customer care.

DOO actually has other operational benefits, especially in an urban context. With modern train safety systems able to stop the train if anything happens to the driver, the provision of a second person in the cab can lead to less, rather than more, safety, as distractions can occur. At station stops, the involvement of a second train-based member of staff during despatch also leads to another step in the process, and hence a delay of several seconds. Giving the driver full physical control of the train, both when it is moving and when it is stationary, is operationally most efficient, even if (for good customer service or revenue reasons) there is a second staff member on the train.

For freight, consideration is also needed of the other duties that may be required en route. Checking brakes before yard departure or operating level crossings en route will necessitate someone to give the driver assistance, whether they are train- or locally-based.

One of the other periods when staff are not entirely productively employed comes at the ends of the line, when trains are laying over between duties. Many suburban trains would have booked turnrounds of about 10 minutes, which may enable service recovery but leaves insufficient time for the staff to do anything else. On the other hand, longer layovers (which are less efficient for the rolling stock) can enable traincrew to take their designated meal breaks, although difficulties can arise if late arrival means that insufficient time is available for the required break.

When turnround times are very short (not only in metro railways, but some very busy urban termini (such as London's Moorgate), a technique known as "stepping back" is used, in order to minimise any delay generated by the driver having to walk from one end of the train to the other (for which an allowance of 4 minutes would be common). Upon arrival of the train, a second driver or full crew is already waiting at the platform end, able to enter the rear cab and take the train out quickly. This can be essential, in order to maximise throughput of services where the provision of sufficient passenger capacity is critical.

This analysis has generally excluded consideration of other customer service staff, although many trains (especially inter-city ones) may have staff with dedicated duties for catering. Such staff may remain at a fixed point (a buffet or restaurant or, in the case of operators such as Virgin, a shop), or may patrol the train providing refreshments from a trolley. Given the relative expense of rolling stock, it is also not uncommon to find cleaners on long-distance trains; such staff are able to collect rubbish before it becomes overwhelming, and also reduce the amount of time required for turnround.

As can be seen, there is a very large number of constraints on planning rail staff rosters which can, for all but the smallest railway, become impossibly difficult to optimise without IT support. Personnel planning systems used at present include those fromSiscog (Portugal, used by Norwegian and Finnish railways), IVU (Germany, used by DB Regio, SBB Cargo, and Trenitalia) and Quintiq (from the Netherlands, although owned by the French Dassault company, and used by TfL among others, including in the logistics field).

5.6 Summary

Personnel planning is a key element of the operational planning process, and is dependent upon a mix of external factors (such as employment law), the structure of the railway (network and timetable) and the amount of spare cover required by the desired level of reliability, which reflects management decisions. Minimising the number of traincrew is likely to mean more complex rosters, but these are likely to be less reliable.

6 Rolling Stock Planning

6.1 The Decision-Making Process

The acquisition, rebuilding and refurbishment of rolling stock are decisions usually taken at a strategic level, while production of rolling stock rosters and maintenance plans will take place both on a tactical and an operational level.

The consideration of appropriate rolling stock needs to include its sheer capacity, its quality (e.g. what proportion of passengers need to be seated), and what facilities are required (for instance, catering, toilet, luggage, or first-class seating for passengers, or whether freight wagons need to be covered to protect cargos such as road vehicles). Infrastructure constraints will impinge too: some lines have restricted axle-weight limits, whilst others have more or less generous structure gauges[1]. Modern wagons are typically larger than their predecessors, and based on bogies which reduce wear & tear on the track, compared to fixed wheelsets. As usual, there are trade-offs: double-stack container trains are run in some countries (e.g. the USA) but the aerodynamic consequences are significant, and vehicles less stable.

Similarly, double-deck passenger trains can provide more seats per unit length than single-deck carriages, but the increased number of passenger movements

Figure 6.1 Rolling Stock to take Advantage of Modern Infrastructure: (a) bogie hopper wagon, Mengen, Germany; (b) double-deck RER stock, Versailles, France

[1] The loading or structure gauge of the line is the cross-sectional area within which trains must fit, if they are not to foul tunnels and overbridges. Technically, the actual limiting factor is the kinematic envelope, since trains move about whilst running, which can take them outside the loading gauge calculated when stationary.

per doorway tends to lead to significant increases in station stop time, which therefore reduce line capacity. At the highest frequencies (c. 20tph+?) appropriate for metros and busy suburban railways, single-deck trains with many doors and open-style interiors are likely to be more effective.

Railway rolling stock has a long lifespan: 30 years is normal, whilst many railways have rolling stock which is 50 years old (even if it has been refitted inside, so that the passenger interior is rather more modern). The oldest carriages (Type B3) used in Norway are from the 1960s, and the oldest multiple units (Type 69 EMUs) are from around 1970. Albeit as an exception, Britain still runs ex-London Underground 1938 stock on the loading gauge-restricted Isle of Wight line. However, 40-year-old High Speed Trains (HSTs) are about to be moved from top-rank inter-city routes in England to regional express services in Scotland.

Figure 6.2 1970s-built HST at Didcot, England: bound for Scotland in 2016?

Even with component replacement, many train characteristics, like weight, acceleration, maximum speed, air resistance and brakes, are difficult to change significantly after acquisition. Choice of rolling stock therefore is important for train service planning over a long period of time. Maintenance plans and maintenance intervals for new rolling stock are influenced by train design, and requirements from the train operator, manufacturer, maintenance company and authorities (Elliott, 2001).The timetable should be taken as a starting point for rolling stock planning. A rolling stock plan (diagram) specifies train movements during a specified period, i.e. which journey legs in the timetable are to be operated by the same train set. In this plan you can also see where the train set is to stay overnight, what distance is to be covered (potentially important for maintenance) etc.

Only closer to the actual day of production will it be decided which individual train (i.e. train set or a combination of locomotive and carriages) that will be used. On a tactical level, the plan is changed only when lasting changes in rolling stock, infrastructure or timetable structure makes an adjustment necessary. Such changes might include interior refurbishment, rolling stock being swopped between routes, long-term infrastructure work on a line (e.g. a change in line speed over a significant section) or a significant timetable change (e.g. service doubling).

6.2 Determining Rolling Stock Requirements

Once a timetable has been compiled, the next step is to allocate physical trains to each train working. One might start with the first train of the day, then evaluate which departure that trainset might work next, and so on through the day, taking account of various constraints (e.g. similar capacity requirements) and planning margins (especially turnround times). Eventually, all the departures in a timetable will have been covered, and a series of 'diagrams' constructed for various trainsets.

Rather than starting from the first train of the day, however, cost minimisation may make it more sensible to start with peak trains, since these determine the capacity required. Longer trains may be run all day on train workings with fewer passengers, but this may be unavoidable (e.g. if trains are run in fixed formations). Alternatively, it may be possible to strengthen peak workings by joining two trainsets together. It may be necessary to leave trains in sidings between the peaks, but this does not help much either in a financial sense, because trains earn nothing whilst stabled. Other complications may arise if not all trains can run on all lines (e.g. for weight or loading gauge reasons). Juggling these possibilities is the province of the train planner, but matters considerably, because of the sheer capital and associated cost of trainsets (as well as the ≈£1.5m purchase cost per carriage, it should be remembered than an extra trainset in service will also need an extra set of traincrew). An example of a vehicle diagram is shown in Figure 6.3. This shows the locations the unit starts from and runs to in its day's work, with arrival and departure times, before being stabled for the night.

Although experienced train planners can assess a timetable by eye to see the number of trainsets required for service, this can be calculated from a formula. The theoretical formula for estimating the number of trains required is:

$N = 2 * (J + L)/H$, rounded up to the nearest integer

where N = no. of trains required,
J = journey time
L = layover (turnround) time
H = headway.

Ideally, one wants rolling stock to be utilised 80-90% of the time, which provides a balance between cost-efficiency and sufficient slack to maintain performance. However, the sheer geography of railway networks can cause problems – for instance, an hourly service on a line taking 61 minutes to traverse will require 3 trainsets in service, even though they are only used for 67% of the time.

Nevertheless, there are techniques designed to minimise the impact of this problem, and these are collectively based on the inter-working of train services. Importantly, though, the way in which train services are packaged together in franchises or concessions can affect the ability of a train operator to use these techniques.

Cross-Forming

The term "Cross-forming" refers to the interworking of two different train services on the same side of a major city. Consider the network shown in Figure 6.4, which roughly replicates the situation in Britain, with Birmingham at the hub of services from Aberystwyth, Chester and Derby. Using the formula shown above, it is easy to determine that 4 trains are needed for the Aberystwyth service if operated individually, and 3 for the Chester service. Both, however, are relatively inefficient (a measure of efficiency can be derived by assessing the proportion of the round-trip time spent in motion). If trains returning from Aberystwyth are instead sent next to Chester (and vice versa), a complete trainset can be saved from the circuit. Given the typical costs of operating a railway carriage (leasing and maintenance costs are each typically c. 10% of the purchase cost per year), and that most trains are formed of several carriages, the impact on cost-effectiveness of saving a whole trainset is obvious. Further

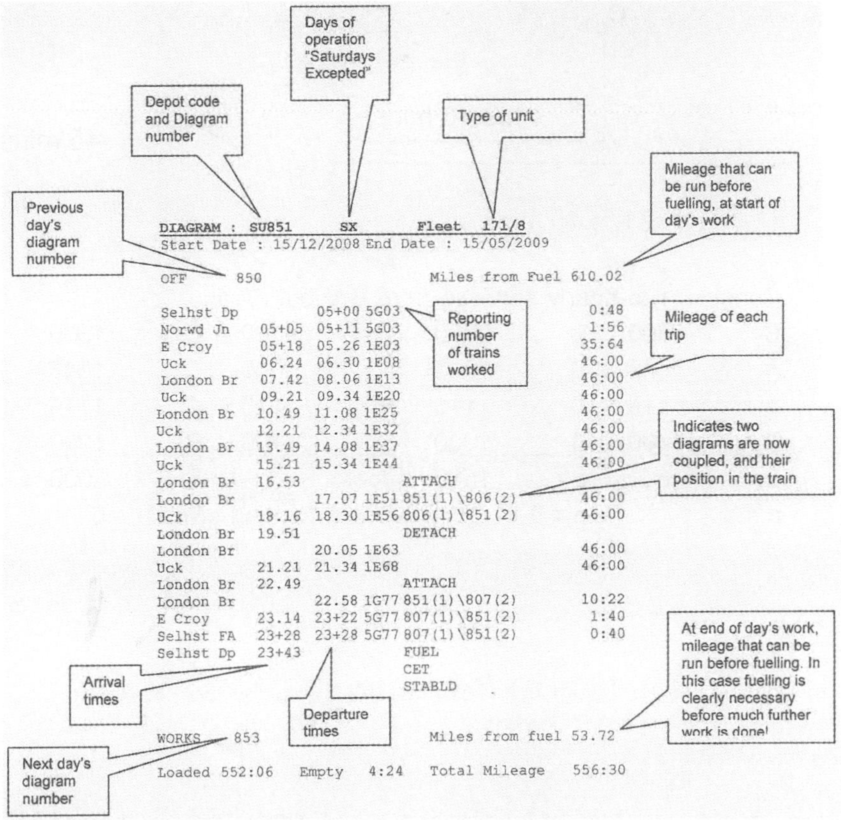

Figure 6.3 Typical Vehicle Diagram for a Diesel Multiple Unit
This shows the locations the unit starts from and runs to in its day's work, with arrival and departure times, before being stabled for the night.

savings can be achieved from a reduction in traincrew, whilst fewer trains in the system also reduces potential congestion and hence knock-on delays.

However, there is one significant disadvantage with cross-forming, namely the spreading of delays around the network. A problem on one line very quickly manifests itself in problems on the other lines with which the rolling stock is shared. There is a clear balance here between cost-effectiveness and train service punctuality.

This use of cross-forming is designed to address the problem of the inefficient use of rolling stock, a problem which becomes more acute, the less frequent

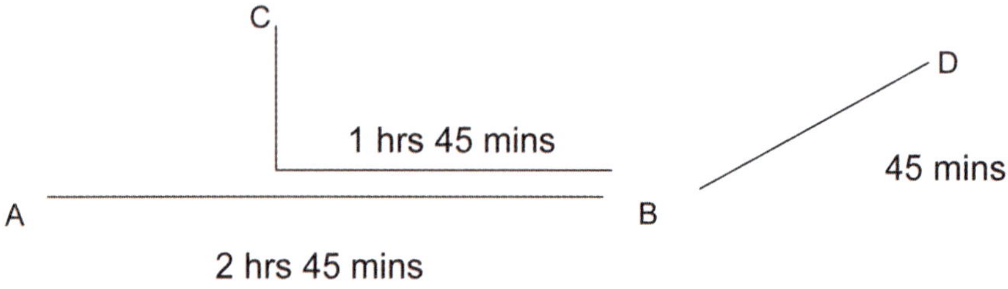

Consider two-hourly services from B to both A and C:

B	0800	B	0900	B	0800	B	1500
A	1045	C	1045	A	1045	C	1645
A	1115	C	1115	A	1115	C	1715
B	1400	B	1300	B	1400	B	1900
B	1600	B	1500	contd.		B	2000
n = 4		n = 3		Cross-forming gives n = 6			

Figure 6.4 Cross-Forming to save Trainsets

the train service. For instance, it is essential for the sparse services North of Inverness, where the Kyle line has only 2-3 tpd; if not used, trainsets could be required to stand idle for hours.

Nevertheless, cross-forming can also be required in order to overcome infrastructure constraints, notably a shortage of platforms: consider the example shown in Figure 6.5. Southern suburban services out of London Victoria only have 3 platforms, but each of the three routes operates a 4tph service. Given the run-in/run-out times of trains at Victoria, the maximum time that a train could possibly spend at Victoria is 15 minutes (the headway) less the run-in and run-out times (as far as the signal protecting entry to the station) (about 2 minutes each). However, there are other constraints on the network, which prevent trains crossing exactly as needed, so trains are unable to return to the branch from which they have originated.

Through-Running

Another method of inter-working train services is through-running. Consider the same cities in the British railway network, but with a slightly-revised timetable specification, this time with hourly services between Birmingham and both Aberystwyth and Derby.

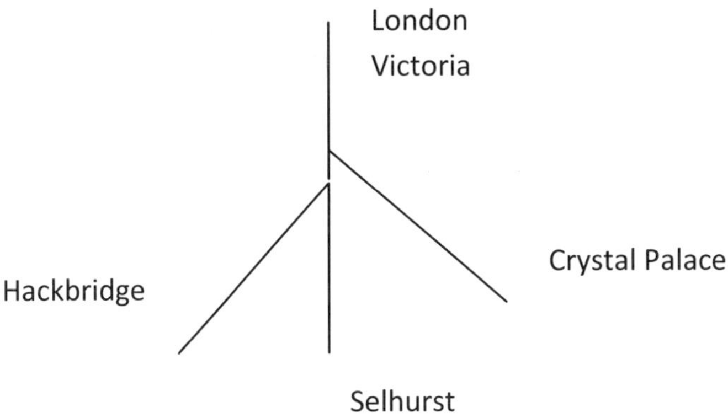

Figure 6.5 Cross-Forming to save Platforms

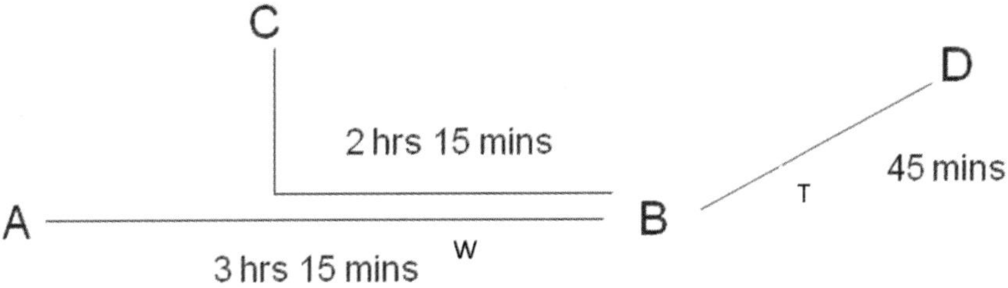

Consider hourly services from B to both A and D:

B	0800	D	0715	D	0715
A	1115	B	0800	A	1115
A	1145	B	0815	A	1145
B	1500	D	0900	D	1545
B	1600	D	0915	D	1615
n = 8		n = 2		Through-running gives n = 9	

Figure 6.6 Through-Running to save Trainsets

The inter-working of train services may not be quite as simple as it appears, however. In practical terms, matching up demand levels (hence train sizes) between different services is rarely likely to work exactly, with compromises having to be made. Demand may not quite be equal in volume – or, if it is, may be comprised of different market segments e.g. different proportions of first-class traffic. Through-running also needs to take into account the impact of maximising the demand or revenue for the new, direct, service – which our theoretical background (section 2) has already highlighted should be a reflection of the net improvement in generalised cost (passengers x journey time saving), not just the greatest number of passengers benefitting.

The removal of an interchange by through-running increases demand, as explained by generalised cost theory. However, that theory also implies that the proportionate increase in demand is greatest for shorter journeys (in the example of Figure 6.6, between Wolverhampton (W) and Tamworth (T), not between Aberystwyth and Derby (which, being further apart, are also likely to have fewer trips in the first place)). This means that train loadings over the central section are likely to rise, potentially above the capacity of the existing service. Options for dealing with this are all unsatisfactory, in one way or another: the provision of extra train capacity adds costs, whilst the failure to do so increases crowding, potentially to an unacceptable extent.

6.3 Rolling Stock Diagrams

A rolling stock diagram shows how to operate planned train services with rolling stock. The diagram shows how many train sets are needed, and which type of rolling stock shall be used for which train departures. Rolling stock plans must ensure that all planned train services are covered within available rolling stock, and with sufficient capacity (e.g. train seats or freight volume) according to demand. The rolling stock diagram should also demonstrate sufficient time for all necessary activities to keep the rolling stock ready for daily operation (including turnround time, the joining or splitting of train sets, cleaning and maintenance breaks). The diagram is based on what is available from the maintenance depots. The goal of rolling stock planners is to find feasible plans that do not unnecessarily drive personnel and maintenance costs, also taking into account the practicalities of operation and expected robustness.

In connection with strategic plans, and as suggestions for timetable plans, simplified diagrams are often made, which give a preliminary picture of rolling stock demand. As a quality assurance to ensure that sufficient rolling stock for the timetable is available, a preliminary diagram may be made, one that for example does not include empty train movements.

A more specific rolling stock plan depends on an established timetable. Even if the train service planners must consider available rolling stock, the process of detailed rolling stock planning often only starts after the requests for train paths have been sent to the infrastructure authority. When the rolling stock plan is settled, the rolling stock planner takes a timetable as a starting point. This timetable must be workable as to track access, so that the planner knows that it is feasible. The timetable contains all train services to be produced, and the planner therefore must provide them with rolling stock. Yet rolling stock planners may suggest changes to the timetable coordinator that are necessary to obtain a feasible rolling stock plan, or may mean considerable improvements to the rolling stock plan. The seat capacity allocated is mainly based on requirements from the marketing or planning department, who should have the best demand knowledge.

All train services in the train graph get allocated by making rolling stock plans (diagrams). The diagrams show train positions in distance and time, in a way similar to a train graph. Figure 6.7 shows movements for two train sets.

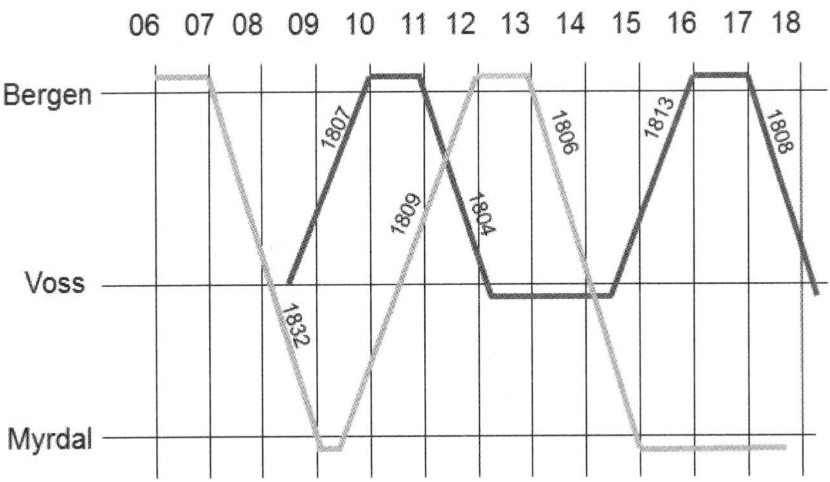

Figure 6.7 Rolling stock schedule in graph (diagram) format
Numbers are the train numbers for the respective journeys

This can be done either manually or in an IT-based planning tool. A complete plan for one day is called a day plan. As well as a standard plan for weekdays, separate plans are usually required for Saturdays and Sundays, but also for Mondays (when trains may start from different locations) and Fridays (when they may finish at different locations). The rolling stock scheduling plan will also need to take into account cleaning requirements (e.g. not all overnight stabling points may have toilet-emptying facilities available), fuelling requirements (most diesel trains have a fuel range of c. 1500kms, which they are likely to cover within 2-3 days), and maintenance requirements (which may be either on a time-based or distance-based regime). However, exactly which individual train is going to run which service on what day, is only decided later on.

Several restrictions must be observed for a rolling stock schedule to be feasible. Naturally you cannot plan for more rolling stock than is available. This may sound obvious, but in practice it is a question about how much of the train fleet you want as a reserve, and this depends upon the type of train and capability of the local maintenance teams: over 90% is achievable for electric multiple units in developed countries, but DMUs will probably only reach 85%, whilst in the developing world (where spare parts may be difficult to source) availability of as low as 50% is not uncommon. The trains must be serviced at defined intervals. The rolling stock schedule must be arranged so that trains arrive at the maintenance depots at these intervals, while at the same time utilizing as much of the defined maximum mileage. This is not as straightforward as it may seem, as there may be relatively few depots and/or not all of them may have the required capability e.g. some may only deal with diesel trains, whilst wheel lathes for reprofiling wheels are expensive and may not be available at all depots.

Indeed, not all locations can be used as train depots. Even where a location does have maintenance facilities, there may be limitations on how many trains may be stabled in stations or depots/sidings, and how long they may be. Strategic changes to the rolling stock fleet therefore may need to be accompanied by investment in stabling facilities. For instance, London Overground lengthened its trainsets from 4 to 5 cars during 2014-15, and this required a new set of sidings to be constructed at Silwood, as the existing depot at New Cross Gate did not have sufficient capacity to accommodate the longer trains.

This can lead to a need to have empty train movements if a train ends up in a place without available depot/sidings facilities. This demand often comes at the end of morning or afternoon peak, and at the end of the service day. These requirements may also change with changes in the fleet. For instance, one of the line ends of the East London Line, at Crystal Palace, has platforms which take 8 cars. In the early days of operation of the ELL with 4-car trains, the last two trains were coupled up in the platform before running back to the depot. When the trains were extended to 5 cars, each had to be run separately, because a 10-car train formation no longer fitted into the platform.

For empty train movements you must ensure that track capacity is available for the actual distance during the period available. During peak hours this may be difficult, because of line capacity; empty train movements during peak hours (at least in the peak direction) are therefore unusual. On the other hand, many infrastructure authorities impose white periods overnight, so that maintenance work can be undertaken. Empty trains may need to be run outside the normal period of service operation, so there can be conflicts with that maintenance activity.

72 - Sundland – 158.2 Grunnplan

Tur	Mandag	Tirsdag	Onsdag	Torsdag	Fredag	Lørdag	Søndag	Til Tur
1	72-0001 508/2 - 513/1 518/2 - 523/1 - 530 - 535 - 538 <EVL>	72-0005 507 - 512 - 517 - 522 - 527 - 532 - 537 <KBG>	72-0022 504/2 - 509/1 - 524/2 - 529/1 - 12264 <DRM>	72-0007 12253/2 - 506/1 - 511/2 - 516 - 521 - 526 - 531 - 536 - 541 <KBG>	72-0004 504/1 - 509/2 - 514 - 519 - 524/1 - 529/2 - 534 - 539 - 12284 <DRM>	72-0601 Vedlike (DRM) <DRM>	72-0716 (DRM) <DRM>	2
2	72-0002 12253/2 - 506/2 - 511/1 - 520/2 - 525/1 <KBG>	72-0001 508/2 - 513/1 - 518/2 - 523/1 - 530 - 535 - 538 <EVL>	72-0005 507 - 512 - 517 - 522 - 527 - 532 - 537 <KBG>	72-0022 504/2 - 509/1 - 524/2 - 529/1 - 12264 - Vedlike <DRM>	72-0007 12253/2 - 506/1 - 511/2 - 516 - 521 - 526 - 531 - 536 - 541 <KBG>	72-0607 508 - 513 - 518 - 523 - 528 - 533 - 540 - 11656 - 11586 <FIL>	72-0712 (FIL) <FIL>	3
3	72-0013 11151/1 SKØ - 11151/2 - 1151/2 - 1110/1 - 1111/2 - 1120 - 1119 - 1128/1 - 1131/2 - 1136/1 - 1139/2 - 1144 - 12202 <FIL>	72-0013 11151/1 SKØ - 11151/2 - 1151/2 - 1110/1 - 1111/2 - 1120 - 1119 - 1128/1 - 1131/2 - 1136/1 - 1139/2 - 1144 - 12202 <FIL>	72-0013 11151/1 SKØ - 11151/2 - 1151/2 - 1110/1 - 1111/2 - 1120 - 1119 - 1128/1 - 1131/2 - 1136/1 - 1139/2 - 1144 - 12202 <FIL>	72-0013 11151/1 SKØ - 11151/2 - 1151/2 - 1110/1 - 1111/2 - 1120 - 1119 - 1128/1 - 1131/2 - 1136/1 - 1139/2 - 1144 - 12202 <FIL>	72-0013 11151/1 SKØ - 11151/2 - 1151/2 - 1110/1 - 1111/2 - 1120 - 1119 - 1128/1 - 1131/2 - 1136 - 1139 - 1144 - 12202 <FIL>	72-0608 12203 - 1107 - 1116 - 1115 - 1124 - 1125 - 1132 - 1135 - 1140 - 2298 - 1145 <MOS>	72-0711 1110 - 1111 - 1120 - 1119 - 1128 - 1131 - 1136 - 1139 - 1144 - 12202 <FIL>	4

Figure 6.8 Example of rolling stock schedule in table format

6.4 Stabling Trains during Day and Night

Local train services are characterized by big variations in number of passengers over the day, largely as a consequence of the demand for work commuting trips during the morning and evening peaks. Therefore there is no need to use all trains in the offpeak periods; and trains need to be stabled (parked) somewhere. The demand for stabling depends on the level of train service provision over the day, with low production giving an increased demand for stabling. The demand for stabling is greatest at night, but stabling also takes place at midday, early in the morning and in the evening. A typical example of train production for a weekday is shown in Figure 6.9.

In Figure 6.9, maximum utilization of rolling stock is planned for the period 07.00 - 09.00 and 15.00 – 17.00. In the period between those two peaks there is a demand for stabling trains. The demand for inter-peak stabling includes both trainsets used for extra peak hour departures and also those trainsets used for doubling train lengths, as it can be helpful to run multiple trainset services during peak periods, but form them of only one trainset offpeak.

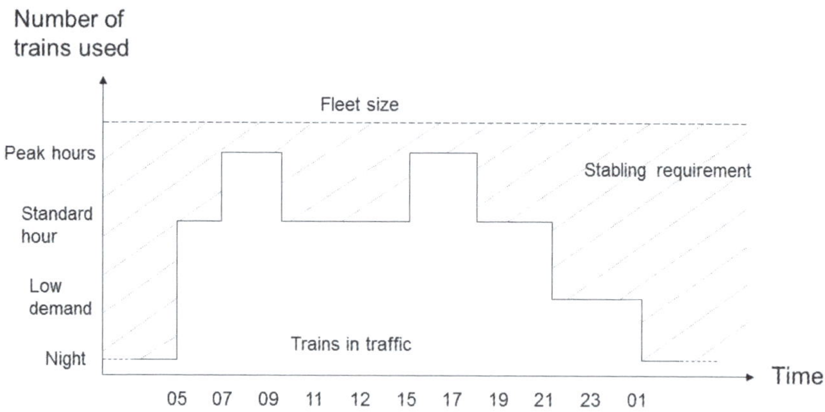

Figure 6.9 Illustrative Daily Profile of Train Service Production and Demand for Stabling

Figure 6.10 Trains Stabled at Macdonaldtown Sidings, Sydney, during the Inter-Peak

Extra peak hour trains may be run for 2-2.5 hours during each peak but it can be the case that they are only required for one journey in one direction; this peakiness incurs substantial costs/loss of profitability to the railway but can provide substantial social benefit, in reducing peak-hour road congestion. During the day, the extra trainsets will ideally need to be stabled somewhere near key city centre stations. However, this is not without its problems, because land is expensive and could be used for other purposes. Because of the willingness to pay for land in city centres, the railway is under pressure to limit the land used for stabling. In the most densely-developed cities (such as Hong Kong), property development over the depots may be considered, whereas in medium-density cities, the railway may resort to unproductive train movements e.g. in London, some trains into Victoria are returned to Brighton (80kms away) during the interpeak, because there is nowhere else to put them.

During the night, it is preferable for trains to be stabled at the end stations of the line, so that they are ready for the first departures to the main city in the morning; this minimises empty train running. The maximum demand for stabling comes during the night, and may include a demand for stabling trains not in regular use.

6.5 Planning the Maintenance Requirements for Rolling Stock

However, the strategy for stabling trains should also take into account the possibilities and requirements for maintenance. Planning must ensure that trains are maintained at the right time, in the right way, according to technical specifications, according to approved work orders, and considering the type of service they are used for (for instance, trains travelling at higher speeds would typically have components maintained to smaller tolerances). Each rolling stock type has a maintenance regime, which may be based on:

- emergency failure;
- distance run since last inspection;
- time since last inspection;
- reliability-centred, based on expected component life.

The first of these is generally viewed as unacceptable, as it leads to failures in traffic and unreliable service (although this may be satisfactory for minor, non safety-critical, defects such as light bulbs). The remaining approaches are all based on some kind of plan, where engineers indicate in advance when they need the trainset back in the depot. The second and third options are predictive, based on standard rules, whereas the last involves a greater degree of analysis, However, all three require train planners to ensure that trains are sent to depots at an appropriate time, for works of different durations: heavy maintenance means larger and more time–consuming operations.

From a train service point of view, rolling stock should be serviced when it is not required for production. In practice, that means evenings, nights, holidays, and partly in the inter-peak period between the morning and evening peaks. A key disadvantage is then that doing maintenance work is more expensive in evenings, nights and holidays than during the daytime, as staff have to be paid more for working anti-social hours.

However, especially as trains become more modular in their construction, a range of activities can conveniently be carried out in the inter-peak periods e.g. cleaning, inspections, and swops of air conditioning equipment or even bogies. Night-time affords even greater possibilities for maintenance, as there is likely to be about 10 hours between the end of the evening peak and the beginning of the morning peak the following day. The level of peakiness of the railway depends upon the range of journey purposes of its passengers, and the impact that any fares policy may have in smoothing demand. Inter-city operators using market pricing can often flatten the trainset resource profile considerably, leaving minor maintenance to be wholly undertaken overnight/ at weekends, with depots undertaking major maintenance during the day, on specific trainsets on taken out of traffic for several consecutive days. On some routes, demand may be highest on Friday and Sunday afternoons, and this gives the opportunity for very major maintenance to be undertaken between Monday morning and Friday morning, still leaving the trainset available for the weekend peaks. This minimizes the total number of trains required to run the service, and adds to profitability.

However, whatever the specific process, rolling stock must be taken out from the schedule when heavy maintenance is to be done. This implies that you have either to have spare rolling stock, or that you can (temporarily?) run the service with a reduced amount of rolling stock.

6.6 Summary

Because trains are relatively expensive, planners need to minimise the requirement for them. Although there are a number of techniques for doing so, these have other implications e.g. on service reliability and passenger demand. The timetabling needs of rolling stock also need to be considered, at least from time to time, in conjunction with the more strategic issues of depot location and train maintenance practices.

7 Performance

7.1 Definitions and the Importance of Performance

Safety should be the over-riding priority in railway operation, but signalling systems and safe railway operating practices have developed over the years, so the potential impact of planners on safety is perhaps limited. However, an exception might be a timetable which meant it likely that train drivers would continuously encounter adverse signals which, human factors analysis suggests, might in due course provide an unnecessary risk.

After safety, punctuality is probably the most important quality factor in railway operations (Fahlén and Jonsson, 2005; NEA, 2003; Seco and Goncalves, 2007). Railway companies underline the importance of punctuality in their visions and goals. That punctuality is a very important quality factor is also confirmed in customer satisfaction enquiries when railways communicate with stakeholders (Gelders et al., 2008). Punctuality is, however, only one among several factors defining transport service quality. For example, Metz (2005) defined journey quality in passenger transport as a function of comfort, predictability, safety and security (presumably after the basic generalised cost-driven elements of journey time and frequency have been satisfied).

Good railway performance is often measured by the two key criteria of punctuality and regularity (as in the proportion of the actual service delivered). These are comparative measures between planned and actual train service. They measure if you gave the customer what he or she has paid for, and if they got their transport at the agreed time. There are several definitions of punctuality in transport. We define punctuality in railway operations as:

Punctuality in railway operations is that train traffic runs according to the timetable

In most countries punctuality is followed up both by railway companies and authorities. Among other things there may be incentives based on punctuality measurements where train operating companies and infrastructure providers must pay compensation if they cause delays. Punctuality may also be a factor in contracts between public authorities and train operating companies (public procurement, "offentlig kjøp").

Good punctuality is important both for passenger and freight rail transport. There is, however, a difference between the two, because most freight customers are at a terminal station, and therefore are most concerned that the goods can be picked up there at the agreed time. In passenger transport, however, customers may face delays en route, and there is more likely to be passenger exchange at intermediate stations.

Delays can be primary or secondary delays. Primary delays are caused by specific incidents, like infrastructure failures, rolling stock failures, weather or the absence of personnel. Secondary delays are knock-on delays caused by other delayed trains through interdependences in the timetable and infrastructure. The exact allocation of cause can be important when it affects monetary compensation, but many delays may be multi-causal e.g. a station stop time was too long because the previous train had been cancelled due a rolling stock fault, so there were more passengers than expected; or a service was incorrectly regulated because one train was running at the wrong time.

Nevertheless, both passenger and freight operators are concerned with the way in which a small delay may lead to other, larger, ones. Typically, as (even quite small) primary delays build up, trains which might have been timetabled to pass in parallel across double junctions may arrive out of course, and have to wait for conflicting moves, creating a further delay. Another example might be when late train arrivals lead to knock-on delays for trainsets, drivers and/or conductors – a complex plan could lead to three late departures resulting from one late arrival, hence our recommendation in chapter 5 for "full-crew" working.

7.2 Why does Performance Falter, and how can Planning Mitigate This?

It is easy to construct train graphs in which the lines do not cross or merge. However, that is an entirely insufficient criteria of success for the timetable planner. It should be remembered that these lines represent the front of where trains are supposed to be but, in reality, they are likely to be several minutes later – or occasionally before.

Delays on a railway typically follow a Weibull distribution (see, for instance, Yuan, in Hansen & Pachl (2008)), with relatively few trains running early (and not by very much), but a significant 'tail' of late trains, ranging far beyond a typical average lateness of 3 minutes into occasional delays of hours (or, apocryphally, days).

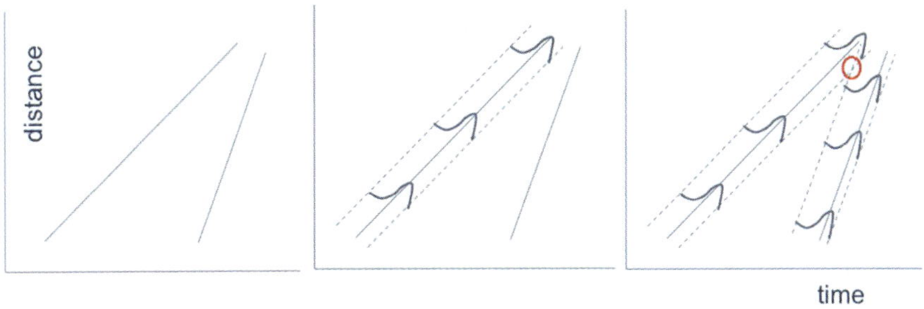

Figure 7.1 Knock-on Impacts of Variable Train Performance

Many timetables include plans which should work in theory but are less likely to do so in practice. Figure 7.1 is a classic example: the two lines on the train graph appear quite separate but are actually likely to interfere with each other from time to time (e.g. weekly). The required inter-working of fast and slow trains on the same track is a key reason why performance may disintegrate, and ratios of output: input delay multiply.

On other occasions, planners may not have thought through the implications of the infrastructure clearly enough. For instance, there may be indirect conflicts at junctions where timing margins are insufficient – or have not been considered at all. As the operation of the railway is organised to be fail-safe, this can lead to knock-on delays.

Because of space limitations, the new platform 5 at Crystal Palace has led to an insufficient overlap for trains entering platform 6. When delays occur to the LOROL departures from platform 5, trains booked to use platform 6 may be unable to enter the platform, because the proximity of the pointwork to the end of the platform provides an inadequate overrun; trains are therefore held at the preceding signal, taking further time to enter: delays are multiplied.

7.3 Follow-up and quality improvement of Train Services

All railway organizations undertake checks, reporting and analysis to see if the train service is being delivered according to the timetable. Information from this process is, among other things, fed back to production plans made during the planning process. There will be an interface to the planning process, because this information is input when plans are revised or made. Follow-ups of train traffic are important for identifying problem areas and improvement activities, and to show the effect of public investment in railways.

Train service quality can be examined by several metrics:
- Required quality (by customer)
- Planned quality (the goal)
- Produced quality (by TOC)
- Perceived quality (by customer)

It is not necessarily the case that all quality aspects are perceived in the same way. Planned quality may differ from required quality for a whole host of reasons, such as a lack of resources to provide what the customer really wants.

Railway performance may also be challenged in other ways. A usual way to for follow-ups of businesses is to look at these three dimensions:
- Internal efficiency – are we doing things correctly?
- External efficiency – are we doing the right things?
- Effects on society

Performance is something done or achieved by an organization that can be measured quantitatively, and then compared to other measurements so that useful assessments can be made. At its simplest train production may be seen as transportation of passengers or freight. Therefore passenger kilometres and tonne kilometres are the usual starting points for measurement of train production, although technically these are only intermediate outputs reflecting the efficiency of the railway, and not its effectiveness to customers. Because of bottlenecks and overload, and limited possibilities for expanding existing network, an efficient exploitation and usage of infrastructure and infrastructure management have become all the more important.

Within the railway industry there is an established tradition for economically-based performance measurements both at an aggregated and at a more detailed level – for instance, cost/train kilometre In addition there are more comprehensive follow-ups and benchmarking studies of punctuality where the aggregated results (e.g. % of trains on time) get particular attention. Comparisons of statistical figures for railway operations of various countries are common, with a gradual trend also to include more "soft" indicators (e.g. % of customers satisfied or very satisfied). Quality in railways is therefore not normally defined in economic terms.

Two main approaches have developed to 'after the event' analysis of train services. Six-sigma lean philosophies concentrate on analysing major outliers in performance (which, in railway terms, usually means incidents or very significant delays), whilst the current authors have usually concentrated on sub-threshold delays, on the basis that these happen much more frequently, and often go un-noticed. But, whichever approach you take in following up train service quality ("forensic train service planning" – see, for instance, Harris et al, 2014)), it is important both to see the big picture and in detail what happened in any deviations from plan. There is therefore a demand for a broad perspective in the follow-up of train production and its consequences, and a demand for good measurements with high resolution. This includes following follow specific train services (train numbers) over a line, and examining any deviations linked to place, train number, cause and infrastructure component.

Several circumstances contribute to making the analysis of railways complex (Nash and Shires, 2000). Activities within railways are multi-faceted, and there are many types of transport services and operational activities. In addition, railways and railway traffic are themselves very complex systems, which give a multitude of information, cost types, and ways of distributing costs. Lastly there are great variations in operational environments within a country, but especially when making benchmarking comparisons between different countries. Among other things, geographical factors and the degree of government involvement are important determinants of performance (as discussed in chapter 2).

7.4 Measuring Performance

Historically, *punctuality* was recorded when staff in signal boxes or stations wrote down actual train timings, to the nearest minute, in a log. Nowadays, the vast majority of punctuality data is automatically gathered, accurate to the nearest second, as trains pass over particular track sections which correspond to timing points. In theory, this means that we now have a higher volume and better quality of punctuality data; however, measurements may need to be calibrated if track circuits do not align exactly with the point at which measurements are supposed to be made. In one example known to the authors, train services arriving at a London terminus were recorded as arriving 53s earlier than in reality because the time recorded was actually of the train entering the platform, not when it actually stopped in it (and certainly not when the doors opened).

Punctuality is normally calculated by comparing trains arriving at the terminal station relative to the timetable. Trains are defined as "non-punctual" when they are more delayed than a certain time limit. A typical value for this limit is five minutes in Europe (Nyström, 2005). The magnitude of this time limit varies, however, between countries and between train products within a country. For instance, in Norway the limit is five minutes (actually 5 min 59 sec) for freight trains and long distance trains, and three minutes (actually 3 min 59 sec) for local trains, Intercity trains and Airport Express trains.

Delays are a concept closely connected to punctuality. In train operations, a delay means a deviation between planned and actual train time (Gylee, 1994). In data collection terms, it is the difference in train punctuality between point x and point (x+1). This means that you may have positive and negative delays, but the latter is often said to be "arriving ahead of time". Delays are often used as an indicator in following up punctuality, often with all delays for a train, a line, a region or country being summed up in delay hours and minutes. However, just because a train is delayed does not necessarily mean that it will be unpunctual, because of the additional time put in timetables specifically to recover from delays.

We have already seen that some delays create others. One way in which this may be measured is by examining the secondary: primary delay ratio of services, either in practice or through simulation (Haugland, 2006). However, the quantity of secondary (knock-on) delays is affected not also by the proportion of capacity used (Network Rail note an exponential increase from a capacity utilisation ratio of around 60%) but also by the complexity of the timetable: for instance, if trains are supposed to overtake, pass, split from or connect with each other. Overall, a reasonable target might be that the secondary (knock-on) delays from a particular incident were no greater than the initial delay (i.e. 1:1), but incidents on congested networks can degrade significantly – we have even seen reports of knock-on delays being 1000 times the original.

A particular indicator focussed on by Jernbaneverket, and used to follow up infrastructure quality, is route availability. This is a percentage calculated thus:

$$\text{Availability} = \frac{\text{hours when line supposed to be open}^{1} - \text{hours not available}}{\text{hours when line supposed to be open}}$$

"Hours not available" in the formula above means the number of hours attributed to infrastructure failures (based on attributions made by Jernbaneverket).

Regularity in railway operations is a measurement to show if the service planned in the timetable is actually produced. This means that regularity drops if a train service is cancelled. Regularity is often coupled to punctuality;

[1] 24 hours per day, less pre-planned white periods

because both relate to the issue of whether the train service has been run according to plan. Sometimes there is also no distinction between punctuality and regularity in the statistics (a cancelled train is counted as delayed). However, there are trade-offs which can be exploited, if incentive regimes are not carefully-calibrated: sometimes operators have a choice, and can either run a train to its destination late, or cancel it.

7.5 Registering and Attributing Delay Cause Data

In addition to time-based punctuality registrations, different causes for delays are usually registered. These are manually-determined, and the code systems used varies from one country to another. For example, Norway uses 15 codes (Jernbaneverket, 2006a), but Sweden 100 (Banverket, 2003) and Britain about 270 (as per the latest version of the 'Delay Attribution Guide'). In most cases staff at stations, signalboxes or train control centres register the cause according to the information available to them, but the shortest delays (e.g. under 1 minute) often go unattributed, since there are simply too many of them. Cause data are presented as the number of instances a delay is registered, categorised by the various codes. Often cause data are coupled to time data in presenting the aggregated time loss (delay) registered for each code. Table 7.1 shows the cause codes used in Norway.

Infrastructure	Traffic	Train Companies	External
1. Permanent way 2. Signals 3. Power 4. Planned works 5. Rolling stock blocking	7. Traffic	81. Rolling stock failure 82. Rolling stock late 83. Personnel absence 84. Station stops 85. Planning prerequisites changed	91. Delayed from abroad 92. External 93. Incidents 94. Unwanted incidents

Table 7.1 Delay codes used in Norway split by main categories (source: Jernbaneverket)

The distinction between delays caused by external causes, and those by infrastructure or equipment failure, may also be more blurred than it may appear. For instance, a failure to maintain trackside drainage properly can lead to subsequent land-slips after heavy rain. Increasingly-extreme weather events are also having impacts on railways; environmental mitigation is becoming important if the railway is to be resilient in the future (Lustig, 2015).

Many question the accuracy of such cause registrations, and how they can be used, and they are often considered to be inaccurate (see for example Lundin et al, 2005; Veiseth and Bititci, 2006). There are several reasons for this. Among other things, there are limitations in the code system itself because the codes used may be characterized as collections, containing many different types of causes. Another problem is that those doing the registrations do not have the total overview of all causes leading to delays. Delays are therefore coded according to the perception of what is the cause based on available information. This is one reason why cause registrations are said by many to be "symptom registrations".

Punctuality statistics for different countries, lines or train services are often compared. However, several factors are making it challenging to compare punctuality figures. First and foremost this is because the way punctuality is calculated varies, and because different time limits are used to define if a train is punctual or not. Whether or not cancelled trains are included is important, as is how averages are calculated. In addition there are differences in the ways data are collected (manually or automatically), and how they are processed, for example if they are rounded up to the minute (NEA, 2003). Comparing cause data between countries is even more challenging because of the different coding systems used. This is both dependent upon which specific codes are used, but also has structural differences e.g. if it differentiates between primary and secondary delays or not.

7.6 Factors influencing Punctuality

There are many different factors and processes influencing punctuality. Olsson, Sætermo and Røstad (2002) distinguished between technical factors (e.g. how the timetable is designed, and the reliability of rolling stock and infrastructure), and "soft" factors such as culture, behaviour and communication. There are also three generic types of delay by cause: delays caused by the train companies, delays caused by the infrastructure provider and external causes where perhaps no one in the railway can be blamed. In Norway and in Britain the train operating company ("self-on-self") delays are often only around 30%, whilst the external delays may comprise 20% (see http://www.networkrail.co.uk/ about/performance/).

Figure 7.2 Risk to both Safety and Performance: Level Crossing: Midgham, Britain

The delay causes recorded give specific insight in what is influencing punctuality. However, several authors have discussed this in more in detail. Both Gylee (1994) and Lindfeldt (2001) split delay causes between primary and secondary causes. As noted above, primary delays reflect the root cause (for example a locomotive failure) whilst secondary delays are delays caused by other delayed trains, for example from crossing movements at passing loops. Gylee (1994) in addition split the causes in "circumstances within and outside company control". This is similar to the principles used in the cause code registration systems used by Jernbaneverket.

Fahlén and Jonsson (2005) pointed to communication and decision processes as fundamental causes for delays, both inside railway organizations and between them. The latter is especially a problem between infrastructure provider and train operating companies, and they found that this is more critical the more TOCs there are. They also underlined the importance of routines for communication and that these are the same for all parts of the railway network. They also pointed to the organisation of the railway industry and access to information as underlying explaining factors. Thus punctuality is also explained from the circumstances in each country, including the conditions of the railway system, but also for institutional, organizational and cultural differences between countries.

The timetable has a special position as to factors influencing punctuality. Casson (2004) for example states that the timetable is the key to optimize performance in a railway network. When punctuality and timetable are discussed, the theme is often how much slack or buffer should be included, and where to put it in the service. During timetable construction, time is added on top of the theoretically calculated run time to compensate for differences in locomotive performance, weather conditions, driving style; and to prevent small delays leading to secondary delays (Hooghiemsta and Teunisse, 1998). Adding slack to the run times leads to longer travel times, which is not desirable from a marketing or demand perspective, although passengers respond about three times less favourably to a minute of delay than to a minute of scheduled journey time. Ackermann (1998) therefore stated that there is a trade-off between speed and punctuality and in timetable planning you should try to find a common optimum for delays and travel times. On the other hand, this does not mean that the more slack, the better punctuality. Examples have shown that punctuality does not necessarily improve by adding time in the timetable, perhaps through its impact of creating a slack culture amongst staff.

It is a widely-held belief that high utilization of infrastructure has a negative influence on punctuality. The recommended capacity utilization defined by the UIC (2004), is therefore 75 % of theoretical capacity during peak hours and 60 % off-peak for lines with mixed traffic. However, limiting utilisation to this may not be possible if the sheer demand for capacity is higher; Britain has many lines operating at over 90% capacity in the height of the peak – with the consequent impact on performance.

Several empirical studies have been made to see how capacity utilization influences punctuality. Gibson et al. (2002) found that a high capacity utilization mainly contributes to secondary delays, but does not itself creates delays. Olsson et al. (2002) also found a negative correlation between punctuality and capacity utilization, though relatively weak.

This may be because only specific elements of capacity have a direct impact on poor punctuality. For instance, the measurement of junction capacity is less well-understood than of line capacity, whose impact may only be secondary. It is also particularly helpful to have 'bolt-hole' platforms or sidings in which to put trains during times of disruption, in order to improve resilience, since trains can quickly be 'got out of the way'.

Much research is done on timetable planning and punctuality. There are different types of models for the evaluation of timetables, and many tools for the simulation of punctuality and delays. Such models may be used to examine how secondary delays spread in a railway network and, in this way, enable the examination of the robustness of different timetable alternatives. The simulation of delays may also be used to foresee the influence of alternative infrastructure designs on punctuality and traffic in general. Important detailed infrastructure factors include speed restrictions over points and the release times of signalling equipment.

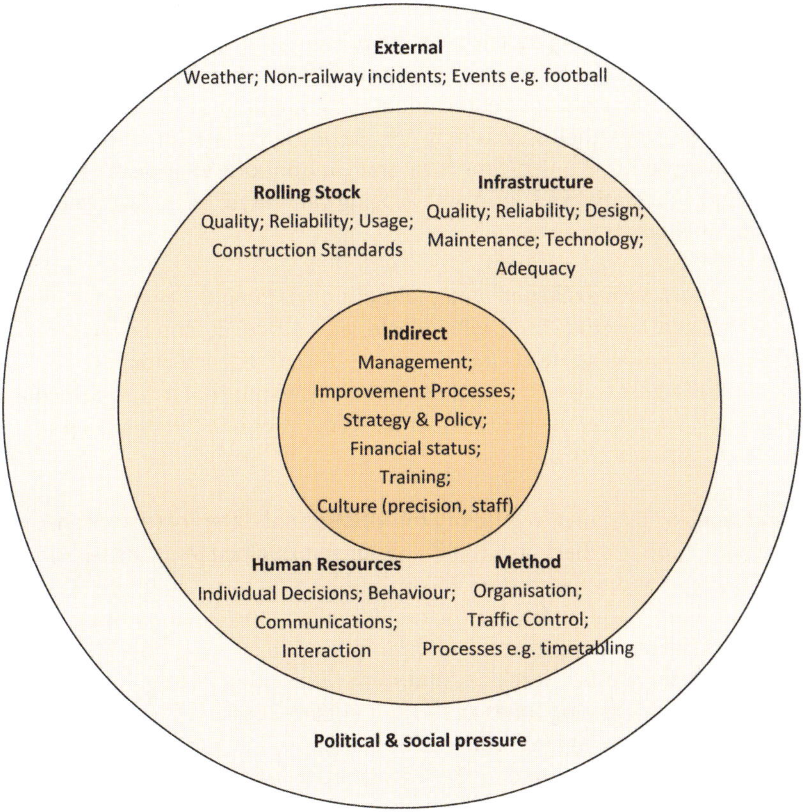

Figure 7.3 Factors explaining punctuality (adapted from Veiseth, 2009)

Operational priority rules may influence punctuality for trains getting higher and lower priority. Priority rules state how train control shall give priority to trains when delays occur. In Norway the "trains-on-time" principle has been used for several years. Trains running on time have priority and, as far as possible, keep their allocated train path. Here a train is on time when it is within the "critical delay" for the actual line. What is defined as the critical delay will vary between lines. The critical delay is often larger on single track lines with a long distance between passing loops than on double track lines or lines with good crossing facilities. There may also be local, more specific definitions of how to prioritize between delayed trains. For instance, in Norway, trains in transit through Oslo or trains with Oslo S as terminal station have priority among delayed trains. With delays in the central Oslo area, local trains and Airport Express trains have priority.

However, there are other possible rules for prioritisation. On railways where multiple train operators run over a common infrastructure, legal reasons may require that all operators are treated equally, so that at least the principles are consistent. Nevertheless, this may not maximise the performance of the overall railway: putting an on-time local train in front of a long-distance one may lead to substantial knock-on delays being generated, hours later and hundreds of kilometres away.

Several authors have explained punctuality through punctuality models. One example is Veiseth (2009), who developed a model describing factors influencing punctuality. He divided the factors into direct and indirect explanatory factors (see Figure 6.4). Veiseth pointed out that it is of particular importance to focus on the indirect factors if you want to achieve lasting punctuality improvements.

Several studies have tried to quantify the influence of different factors on punctuality. Among others punctuality has been explained from the factors

- Train length and distance run (Harris, 1992)
- Temperature, precipitation, number of travellers, and dwell times at stations (Riksrevisionsverket, 1986)
- Station, train number, week day and week (Banverket, 2001)
- Alighting and boarding times at stations (Heinz, 2000)
- Rolling stock type/age/utilisation (FE/RCL, 2005)
- Network use (as measured by the Capacity Utilisation Index) (FE/RCL, 2005)

In Norway, several analyses were carried out in the period 2002-2003 to find correlations between delays/punctuality and the following factors:

- Number of passengers
- Load (number of passengers / number of seats)
- Track capacity utilization

- Cancellations
- Speed restrictions
- Track construction work
- Departure and arrival punctuality
- Rules for disruption management

The studies were summarised by Olsson and Haugland (2004). The strongest correlation showed punctuality to be a function of number of passengers, train load and departure punctuality. Many of the studied factors give the impression that there is no linear influence on punctuality, but that there are threshold values. If threshold values are not exceeded, the effects of these factors may be hidden in the "noise" from the other factors.

Olsson et al. (2010) analyzed the causes behind a decrease in punctuality in Norway from 2005 to 2010. They concluded that the increase in delays was a combination of three causes:

- Increased failure frequency of infrastructure and rolling stock
- Increased work in and around tracks because of investments and increased maintenance
- An inability to handle normal weather variations

Further it was argued that these causes taken together have given a reduced robustness in the railway system. The reduced robustness means that even minor increases in traffic volume and rule changes for train production may give comprehensive delays. The load on the railway system has increased, but the ability to handle its load has not increased correspondingly. It was put forward as a paradox that new lines and new rolling stock have not given a marked improvement for the railway.

Lastly, it might be argued that, as railways are a system, then all the components of that system are likely to impact on punctuality and, generically, those components are:

- fixed infrastructure;
- rolling stock;
- timetabling and other planning processes;
- train service regulation and control;
- platform management;
- staff (especially traincrew); and
- passengers.

A holistic approach to the improvement of punctuality (e.g. Harris, Mjøsund & Haugland (2014)) might therefore reasonably look at all these areas.

7.7 Effect of Delays and Poor Punctuality

Both customer satisfaction surveys and literature about railway operations quality underline the importance of good punctuality (for example Fahlén and Jonsson, 2005; Seco and Goncalves, 2007; Gelders et al. 2008). This is because customers are affected by delays, and that they have consequences for them. For example it may lead to being late for work or meetings, too late for picking up children from school, or that goods are delivered too late to customers. It is therefore an assumption that punctuality and delays influence train companies by encouraging customers to choose other modes of transport. This is supported by studies of the willingness to pay to avoid delays, showing that customers appreciate good punctuality more highly than reduced travel time for example.

There are, however, many other effects of delays and punctuality than individuals choosing other transport modes because of experienced delays. One of them is the public opinion's perception of the railways. Delays and bad punctuality get a lot of media attention. This especially true in areas where many depend on trains in their everyday life. In Norway the Oslo area stands out, which because of high train density and many passengers, is particularly vulnerable to train service disturbances. Big and frequent disturbances in this area often lead to a national debate about the bad situation in railways; even if punctuality in many other parts of the country may be very good and/or the overall situation is not that bad anyway. Such a negative image may by itself make people choose another transport mode, and it makes recruiting new customers more difficult. This may then influence possibilities of achieving the goal of moving transport from road to railway. A bad image may also make it more difficult to get access to needed competence because it becomes less attractive to work in the railway industry.

Delays and reduced punctuality also influence the ability to carry out planned maintenance and renewal activities. It is normal that infrastructure maintenance is done during what is called "white periods", times when no trains are supposed to run. Delays in train traffic can mean that the duration of "white periods" is reduced, which may lead to all or parts of planned activities not being done as planned[2]. This is a waste of resources, and it may lead to more delays because failures are not repaired, or an increased risk that new failures occur. As for rolling stock, delays may lead to disturbances in rolling stock plans, so that maintenance cannot be done according to plan – trains

2 This is particularly likely when it is remembered that, at the beginning and end of each work task, there are typically significant equipment set-up/dismantle activities, which take the same length of time, irrespective of the actual amount of maintenance carried out

either may land up at the depot too late for remedial work to be undertaken, or may not even reach the depot at all. Delays also mean increased costs for the railway organizations because of demands for more rolling stock, personnel, refunds and price reductions to customers, and greater use of buses and taxis in disruption management. Delays also influence safety; this is because any deviation from plans, which is what a delay means, represents a safety risk.

In order to include punctuality in demand forecasting models and cost/benefit analyses, delays, or the probability of delays, are given a value. This is often called non-punctuality costs or value of delays. There are many studies presenting such values, and most of them are based on Stated Preference (SP) analyses. In this type of studies travellers are asked what they are willing to pay to avoid delays. Such studies show that the travelers typically are willing to pay between 1.5 and 3 times more to avoid 1 minute of delay than they would pay to reduce travel times by 1 minute. This means that delays are considered to be a greater disadvantage than travel time. From these studies you also find that business travellers and commuters are willing to pay more to avoid delays than other passengers, and that high income passengers are willing to pay more than those with a lower income. Airport-bound passengers are the most willing to pay to avoid delays (perhaps 5x the normal value of time). Longer delays are also valued more highly than shorter ones; recent research from Britain shows that delays of under 5 minutes may only be weighted 1:1 relative to in-vehicle time, but delays of over 30 minutes are often weighted >3:1; this is thought to be because those sorts of delays are likely to have bigger consequences, and so Network Rail has been specifically charged with reducing the quantity of these longest delays. In addition, Lind and Widlert (1989) showed that the delay disadvantages are considered to be bigger for passengers waiting in stations than for those already on board the trains.

For freight trains there is also often set a value or a cost on delays. Jernbaneverket (2001) calculated for example that delays cost 72 NOK per ton per hour (figures from 2000).

In SP studies the willingness to pay is measured in two ways: willingness to pay to get an advantage in today's situation, and claim for compensation to accept a worsened situation. Different methods do not usually give the same result, and one must find out what is more relevant for further use of the values. Usually the respondent will express higher values in a worsening situation than in an improving one (Finans- og tolldepartementet, 1998).

Most literature discussing the value of delays focuses on the costs for railway customers. However, delays also mean costs for the railway industry. Nyström

Source	Importance of delay time / travel time	Comments
Jernbaneverket (2006b)	3.0 (short journeys, < 50 km) 1.5 (long journeys, > 50 km	Used in Norway
HEATCO (2006)	2.5	EU recommendation
SIKA (2008)	2.0	Used in Sweden
Department for Transport (2007)	3	Used in UK

Table 7.2 Weight of delay time vs. travel time for passenger travels

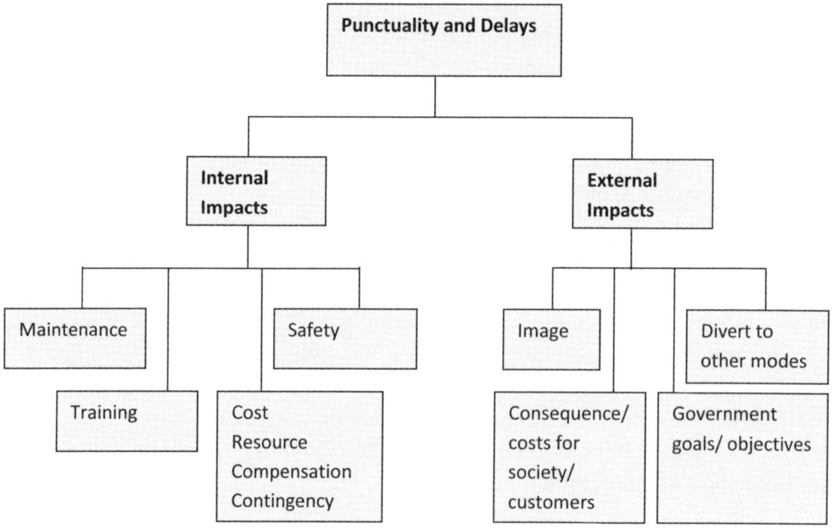

Figure 7.4 Effects of punctuality and delays (source: Veiseth, 2009)

(2008) therefore suggested dividing non-punctuality costs into external and internal ones. He meant that the external non-punctuality costs hit passengers and freight customers outside the railway industry, while the internal costs impact the rail industry directly, as examples of which he mentions secondary delays and reduced time for infrastructure maintenance. Veiseth (2009) also splits the internal and external effects of punctuality and delays, and sums up his discussion of the subject in a model illustrating various categories of such effects (Figure 7.4).

Figure 7.4 illustrates that punctuality and delays have both internal and external effects. Even if external effects are those most often focussed upon, both dimensions are important when looking at consequences of disturbances. The same is true when estimating the costs connected with delays and punctuality.

7.8 Improving Punctuality and Regularity

Because punctuality is influenced by many different factors, it is important to have on-going improvement activities in all parts of all organisations involved in railway operations. Analysing causes of punctuality problems, coming up with improvement activities, and then implement and follow these up, should be a continuous process and a natural part of improvement work in all railway organisations.

Given the importance of punctuality, Performance Improvement Programs are relatively common on railways, and typically comprise a cross-organisation group of staff seeking to analyse and address delays across a range of elements of the railway system, including:

- How the timetable is constructed, and what parameters are used in its construction;
- the priorities chosen when planning maintenance and renewal activities for both infrastructure and rolling stock;
- Ensuring appropriate incentives between different organisations (e.g. TOCs may have a view on when it would disrupt traffic least, for works to be carried out, and might be prepared to forego penalty payments they might otherwise have expected to receive from an infrastructure owner for non-availability of tracks);
- How operating problems (large and small) are dealt with (see chapter 8 on contingency planning);
- Staff training;
- focus, commitment and management support (management commitment and broad involvement are seen as success factors for quality improvement (Evans and Lindsey, 2005)).

To work systematically with delay reduction, all railway organisations should define and describe the punctuality process they will use. The punctuality process describes the main activities in punctuality work, and how to they are executed. As to which activities should be included, this will vary depending on the railway organisation. There will, for example, be differences between an infrastructure provider and a train operating company here, although that can cause problems in an inter-disciplinary system such as the railway. This was recognised in Britain about ten years ago, when Network Rail was given overall responsibility for maximising the performance of the railway. Figure 7.5 gives an example of a punctuality process.

Station stops in Norway:
The accuracy of stopping at stations matters in intense urban rail operation. Trains may be considerably shorter than the platform, either during quieter hours of operation, because platforms were designed for a different type of operation, or because they give access from multiple locations on the street. However, if trains do not stop in a position to match waiting passengers, there are two sources of delay. First, passengers may have to walk/run to the nearest door of the train, creating a delay before they can even board. Secondly, the distribution of passengers between doors is likely to become sub-optimal, with an excess number of passengers at the end door of a train, thereby creating a further delay whilst they board. Each of these problems can easily add 2-3s to the stop of every train which, at 20tph, could be a minute lost at a specific location.

This problem may need to be addressed in two ways. First, information systems to passengers should provide sufficient information about the incoming train, that they can stand at the appropriate places along the platform. Secondly, stop boards for drivers can explicitly mark the correct stopping position of trains of different lengths/types

Figure 7.5 Train Stopping Position Information for (a) Passengers, Nationaltheatret and (b) Drivers, Lillestrøm

The punctuality process is divided into four major parts. They are explained briefly below.

- **Follow-up:** Collecting and analyzing operations data to study and communicate if trains are running according to timetable, and explain deviations.
- **Improvement:** Identify causes to punctuality defects and execute improvement actions according to these
- **Evaluation:** Evaluate production plans as to punctuality to make more robust production plans in the future
- **Development:** Maintaining and developing methods, systems and competence used in punctuality work

PIMS method

Sometimes, organisational inertia or a lack of incentives can make it relatively difficult to implement specific measures designed to improve operational performance. Different railways have tried different methods to achieve success. London Underground created the posts of Service Performance Improvement Manager to provide a focus for work; importantly, these managers also had (small) budgets for minor works (e.g. moving a signal 5m, or redesigning staff instruction booklets) so that subsequent recourse for monetary authority was not a delaying factor.

In addition to the daily punctuality work, however, improvement work on punctuality may be organized through specific projects. Formal processes and projects can be helpful in delivering performance improvements. Through the research project PEMRO (2005-2008) a method was developed to support work in such projects in Norway. The method was called PIMS: "Punctuality Improvement Method System". PIMS was built from general work quality principles, and developed by testing in practical situations (Veiseth, 2009).

The PIMS method consists of five steps attached to the day-to-day follow-up of punctuality. Within each step a procedure was described, and behind the steps there were a set of improvement tools to support this work. This includes general quality improvement tools and more specific tools for the analysis and presentation of punctuality data. The method is focused on the connection between analyses of punctuality data and knowledge based on experience, and on the interaction between the project organisation and the line organisations. Figure 7.5 illustrates the steps in PIMS, which is summarised in a handbook (Veiseth et al., 2008).

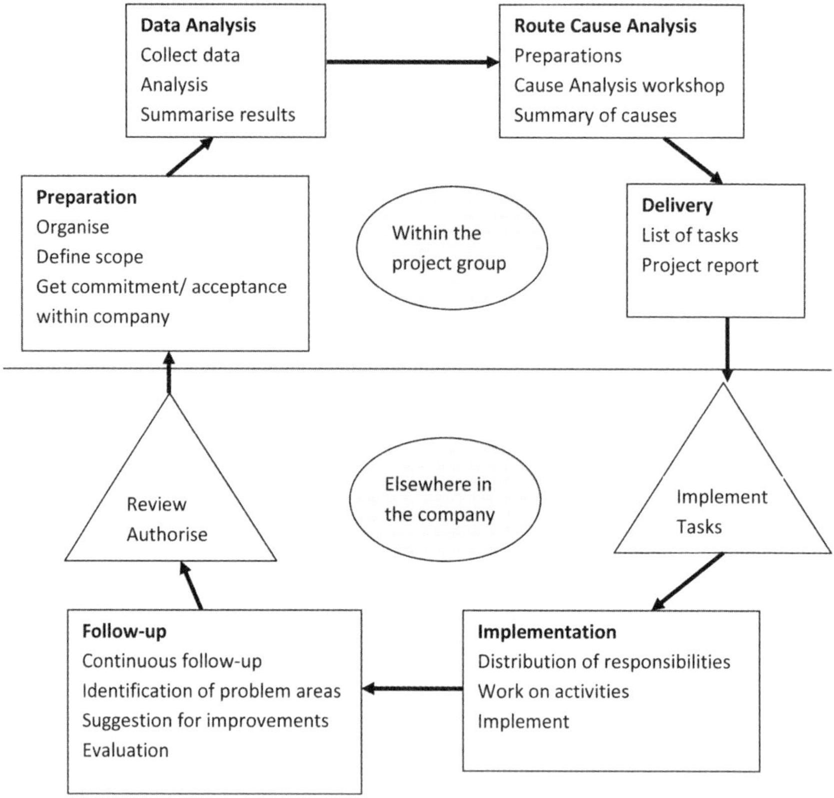

Figure 7.6 PIMS Method
Adapted from Olsson &Veiseth

Punctuality Activities

As many different factors influence punctuality, there are also many different punctuality activities. To achieve a stable and high level of punctuality, a broad spectrum of activities is important. You must, for example, have activities ensuring a high focus on punctuality within the organisation, and activities so that uncovered failures do not appear, nor existing types to happen again. Generally you should have activities aiming at avoiding delays from happening in the first place (primary delays), and activities to prevent delays spreading across the system (secondary delays).

Examples of activities to avoid delays from happening may be to:

- Avoid or remedy failures in infrastructure and rolling stock
- Manage many passengers / long station dwell times

- Adapt timetables to circumstances
- Manage seasonal variations (e.g. snow, autumn leaves, rails buckled by excessive heat)

Examples of activities to prevent delays from spreading may be to:
- Provide extra turnaround times for rolling stock at terminal stations
- Remedy failures in rolling stock and infrastructure
- Manage seasonal variations (e.g. snow, autumn leaves, rails buckled by excessive heat)
- Cancel services / turn them back before terminal stations
- Provide infrastructure activities as crossing facilities on single track lines, distance between passing loops, length of passing loops, manning of stations/central train control, simultaneous entry into stations and speed over points.

A way to categorize punctuality activities is to divide them in two different strategies: slack or precision. The slack strategy means that you build in buffers and reserves in the system, so that the vulnerability to delays is reduced (the propagation of delays is prevented). Examples of buffers and reserves are spare rolling stock units, extra personnel for shunting, extra run time etc. The slack strategy is basically reducing railway efficiency because extra resources are added. In a precision strategy the focus is on reducing buffers and reserves. The idea is that a focus on precision in the organisations shall increase when margins are reduced, and that this shall lead to reduced delays. The precision strategy assumes good operations reliability in infrastructure and rolling stock, and a changed attitude towards punctuality.

Precision will probably give lower operating costs, but requires investments and continuous maintenance. On the other hand, a slack strategy is expensive. In logistics generally, recent developments are clearly in direction of precision. In the long term, the most resource effective strategy is probably to strive for precision, with associated obligations for maintenance and a preparedness to ensure quality in infrastructure and rolling stock. In practice, the strategy will be something between slack and precision.

Table 7.3 gives examples of activities introducing slack in the railway system, and activities giving higher precision. It also tells if activities are giving reduced primary or secondary delays.

The SWT 2004 Timetable

The South West Trains (SWT) franchise runs inner- and outer-suburban services from a terminal at London Waterloo. In the peaks, over 60tph link Waterloo to key destinations including Portsmouth, Southampton, Bournemouth and Reading. It is one of the largest franchises, in 2013 having around 10% of the national total of services (40m train-kms), demand (240mppa) and revenue (£850m p.a.). In the early 2000s, on-time punctuality (measured to within 5 minutes) was hovering only just over 70%, despite the provision (in the 1930s) of six grade-separated junctions. Management embarked on a complete re-write of the timetable, based on what was considered to be the main conflict point, the flat junction at Woking. Starting from parallel train movements of Portsmouth line services over Woking Junction, the planned service was developed across the network, to provide regular (although not strictly Taktfahrplan-standard) services.

Figure 7.6 450016 at Woking

Controversially, many journey times were lengthened, in order to improve service robustness, which duly improved – by around 10%, immediately over the weekend of the timetable change. The extra time (of up to 10 minutes on the longest-distance services) was initially criticised in the media, but subsequent analysis showed that there were reductions in generalised cost for all lines, both in peak and offpeak periods, since the increase in planned journey time was more than outweighed by the reduction in delayed journey time, which passengers typically value three times more highly. The only exception was on the local Southampton – Portsmouth route, where one minute was subsequently removed from journey times, to ensure that all services and passengers were indeed better off.

	Slack	Precision
Avoid delays to occur (primary delays)	◆ Timetable allowance ◆ Longer station stops in timetable ◆ Personnel reserve ◆ Rolling stock spares at terminal station	◆ Maintenance/ reliability of infrastructure ◆ Maintenance/ reliability of rolling stock ◆ Timings adapted to actual run times ◆ Departure on the second ◆ Guiding passengers quickly off/ on ◆ No Temporary Speed Restrictions (TSPs) ◆ On-time departure more important than customer service
Avoid spreading of delays (secondary delays)	◆ Ample turnaround times ◆ Lower capacity utilization ◆ Many manned passing loops ◆ Rolling stock reserve on route ◆ Pragmatic enforcement of priority rules	◆ Remote train control ◆ Quickly redirect signalman if changed crossing ◆ Strict enforcement of priority rules ◆ Uniform punctuality requirements for all products/lines ◆ Cancel/turn trains before terminal ◆ Follow-up of "problem trains"

Table 7.3 Examples of Performance-Improving Activities

7.9 Summary

Railway operational performance is measured in a variety of ways, but many of the simpler metrics (e.g. % of trains on time) are not really sufficient to support high-quality rail operation. Performance failures are often due to poor planning, including weak assumptions and an inadequate understanding of the detailed impacts of the infrastructure's capability. Analytical work ("forensic train planning") may be required, in order fully to understand the types and relative importance of factors driving poor performance, the impacts of which are very substantial, in commercial as well as operational terms.

8 Station and Terminal Planning

8.1 Station Design Principles

It is important to start by remembering that stations have four principle functions which are, in descending order of importance:

- circulatory;
- operational;
- beacon;
- commercial.

The main aim of operational planning at stations should therefore be to maximise their contribution to these objectives.

Stations are those places where passengers access, and egress from, the railway network. Good pedestrian *circulation* is therefore essential. Generalised cost theory reminds us that railway planners need to consider the journey from door to door, and this means ensuring that stations are easy to access. The first task is then one of station planning – can we get stations as near as possible to places with high footfall, whether these are office blocks, shopping centres or sports stadia? Many old cities in Italy forced train stations to be outside the city walls (in order to take care of their cultural heritage), whilst Cambridge University wanted to keep the 'new-fangled' railway well away from the students in the 1840s, but these decisions leave disbenefits in perpetuity. On the other hand, some stations are clearly within areas of extremely-high trip density e.g. in Hong Kong (see Figure 8.1).

Because the railway is a high-volume mode, it needs to be supported by high-volume access, so priority should be given to those arriving/departing by public transport modes such as metro, tram and bus, if passengers cannot walk or go by bicycle to/from their destinations.

Street-corner locations and the double-ending of platforms are both measures to minimise access times from passengers' real origins to the train, whilst constrictions to enable better revenue protection can do the opposite – there are always trade-offs. However, in recent years, technology has developed remotely-controlled gate access points, which may provide the optimum answer to both (see Figure 8.2).

However, as the railway becomes more popular, its catchment areas will increase, and attention needs to be given to those accessing by car. Creating

Figure 8.1 MTRC Train Approaches Kowloon Bay, Hong Kong

Figure 8.2 Remote Ticket-Checking/ Passenger Access Point, Oxted, England

double-deck car-parks in old goods yards can help, but this does not improve the carbon footprint of the overall journey, and measures such as through-ticketing to/from bus (e.g. the PlusBus product in Britain), improved

Figure 8.3 Bicycles outside Groningen station, the Netherlands

Figure 8.4 New Park & Ride Station at Schofields, New South Wales, Australia

information about bus services, and the provision of cycle racks will also be needed. Here, Germany and the Netherlands probably lead the way (see Figure 8.3).

Where stations do function as park & ride stations, however, bus access and kiss & ride drop-off points do need to be located nearer to the station building, since these provide the higher volumes of trips requiring less time and space to accommodate.

The most important part of the circulatory function is egress, which should have sufficient capacity to enable speedy evacuation in the case of emergencies, and should similarly be straight and direct; this also helps the visually-impaired (see Figure 8.5).

Figure 8.5 Direct egress from Gare de l'Est, Paris, with floor markings for the visually-impaired (although a contrasting colour would have helped too)

On the way in, planners should ensure that the layout of facilities follows a logical sequence that a passenger might want to take e.g. buy ticket, see departure board for time of train, buy coffee, go through ticket barrier, get directions to platform. Too often these tasks may need trekking to and fro across the concourse, creating unnecessary pedestrian conflicts.

Planners in particular need to consider the location and presentation of information – not only is this part of the 'sales' process of the railway, but it is also a key element in minimising time and reducing stress, enabling passengers to find their train (and potentially their carriage) easily.

The station also needs to provide *operational* support for the railway and its passengers. If traincrew are to change here, or catering trolleys replaced, then facilities for these need to be available – quite close to 'the action', but not actually in the way. Upstairs rooms or the ends of platforms can be appropriate here. Ticket offices might be on one side of the main entrance passageway not, as recently installed at Newcastle Central, 100m off down one platform.

Figure 8.6 New Information Board at Oslo S – but how does one find out information about travel to smaller, intermediate stations?

The *beacon* function of the station is in its ability to advertise the presence of the railway within the local environment, so prominent displays of logos, linked to direct access to entry points (as in Figure 8.7), should be part of the wider planning and marketing of the railway. Some stations are remarkably difficult to find.

Commercial considerations, however, can lead to the imposition of obstacles blocking sight-lines, preventing the free flow of passengers or requiring deviations in minimum distance/time to the platform. The extra income from retail can be a misleading source of income, if it indirectly makes the main purpose of a station (i.e. boarding and alighting from trains) more difficult but, suitably placed around the periphery or upstairs, it can indeed form a key element of making a railway more commercial. The concourse at London's Waterloo station (Figure 8.8) has generally been cleared, with retail space being made available within buildings and at a mezzanine level.

Figure 8.7. The London Underground roundel provides a beacon effect for even its smaller stations (as here, at Chiswick Park), giving potential users reassurance about the level of service likely to be provided.

Figure 8.8 Even the Siting of Passenger-Relevant Facilities (such as this Information Kiosk at London Waterloo) needs to be considered carefully, in the context of maintaining passenger flow

8.2 Arrangement of Platforms

Track layouts need to be planned to enable the expected train movements, both in terms of quantity, but also type – for instance, if trains are to be reversed, or joined and split. The arrangement of platforms within stations can also either provide or inhibit easy passenger movement. Side platforms enable buildings and bridge piers to be set back, and allow level access from the street (see Figure 8.9). Island platforms enable step-free transfer between mainline and local services, whilst bay platforms in the middle of larger islands can prove ideal for centre reversing (see Figure 8.10), where passengers can be afforded same-platform interchange whilst minimising the number of conflicting train movements.

On the other hand, multiple platforms enable the segregation of flows and destinations by platform: if preferable, all services to the same destination should leave from (either side of) the same platform. At the extreme, one can have dedicated platforms for particular train services: this is good practice from a customer point of view, but can lead to the inefficient use of platforms, so is often limited to airport express services, where the special requirements (e.g.

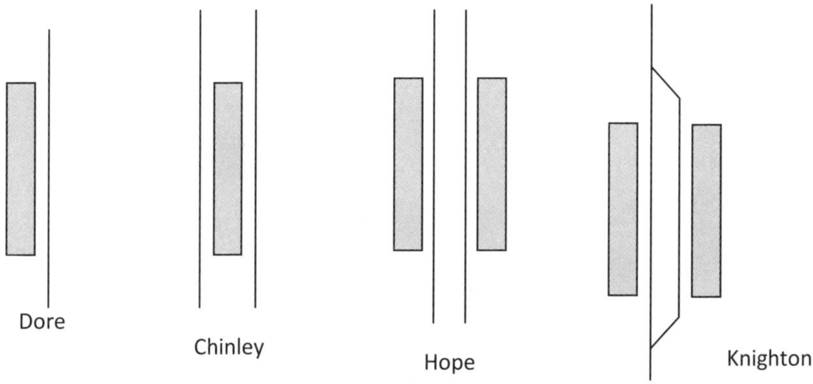

Figure 8.9 British Examples of Different Platform Arrangements for Through Stations

luggage, passenger unfamiliarity, special ticketing) may warrant it (see Figure 8.11).

Where trains are longer, the time taken to access a single footbridge or subway from the ends of the platforms, and the excessive number of people trying to do so, may effectively necessitate multiple facilities for doing this. Many German railway interchanges (e.g. Mannheim, München Ostbahnhof) have multiple subways. However, provided that operational procedures or appropriate signalling facilities are in place, such longer platforms can also enable the usage of the same platform face by several shorter trains, enabling same-platform interchange and/or the coupling of longer trains to provide peak capacity.

Although these considerations may seem to be the longer-term responsibility of the infrastructure operator, they do impact upon day-to-day operation, and can be affected in the short-term by the way in which the timetable is written. For instance, the Taktfahrplan approach described in section 3.3 tends to lead to a need for greater simultaneous platform occupancy, interspersed with periods of fewer (passenger) trains. Stations need to be sized adequately to cope with these intermittent greater passenger flows. An alternative approach might enable passengers to change between trains by remaining at the same platform face for a following service.

Similarly, timetables providing passengers with through trains may require fewer platforms than those requiring interchange, although the circulation space available on those platforms may have to be larger, if opportunities to travel are less frequent. This is a particular problem for platforms which are

Figure 8.10 Connecting Service to Lebach-Jabach in a Bay Platform at Saarbrücken

Figure 8.11 Dedicated Platforms for the Gatwick Express, London Victoria

underground, where the (construction) cost of providing circulating space is relatively expensive. However, that space is needed, for the safe movement and evacuation of passengers (see below).

Larger stations may also need to be provided with sidings for trains, if some of these are expected to remain there for several hours (or overnight) (see Figure 8.12). If this is not the case, long-distance empty coaching stock (ecs) train movements may be required, which can be costly. Whilst understandable (in the context of high land values in, and peak rail demand to and from, Central London), running empty trains to/from Brighton (50 miles away) is expensive. It may, however, enable minor maintenance between the peaks, whilst allowing another loaded train into a critical platform as soon afterwards as possible, without needing to take into account the needs of contra-peak passengers.

Where trains terminate at stations which are not termini, the provision of separate sidings *beyond* the station can be helpful (as opposed to extra tracks *within* the station, also shown in Figure 8.12). It may be easier to split and join trainsets 'offline', without passengers, especially if cleaning is also to be undertaken at the same time.

It can also be helpful to provide through or bypass lines (see Figure 8.13), to enable freight trains to pass through the area without conflicting with passenger trains *in* the platforms, or providing a potential safety risk to passengers *on* the platforms. This was a common policy on the Continent, but is relatively rare in Britain.

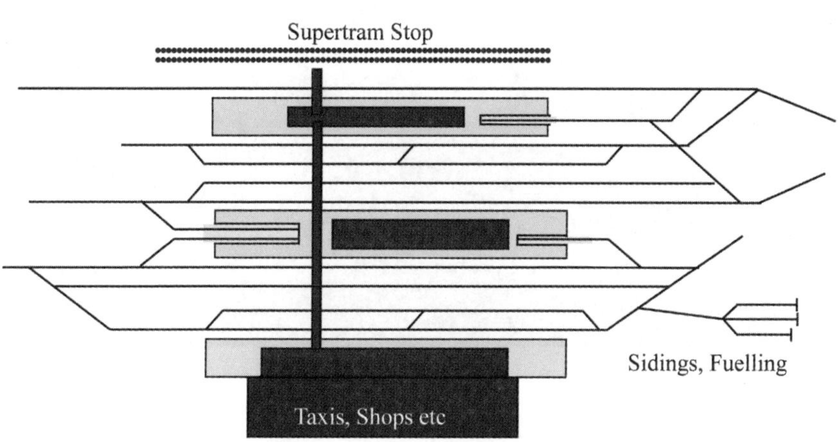

Figure 8.12 Station Layout for a Complex Through Station, Sheffield (Midland), Britain

In line with the volume of demand, and the functions of the station, appropriate facilities need to be provided for several purposes: shelter, ticketing, information and retail. Many railway networks have standards for the appropriate level of these at stations of a defined size; for instance, for many years Britain's Network Rail has used a classification system from A (national hub) to F (local halt).

8.3 Pedestrian Capacity

The basis of modern quantified pedestrian planning work is the seminal work of J J Fruin (1971), who observed different categories of passenger flow corresponding to differing levels of crowding. Speeds fall with increasing flow rates (see Table 8.1) before passengers become completely blocked-in, a situation which it is essential to avoid for safety reasons.

However, despite a wide appreciation of Fruin's work, and its use in major new station schemes, many of its detailed implications do not appear to be applied on a day-to-day level. For instance, it can be observed that passengers

Figure 8.13 Voyager at Durham, England: note the through track available for freight and non-stop Northbound passenger services
N.B. There used to be a similar Southbound through track, but this was removed, in order to permit higher line speeds

	QUEUING AREAS		WALKWAYS			STAIRWAYS		
measure	**Pedestrian Density**	**Ave. Inter-person spacing**	**Pedestrian Density**	**Flow**	**Average Speed**	**Pedestrian Density**	**Flow**	**Average Speed**
units	m^2/ped	m	m^2/ped	Ped/m/min	m/min	m^2/ped	Ped/m/min	m/min
Free circulation	> 1.21	> 1.21	> 3.25	<23.0	> 74.8	> 1.86	< 16.4	> 30.5
Uni-directional flows & free circulation. For reverse and cross flows with only minor conflicts	1.21-0.93	1.21-1.07	3.25-3.30	23.0-32.8	74.8-75.4	1.86-1.40	16.4-23.0	30.5-32.2
Slightly-restricted circulation due to difficulty in passing others. For reverse and cross flows with difficulty	0.93-0.65	1.07-0.91	2.30-1.39	32.8-48.2	75.4-68.4	1.40-0.93	23.0-32.8	32.2-30.5
Restricted circulation for most pedestrians. Significant difficulty for reverse and cross flows	0.65-0.28	0.91-0.61	1.39-0.93	49.2-65.6	68.4-61.0	0.93-0.65	32.8-42.6	30.5-27.7
Restricted circulation for all pedestrians. Intermittent stoppages and serious difficulties for reverse and cross flows	0.28-0.19	< 0.61	0.93-0.46	65.6-82.0	61.0-37.7	0.65-0.37	42.6-55.8	27.7-20.6
Complete breakdown in traffic flow with many stoppages	< 0.19	Close contact	< 0.46	0-82.0	0-37.7	< 0.37	0-55.8	0-20.6

Table 3.1 Pedestrian Planning Values
Source: Fruin (1971)

tend not to walk immediately next to passageway walls, thereby reducing the effective width of walkways by 30-50cms. These "edge effects" mean that the minimum width required to achieve a reasonable flow is about 3m (i.e. 1m for pedestrians in each direction, plus the edge effects), but narrower facilities are still sometimes provided. Edge effects can be particularly pronounced where there are changes of direction, so curved passages (see Figure 8.14a) are to be preferred to 90° corners. Similarly, if (as is known) pedestrians are slower in going down (and particularly up) stairs, then the widths of stairways need to be greater than the widths of the passages connecting them, but the opposite is relatively common.

Figure 8.14 Best Practices:(a) Curved Passageways (Green Park, London); (b) Unevenly-split Stairs (Shin-kiba, Tokyo)

As passenger alight from trains and therefore leave stations in large groups but enter stations in small groups (if not individually), then capacity is more quickly used up for exiting than entering flows. Despite the added factor that evacuation during emergencies is critically-important, very few stations are organised to provide a greater width for facilities (passageways, stairs) on egress than on entry (as in Figure 8.14b).

Pedestrian planning at bigger stations (especially those with associated (e.g. retail) developments) has evolved from the use of static models using average parameters (e.g. walking speeds) within elements of the station (models such as PEDROUTE) to those using artificial intelligence approaches (e.g. LEGION). Here, passengers are allocated characteristics (e.g. luggage) which then affect their behaviour through the system (for instance, in walking more slowly, and being more reluctant to move along the platform). Outputs from network models need to be used as inputs for station pedestrian models, in order to ensure that the quantities of passengers expected can fit into the infrastructure at the desired congestion levels.

8.4 Station Stop Management

We have already seen (in section 3.7) that adequate time allowance needs to be made for trains to stop at stations. However, good station stop management is a multi-disciplinary skill which requires a range of actions to be taken not only on the day, but also beforehand, in the disciplines of:

- station design;
- information and route-finding;
- signalling;
- timetable development;
- train control and regulation;
- platform management.

Station Design

Importantly, the timetabling and operational processes are insufficient to solve this problem, if inadequate provision has been made in the first place. The planning of station stops needs to start in the design phase.

The biggest single thing that station planners can do to help high passenger volume station stops is to provide separate platforms for boarding and alighting. This is occasionally done during system construction (e.g. in Sao Paulo, Munich) but (especially if at or above ground) can be retro-fitted, as at Stratford for the London Olympics (see Figure 8.15). Although having separate platforms will not generally be necessary (except in conditions of very significant volumes), it provides a reduction of about 40% in passenger flow time, as interactions between boarders and alighters are largely avoided. Failing that, simply ensuring adequate platform width (so that alighters have somewhere to go, when they alight) is helpful: the 3m standard for platform width should be treated as a minimum, not a fixed parameter.

Secondly, station planners should design stations to have a number of entry and exit points, since this is a key determinant of passenger distribution along the platform, itself a key driver of stop times. End access to platforms is not helpful here – although it may be mitigated if access is provided at both ends.

Entry and exit points must have sufficient capacity to deal with the likely passenger flows when trains arrive and disgorge their load. Single escalators have a capacity of only c. 100 passengers per minute, and actually achieving more than 1 passenger per second can be difficult if people have luggage. The relative crowding on escalators is easily seen in Figure 8.16.

Figure 8.15 1992 Tube Stock Enters the New Platform at Stratford, London

Figure 8.16 Through Platforms, Bras, Sao Paulo

Figure 8.17 Gateline, Glenageary, Dublin, Ireland

Capacity constraints can also be built into stations by mistake, as a result of other programmes. We have already seen that attempts to maximise retail incomes can lead to restrictions in passenger flow, but these can also arise from (perhaps more legitimate) attempts to collect all the fares revenue. Passengers are known to dislike ticket gates (for their inconvenience, which may be measured as several pence per trip) but gates can also cause real constraints on flow, especially where they have had to be fitted into older stations (see Figure 8.17).

Information and Route-Finding

As well as structural considerations, details such as signage are important to ensure the station works well. Consistency of colour and font, with easily-identifiable internationally-understandable signs for key destinations such as "Exit", together with colour-coding of access to different lines/services do matter. Confirmation of direction and departure is also helpful for boarders – the last thing rail operators want is potential boarders asking staff or other passengers the destination of the train when it has already arrived. Similarly, best practice is to provide information within the train, for instance about on which side the doors will open, where one might change to, and even where along the platform are the major exit points. And, within the station, if good information is not provided, unfamiliar travellers will often congregate at decision points, in order to assess where to go next, thereby creating an obstacle for others to try to avoid.

Figure 8.18 Route-Finding before and after Alighting from the Train

Signalling

Enabling trains to have a clear run into and out of platforms is essential in minimising run-out/run-in (platform reoccupation) time. The positioning of signals needs to take into account the fact that trains will spend longer in track sections with platforms than those without, so signal sections may need to be shorter around stations. Extra 'closing-up' signals may need to be inserted, in order to reduce block lengths, and enable following trains to approach more closely those in busy platforms.

Timetable Development

As discussed in section 3.7, ensuring that station stops are maintained within the desired times does mean that an accurate analysis is needed of expected durations. These estimates need to take into account both passenger movement time, and the time required for functions (such as despatch). Both the mean and standard deviations of these values need to be taken into account, so that a management decision can be made as to what proportion of stops are likely to be completed within the allowance. And all these calculations need to be revisited from time to time, to take account of changes in passenger demand or operational procedures.

Train Control & Regulation

Whilst controllers may already have competing objectives in terms of minimising train delay duration or the number of delays, their job also needs to be made more complex by considering the impacts at stations, especially busy ones. In order safely to manage crowds, it is important to provide a regular source of egress by train for passengers at stations, even when the service is disrupted, as this reduces the risk of passengers falling off platforms. Contingency planning might therefore suggest the provision of departures to alternate destinations, even if successive trains were originally for the same one. That requirement for regularity should also encourage signallers to enable an even-interval headway, and avoid bunching; that increases crowding which, in turn, leads to a reduction in the capacity provided as the minimum signalled headway prevents higher frequencies being operated to make up for gaps in the service.

Platform Management

High-quality station stop management requires a level of repeatability across a number of procedures. Trains need to stop in exactly the same place, in order to spread passenger loads evenly and avoid time wasted as passengers run to the nearest door; this may require the careful location of stop boards for different train types/lengths.

Conductors may need to be trained, as to whereabouts in the train they should be, if they are to have the greatest impact in guiding and hurrying passengers – or preventing late runners boarding. In this task they may be aided by platform staff, whose duties similarly need to be described and prioritised: for instance, despatch is more important that giving information.

Figure 8.19 Platform Indicator at Arts-Loi, Brussels Metro

Figure 8.19 Platform Indicator at Arts-Loi, Brussels Metro

8.5 Freight Terminals

Freight terminals need to share some of the key principles which are applied to stations – for instance, the smooth flow of goods from origin onto the train at one end, and through to the destination at the other. The requirement to load and unload is a key disadvantage for rail, so minimising this is important. This can be achieved through investing in equipment designed to make transfer from road to rail as easy as possible, whether this be through bottom-discharge hoppers for bulk materials, or reachstackers and gantry cranes for containers. Railfreight is much more competitive when interchange can be avoided completely, because goods are loaded directly onto trains either at the factory or from ships.

The layout of terminals needs to ensure a safe easy flow of lorries in and out, with supporting operational facilities (such as offices, weighbridges etc.) around the periphery of the site. However, one key difference of freight is that (unlike passengers) it does not itself board and alight from trains – this has to be done actively by the operator or its contractors. With lower frequencies, rail freight terminals may need substantial amounts of land on which to

Figure 8.21 Entrance to Chullora Yard, Sydney, Australia

store goods temporarily. Not only is rail good at transporting bulky items (which necessarily take up plenty of space), but services may run relatively infrequently, so goods may be deposited several days before departure, and collected several days afterwards. For other traffics (e.g. power station coal), it may be considered strategically-important to have stockpiles, in case of traffic disturbance, if delivery failure has severe consequences (such as a failure of the electricity supply). Railways are less good at 'Just-in-Time' traffic, not because they cannot provide reliable service, but because they tend to provide very large quantities of goods when they do arrive, which may be beyond the capacity of terminals to process. Shunting, or using wagon- or part-trainload operation, is operationally less efficient.

Supporting operational elements may also require a headshunt (in which the train can be shunted between sidings, without impinging on main running lines) and a siding to put 'crippled' wagons – these may be attended to, on site, by roving maintenance staff, or may subsequently have to be moved to a wagon repair depot. Modern freight terminals also need to be provided with appropriate IT support, so that details of goods can be scanned in, enabling progress to be monitored through real-time tracking.

8.6 Summary

Railway planning sometimes ignores the importance of what happens *at* stations and terminals, as well as what happens *between* them. The main aim in their design must be the subsequent ease of operation of the system, and commercial (e.g. property developments) must *not* be allowed to interfere with this. The principles of generalised cost, and Fruin's pedestrian flow work can provide an appropriate framework within which to plan, provided that these two sets of principles are worked through to their logical final conclusions. Concentrating on station egress improves safety, especially when stations are underground.

9 Contingency Planning

9.1 Possession Planning

Especially as railway networks age, maintenance work on the railway cannot all be done during non-traffic hours. Even if a 5-hour window (e.g. 0030-0530) is available, maintenance engineers cannot get five hours' productive work done in this time, as equipment needs to be transported to the work site, which needs to be made safe (e.g. by switching off electric current) before work can begin; similar processes are needed in reverse before lines can re-open.

Although there may be greater time available at nights over the weekend (e.g. Saturday-Sunday), this time is under pressure in urban areas from the increasing desire to run 24-hour services at weekends. Maintenance work may then be forced back into five nightly periods (Sunday to Thursday), but this can compromise freight traffic. Despite ongoing productivity improvements in maintenance, renewal and electrification, larger items of work (e.g. bridge or junction reconstruction) will necessitate closure of lines. In order to minimise the disruption both to passenger and freight customers, good planning is needed both for the works themselves and for the continuation of part of the train service.

With major rail works generating large volumes of materials for delivery and despatch, the ordering of engineers' trains is important, especially since track capabilities may be restricted during works. Trains may have to be stabled 100kms away, and brought to the site in the correct order and potentially at limited speed, starting many hours before the works themselves are due to begin. Leaving equipment nearer the worksite may help train planning, but may be an unacceptable security risk; nevertheless, most railways have key pieces of equipment (e.g. tampers) and stores of materials (e.g. sleepers) strategically located around their networks.

Network Rail introduced a separate trainload system of ballast transport between regional distribution centres, so a sequence of train movements from a quarry at the other end of the country may be necessary, starting several days before. Within the site, there may be interactions between trains e.g. electric current is likely to be switched off, whilst some vehicles may be out of gauge whilst working, therefore limiting the passage of traffic on adjacent lines.

The impact of possessions can be particularly severe on freight trains. In countries like Norway, where rerouting possibilities are very limited, and most

Figure 9.1 Tamper at Dombås, a strategic location on the Norwegian network

lines single-track, possessions almost inevitably mean closure of the line. As the main commercial proposition for freight traffic in Norway is mainly based on overnight trains between hubs, night closure is a particular problem in this market. Whilst passengers may be transferred to/from substitute buses over key parts of the route (see section 9.8), this becomes impractical for freight, and the temporary loss of routes for engineering purposes can be a key factor in the wider permanent loss of railfreight traffic.

There is also pressure on inspections; one of the alleged reasons for the accident at Grayrigg, Britain in 2007, was that maintenance engineers had insufficient time for visual inspection of the line during the shorter Winter days, given the train service frequency. French mid-day "white periods" (in which services are suspended for a couple of quieter hours in the early afternoon) lead to big gaps in the service during the day, make a regular, high-frequency timetable impossible, and are increasingly untenable as capacity is filled up.

Some countries have managed to develop systems of working in which service trains continue to run on adjacent lines through worksites, albeit at reduced speed. This is dependent upon the nature of the work being done, traffic levels and local safety regulations.

9.2 The Need for Contingency Plans

Things may happen that disrupt a carefully-planned railway operation. Many things can go wrong in a very complicated interaction of infrastructure, rolling stock and personnel. Within infrastructure and rolling stock, lots of components may fail, and sometimes with dire consequences for the train service. Railways include large numbers of humans, either as staff, passengers or external agents; all of these may not act rationally and, sadly in the modern world, a very small number of the last category may seek out to cause problems through vandalism or worse. The best alternative is of course to go for the root causes and prevent trees from falling over tracks or rolling stock components failing, but when disruptions happen, passengers may have serious trouble in getting to work, getting home to pick up children in kindergarten or reaching a train or a plane connection.

Improvising, and dealing with every incident as something new and not planned for, is not the best way in a rigid system with many interdependencies, although many control centre staff enjoy the challenge. Contingency plans are a great advantage when something acute happens, and they may also be useful in dealing with changes made necessary during the timetable period, and lasting for days or even weeks and months. Preplanning can mean that immediate action may be taken in acute situations – ideally no time is needed for internal discussions or coordination when a readymade "Plan B" fits with the situation.

The real need for contingency plans is that, in some ways, the railway is a dangerous place with a wide range of risks which must be managed. Some of these are physical safety risks (such as passengers falling off overcrowded platforms), whilst some are comfort risks (e.g. overcrowding in trains, or long delays) whilst yet others are commercial risks (in that they prejudice existing and future revenues). In order to minimise these risks, clear lines of communication and accountability need to be set up to a nominated manager e.g. the service controller on duty.

In the meanwhile, considering which assets are most valuable and/or those which are most difficult to fix (and enhancing maintenance for such "golden assets") can help to reduce the need for contingencies in the first place. This may include particular junctions, or potentially freight locomotives (since, whilst freight trains may be able to assist passenger trains, the weight of the former usually means that passenger trains are not able to return the compliment).

9.3 Information (staff and customers)

When service disruptions happen, a very important issue is to get precise information over to passengers, either through staff or directly. First of all, they must be informed about the situation and then what is going to happen next. This is essential for passengers to be able to answer the really important question for them: "How do I get to my destination?" In cases of acute disruption (a broken-down train on the line between stations for example), many complaints are about lack of information or misleading information. Today people in a train usually will have continuous access to news media, and are also able to inform family and friends directly about the situation as they see it. Prompt, reliable and correct information to staff is therefore important to prevent unhelpful rumours. For passengers registered with an operator, messages by text or social media may therefore be helpful.

If a good contingency plan is available, it should contain instructions about which information shall be given (for instances whether suicides should be described instead as 'operational incidents' (in order to keep the thought out of people's minds)) and to whom: staff, passengers and, in some cases, also through media to the public in general. Consideration of what to say, and how and when to say it is important: no longer can the railway hide problems.

9.4 Risk assessment

A systematic approach to contingency planning may be to establish a priority table of risks i.e. calculating risk as consequence times probability for specific situations that may happen. This should address not only the accident-type outcomes, but also the impact on train service performance which should (one hopes) be the usual result. Consequences may be measured in train delay minutes or (even better) in passenger delay minutes. Background information here may come from statistics and from experience. Frequent problems with big consequences will end up high up on the list, whilst situations that do not occur very often, and that will not have serious consequences for passengers or service, may end up further down on a priority list, and as not so interesting as candidates for a contingency plan.

Sadly, modern security and terrorism problems also need to be planned for. Table-top exercises need to be complemented by full-scale exercises also involving other transport operators and the emergency services, especially where rail operations are underground. We have already seen that evacuation potential is an important element of station design, but this needs to be

Figure 9.2 Full-scale Metro Evacuation Exercise with the Fire Brigade, Montreal

practiced, perhaps with volunteers and/or off-duty staff. However, thinking through the (partial) withdrawal/ cancellation/ reinstatement of train services is a key element of these exercises, especially since the options for storing trains may be physically limited. What is the service degradation plan?

9.5 What to plan for

Situations requiring a contingency plan are very specific, depending on network, single/double track, platform alternatives, rerouting possibilities etc., and one important goal is very often to get back to normal service as soon as possible. However, because the railway infrastructure is limited, there are not an infinite number of track sections where things can go wrong, and (given some time in advance) it is practicable to consider all of them. Possibilities include:

- running fewer trains;
- simplifying service patterns;
- running branch lines as shuttle services;
- turning back trains before the end of the line;
- not running parts of the network at all.

But changes to the timetable are only one element of the planning required. Passengers need to be informed of these changes, both beforehand (if known) and during any disruption. Extra staff may need to be drafted in (for instance, from office duties), so plans for how this might work need to be considered. Different plans are likely to be needed at night and at weekends, when these other staff may not be available. Information needs to be updated on websites, and (through control centres) on tv monitors and displays, with announcements made.

Physical actions may need to include support for passengers who become stranded; for instance, some longer-distance train operators ensure that trains carry a supply of bottled water. There may be administrative consequences, too – arrangements with bus and taxi companies need to be set up in advance, to be called off when required.

In their contingency planning NSB in Norway uses "action cards", i.e. detailed specifications for operation when a common disturbance occurs. The overall goal is to provide as much transport capacity as possible. This means cooperation with other public transport modes (bus and metro in the Oslo situation). These "action cards" are made by Jernbaneverket (with overall responsibility for train planning and train control) and TOCs involved (NSB, Flytoget and freight operators). Across Norway there are about 50 such "action cards", 2/3 of them in the Oslo area, which reflect detailed instructions for each relevant train number affected. For each "action card" NSB has despatching procedures covering their internal handling of rolling stock, personnel and information for every "action card" situation. In case of train breakdowns or rolling stock shortage, there are priority rules saying which trains to be cancelled if necessary, and which trains to be run with less capacity (for example, single instead of double train sets). The NSB goal is to provide initial information to passengers about what has happened within two minutes, and within 10-12 minutes more detailed information about how the passenger's situation is solved (other trains, bus, taxi etc.). In this situation, everyone involved knows exactly what to do.

It is reported that in the Netherlands there are as many as 500 "action cards", but such a large number could reduce the effectiveness of the process.

However, as a specific example of one, the Munich S-Bahn has a booklet for staff of c. 20 alternative plans (e.g. Störfallkonzept, see Figure 9.3), each of which contains a description of the train service, and detailed maps of stations where passengers will have to change to/from other modes of transport. A whole plethora of things may be affected:

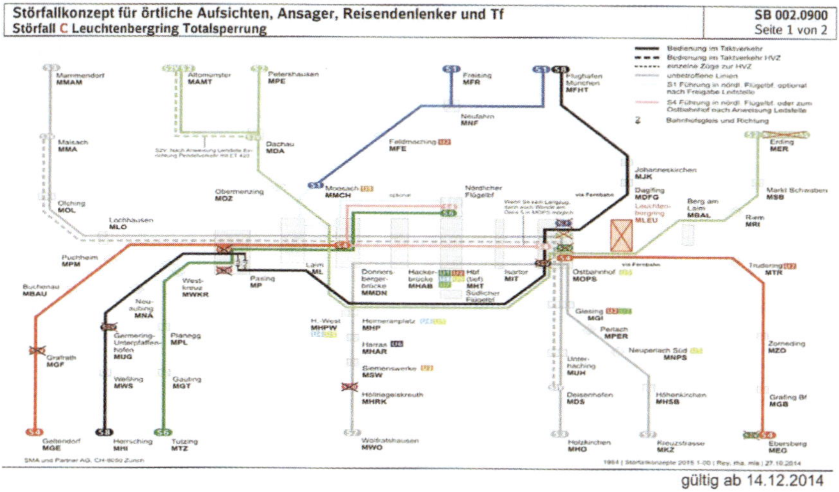

Figure 9.3 Example of Contingency Plan, Munich S-bahn
Reproduced with permission

- power supply if train services are concentrated on another line;
- information to passengers (by all modes: posters, call centre, internet etc.)
- ticketing facilities;
- passenger flow around stations;
- rolling stock maintenance;
- traincrew rosters.

It is also important to recognise that some of these will be affected a long time before and after the event. For instance, if staff holidays are to be suspended during a festival period, not all the staff can then take holidays immediately before or afterwards; in order to ensure cover of the rosters, the remaining leave may need to be spread across an entire year, including starting many months before the event itself.

9.6 Special Events

As well as failures and unforeseen circumstances, railways also need to plan for special events, for instance major sports fixtures, pop concerts and the Chinese New Year. These often attract crowds of 25,000 and more, and it is common for many thousands of passengers to travel by rail. On their return journey, these passengers can all descend on the nearest station at once, completely overwhelming the capacity of both station and train service, unless adequate measures are put in place. Whilst some larger stations may have to deal with bigger crowds, problems also arise where capacity is smaller. For, instance, for the Skarverennet cross country ski event at Finse in Norway, the only way to get there is by rail, and that means 12000 extra passengers on a single track line normally serviced by only three trains a day in each direction.

Planning also needs consider beforehand how much demand there will be from other travel markets, and to what extent this can be prejudiced. Relevant questions include:

- do existing train services have sufficient capacity that they can make a useful contribution to the demand for the special event, or are they already so full that this will not help?
- will many of the 'normal' (e.g. commuting) passengers want to travel to the special event on this particular occasion?
- can other train services run as normal, or do they need to be affected (stop additionally, or be diverted or cancelled)?
- what will the knock-on effects be across the network?

Depending on the frequency of the event, it might even be worthwhile making some allowance (e.g. a longer station stop time) for it in the main timetable if, for instance, it relates to weekly football matches.

A particular problem with events is that the exact end time of the event may not be known (e.g. extra time after football games), so that some flexibility will need to be retained. Some train operators therefore use crewed standby trains, which are kept in sidings as near the event as possible, and brought out as and when directed by the manager in charge.

Special event and contingency planning needs to start a long time beforehand – the first rail planning meeting relevant to the 2012 London Olympics was 6 years earlier. It may be that new trains need to be ordered, or new infrastructure put in place; more simply, it may just mean ensuring that maintenance work is not planned which will interfere. Liaison with sports authorities can be a particular issue e.g. Britain's Severn Tunnel was closed overnight in a weekend which included a Wales v England rugby game, which was then (without consultation with the railway) retimed later to suit television schedules, creating problems for rail passengers.

Events at Crystal Palace:
For many years, Crystal Palace stadium, in South London, has been used for athletics meetings and pop concerts. The normal daily usage of 5,000 - 10,000 passengers can be swelled by up to 35,000 extra passengers, all of whom tend to arrive in a two- or three-hour window before the event, but try to leave immediately afterwards. This creates a number of problems, even at this 6-platform station.

First, alighting passengers arrive in such volumes as to exceed the capacity of the platforms (see Figure 9.4a). This requires station control to be in place beforehand, in order to maintain passenger safety. For instance, liaison with the signalling centre might be required, in order to hold back the following train, until sufficient numbers of passengers have cleared the platform. Platform-based staff (drafted in from elsewhere) are used to answer questions, keep passengers clear of the platform edge, and move people along to the stairs (Figure 9.4b).

Arriving passengers often then exceed the capacity of the normal ticket hall/gate-line egress, so arrangements are put in place to use subsidiary exits normally closed. Not only do these need to be opened, but staff need to be on hand to provide directions, with Oyster readers provided to deduct the appropriate fare from smartcards[1]. Extra signage needs to be provided in this historic station (see Figure 9.5a).

Figure 9.4 Arriving Crowds, Crystal Palace

[1] London's Oyster system applies a penalty fare to those who leave the rail network without touching out, which would clearly be unfair if passengers were directed out of the station through a subsidiary exit, without gate facilities, to relieve overcrowding

Figure 9.5 Preparations for (a) Arriving and (b) Departing Crowds

After the event, passengers may arrive at a rate of 1000 per minute although the capacity of the ticket gateline is only 100 per minute. This requires action, in order to avoid crushing, falls down stairs or overcrowded platforms. However, because the station has multiple platforms, and trains go to a range of different destinations, good practice is to hold passengers in waiting areas at street level (see Figure 9.5b). This enables the segregation of passengers by destination, minimising the amount of potential pedestrian conflict. Passengers can then be counted into groups fitting train capacity, and led down to the relevant platform a few minutes before departure (see Figure 9.6).

Figure 9.6 Departing Crowds, Crystal Palace

With the train plan supplemented by extra services allocated after advance consultation with event organisers, the railway can be shown off to its best, in moving large quantities of people in an urban environment. Although Crystal Palace is fortunate in having multiple platforms, removing 20,000pph in the hour after an event is easily possible for most two-track railways.

9.7 Elements of a contingency plan

As part of the normal plan, spare trainsets and spare personnel should be positioned where they have the best possibility of being helpful in a situation with problems, although the distribution of resources may vary by type. For instance, teams of maintenance staff might need to be spread around the network at key locations, but spare train crew might better be kept all together at one location, to enable crew changes for out-of-order trains. There is then an important link between the plan for normal operation and a contingency plan.

Downscaling service in case of disruptions may be a good strategy, for instance to go from 15 to 30 minute- frequency services to reduce pressure in case of capacity reductions, for example if one track is closed for traffic on a double track line. This is particularly the case because it reduces knock-on delays (either of trains on trains, or trains on displaced train crew). It is also an example of a contingency plan which is easy to communicate to passengers and staff, and it is perhaps identical to a low traffic service (evenings/holidays). Other rationales for service thinning may be only to retain those services which are commercially most important, or those which are most important to customers (e.g. those to/from airports).

A policy about holding connecting services (or not) is also important. Whilst maintaining connections is good for passengers who wish to make the link, it can delay those already on the train about to leave and can subsequently delay many others, if insufficient time is available at termini. In Britain, Anglia (which runs a mainline from London to Norwich, with several branches) have calculated how late each branch line train can leave and make a return trip whilst still making its connection back on the mainline again. It does not hold branch line trains longer than that, so as to avoid missing the connections on the train's return.

9.8 Bus replacement services

Railway passengers have paid to travel by train, and generally want to do so. However, in some circumstances (chiefly associated with network non-availability), operators may have to put on buses instead. Given their smaller capacity, a higher frequency of service may need to be provided, but real value can be added if their stopping patterns do not merely repeat station stops: allowing passengers to alight or board at other transport interchanges or even key traffic origins/destinations can significantly reduce the (negative) impacts of having to change onto a substitute bus. Nevertheless, passengers dislike interchange at the best of times and may have an innate preference for rail. Rail passenger groups in Britain have been presenting this argument very strongly, pointing out that passengers do not like; many long-distance leisure passengers would much prefer a one-hour journey extension with a detour over a different rail line (such as the Settle & Carlisle line) rather than having to change to and from a substitute bus for part of the journey.

Organising the smooth transfer of passengers between bus and train requires some effort, and staff need to be available at the relevant locations, in order to provide physical assistance and information.

Although bus substitution is potentially a good idea for low-traffic lines, buses may not be available in sufficient quantity to handle high traffic volumes during peak periods: a failure of a water main at Croydon in South London in 2012 led to a small landslide onto the track, and Southern estimated that the 51 trains per hour passing the spot would need replacement by over 800 buses which (at over 10% of the total bus fleet for London) was not a realistic option.

Of course, bus substitution isn't an option at all for freight, which therefore can be unduly affected by line blockages or engineering possessions. Only exceptionally is it possible to organise substitute traffic by barge or coastal shipping, and some traffic taken by other modes for the duration of a major engineering project (1 week+) may never return to rail at all.

9.9 Stations

Especially where stations are underground, it is important for the railway to plan how to react when crowding occurs. In big cities where rail has a large mode share, failure of the railway can be crippling to overall transport movement, so plans need to be implemented quickly. This may need to be done either during workday peaks, holiday periods (e.g. Chinese New Year, in

Hong Kong), or potentially at any time if there are severe problems with the service.

Station congestion can be managed by changes either to train services or to the passenger flow within the affected station. In terms of changes to train services, one technique adopted, in order to minimize the impact on station congestion, is for trains to 'non-stop' stations which are suffering overcrowding. Although management of the platform edge may be necessary, if trains are to pass through without stopping, this may be easier than trying to deal with significant numbers of alighting passengers. A completely different technique is for empty trains to be run directly to the station under pressure, ensuring that as many people as possible are able to board them, and leave behind what may be dangerously-crowded platforms. Some very busy metro railways (e.g. Sao Paulo) do this every peak period at stations such as Sé.

The flow within stations may be restricted (for instance, permitting exit only, as at London Underground's Covent Garden and Camden Town stations, at weekends) or even reversed (some stations in the area of London's Notting Hill Carnival are used as exit-only in the mornings, and entry-only in the evenings, on carnival days). Because conflicting passenger movements can cause particular problems, implementing one-way systems within stations may be valuable: this has been made a permanent feature for access to the underground platforms at London Euston. Even though walking distances are increased, times to access/egress from platforms may not be, because smooth passenger flow is ensured, and this is certainly a safer result.

9.10 Summary

Whilst planning for 'normal' operation is, of course, essential, substantial work is also needed if the railway is to operate successfully in degraded or exceptional situations. This work needs to cover conventional planning and rostering, but also must consider the extra risks associated with abnormal operation, especially in terms of crowd management.

10 Economic Perspectives on Railways

Railways can be planned from a wider economic or narrower business economic perspective. Looking at a country as a whole, and the railway as a system, it is natural to use a socio-economic perspective. However, private enterprises often limit themselves to a business economics perspective, even if some want to take some social responsibility. This chapter therefore examines some commercial issues relevant to rail operational planning, with the following chapter dealing with the wider issues.

10.1 Running a railway business commercially

Business profitability has been an underlying goal in much of the description of planning in previous chapters, with a special focus on the optimal use of available resources. It should be noted that optimal here does not necessarily mean minimizing resources, or the maximum exploitation of resources (like available personnel). Optimal use means a balance between an efficient resource usage and appropriately-dimensioned reserves and slack in plans designed to ensure recovery capability and not to make them too vulnerable to disturbances. Excessively-tight plans may end up giving more costs for disturbance handling, overtime and sick leave, whilst too-low resource utilization means increased costs and poor utilization of public and company resources.

Glover (1999) and Samuel (1961) list a number of important principles for efficient railway operations including the following:

- Shorter run times mean that the same rolling stock and personnel can provide more transport services[1]
- Load factor is important
- It is difficult to cover the demand peak in a profitable way
- Short turnaround times are important for having a good resource utilization
- Punctuality is important

For resource utilization, speed and punctuality are higlighted. Shorter run times mean that the same rolling stock and personnel can operate more services. Short turnaround times contribute to a good resource utilization, but also

[1] Although maintenance and energy costs can rise significantly, especially in high-speed operation

require precision and reliability, because slack in turnaround times contributes to the ability to recover from delays.

Load factor is important for income. NSB's regional trains in Østlandet had, according to official statistics, a load factor of 28 – 33 % in the period 2004-2006, whilst we have seen figures suggesting that equivalent figures for Switzerland and Britain are 11% and 37% respectively (the latter including standing passengers on some services). As we have already seen, one of the big challenges in public transport is that it is difficult to cover peak demand in a profitable way. Here, load factors of well over 100% are possible in the peak direction (historically, regulations in Britain try to limit peak load factors to c.120%, although this depends upon rolling stock type) but the peakiness of demand may lead to extremely low load factors (e.g. 5%) in the contra-peak direction. Similar principles apply for freight, although (as different wagon types are often used for different traffics) there is a particular problem in finding appropriate materials for 'back haul' possible using the same wagons. Some freight flows (e.g. containers in Britain) have small margins, as can be seen from the overall profitability rates of British railfreight operators, which have only risen to c.£5m through the operation of longer trains.

Short-term profit motives need to be countered by longer-term market development. In particular, good punctuality is important, if a customer base is to be built over time, so that customers see the train as a reliable transport mode. This is equally important for freight; the impact of landslides etc. has been important for freight in Norwegian railway companies, as lines may be closed for days, and customers desert the railways in search of alternative modes which are still operating.

Profillidis (2006) provided a comparison of income per passenger-kilometre between Norway and three other countries (see Table 9.1), but total income depends of course both upon the quantity of passengers carried and the average fare rate. Both of these elements of the competitive environment are affected by factors outside the railway e.g. the distribution and income of the population, the characteristics of competing modes, and Government policy. Norway has the highest incomes/ passenger kilometre of those four countries, but only a fraction of the passenger density of Japan. Economies of density (increasing traffic on the same network) are a crucial factor underlying the efficiency of railway systems.

Some types of railway operation are inherently more commercial than others. Inter-city services can attract passengers (some of them paying business fares) in both directions throughout the traffic day, whilst commuter operations

	Norway	Germany	Japan (E Japan Railways)	USA (Amtrak)	Great Britain
Per pass-km	0.19	0.16	0.09	0.05	0.10
Per route-km	125,000	378,000	580,000	25,000	240,000

Table 10.1 Income in Euros for railway companies
Source: per pass-km data from 2003: Profilidis, 2006, p. 82. GB estimates by the authors.
The equivalent figures for the British mainline network by 2014-15 were about €0.14 / pass-km and 510,000.

are not only "peaky" but fares may be suppressed for political reasons, and customers inevitably dissatisfied because the journey is to/from work and may be in crowded conditions. On the other hand, airport express services often charge very high fares, even for the leisure market, which is much more profitable and can nevertheless still lead to high levels of customer satisfaction.

Network geography is also an important contributor to railway performance. The Valley lines of South Wales may be branch lines with relatively little contra-peak traffic, but they run along the bottom of narrow valleys, with closely-spaced stations providing easy access to the service. On the other hand, a significant proportion of the once-extensive network of East Anglia has been closed, as traffic between the various market towns was too thinly-spread. Ideally, railways need a "string of pearls" of significant trip generators across different journey purposes e.g. employment centres, shopping centres, sporting venues and residential areas; the Thameslink route, linking Bedford to Brighton via London and Gatwick Airport, is a classic example, returning large premium payments to the British taxpayer.

How then are costs distributed in railways? White (2009) describes that one third of costs for a train operating company in the UK are its own costs for train operation, one third are capital costs for rolling stock and one third are costs for using infrastructure (track access). However, data from TOC accounts (see, for instance, Figure 10.1) show slightly lower proportions for rolling stock and infrastructure, and a large 'other' category including energy, insurance, advertising, etc. Where train operators are profitable, and pay premia back to Government (or dividends to owners), these are effectively an extra cost category, as can be seen in Figure 10.1b.

Figure 10.1 Train Operators' Cost Structure: (a) Subsidy-receiving; (b) Premium-paying
Source: TOC accounts data summarised by TAS

There has also been an ongoing discussion in transport literature about which parts of railway costs are fixed (Coyle et al. 2000). Earlier it was assumed that as much as two thirds were fixed costs, but according to Coyle et al. (2000), about 30 % of the costs are supposed to be fixed. Fixed elements certainly include:

- capital repayment costs of infrastructure;
- some infrastructure maintenance (e.g. periodic track inspections, those relating to weather damage to structures, decorating etc. of office blocks);
- time-dependent rolling stock maintenance;
- some HQ costs (e.g. elements of the personnel, training and admin function)

Another perspective is presented by Wise and Baumgartner (1999) who show that total costs for freight train operation is 21 times the investment costs for locomotives. This is different from private cars, where total costs are five times investment costs. Note that both Wise and Baumgartner (1999) and Coyle et al. (2000) point to American conditions, and thereby include a greater part of infrastructure costs than what is the case in Europe. The figures can, however, give a picture of total costs for railway transport.

Table 10.2 shows how construction costs for a new railway roughly are distributed.

Savastano (2011) states that high speed lines internationally cost from £10 million per kilometre up to £65 million per kilometre, with Britain's proposed HS2 at the upper end of this range. When the railway must be built on viaducts or in tunnels, costs are four to ten times higher compared to building in open terrain. Lower-speed lines have a different cost structure (including stations); for comparison, 10 km of double track between Sandvika and Asker cost c. £350m, including two tunnels and work on both stations (Whist and Christensen, 2011).

	Jernbaneverket (2010)	Profilidis (2006)
Permanent way	25 %	15 %
Power supply	10 %	
Signalling	10 %	18 %
Communications	5 %	
Formation/Structure	50 %	55 %
Planning		5 %
Other		5 %

Table 10.2 Distribution of construction costs for a new railway

In 2000 NSB made a calculation of cost distribution for the production of transport services (Nordlid, 2000); this is shown in Table 10.3. Included in personnel costs are among other things overtime, overnight trips, position trips and extras for staying overnight out of depot.

Although energy costs are relatively small, because they are directly affected by operational planning decisions and directly impact profitability, they are considered separately below.

	Share
Rolling stock (capital costs)	30 %
Personnel	20 %
Maintenance	20 %
Operation costs (diesel, electricity)	5 %
Total	65 %*

*The rest is administration, service in stations etc.

Table 10.3 Cost distribution for production of train services

10.2 Energy consumption

Although railways are energy-efficient compared to other modes of transport, to run a train nevertheless takes lots of energy. Energy costs are a notable element amongst railway costs, and so energy consumption is therefore an important subject. The railway companies have economic reasons for saving energy, but general environmental considerations are also important for railways as a whole. The will in society to use railways is among other things dependent on environmental issues. As long as railways can show that they have lower emissions than other types of transport, interest groups will support railways.

Railway energy consumption (and the associated greenhouse gas emissions) can be split between different processes (Schauplitz, 2008) including:
- train service production;
- train production and maintenance;
- the construction, operation and maintenance of railway infrastructure

Norway's railways are partly operated by electric traction, and partly with diesel, but the diesel proportion is relatively low, whilst the Swiss network uses over 99% electric traction. In other countries, however, the diesel proportion can be much higher; Britain's current electrification programme is intended to increase the proportion of train-kms run using electric traction from only c.40% to over 50% (although the proportion of passenger kms carried using electric traction is already c.60%). Because electric trains do not have to carry round either heavy diesel motors or the fuel to power them, and there are then fewer moving parts, electric trains can be up to 40% cheaper to operate – once the power supply systems have been installed.

According to Toutain et al (2008) electric railways are the most energy efficient transport mode (together with metro and tram). With the same energy usage, railways transport twice as many passengers as petrol driven cars and four times as many as planes. For freight transport, electricity driven railways are the most energy efficient transport mode, with diesel driven trains in second place.

Energy consumption in railway transport is spread out all over the railway system. It is needed for passenger flow (lifts and escalators), heating and air conditioning in buildings and stations (which can be very significant for metro railways in hot climates), for information systems, ticket systems, operation centres, signal systems, and energy for trains.

Figure 10.2 OverHead Line Electrification (OHLE) Equipment at Carlisle: providing cheaper traction power, but only after very significant investment

Energy for train operation can be divided in three (Nag, 2004):
- Train propulsion (overcoming aerodynamic resistance and enabling the train to travel);
- Transmission losses from electric power supply system to train;
- Energy for other purposes than train propulsion, such as heating in passenger compartments, lighting and automatic doors

Energy consumption for comfort and functional purposes is relatively minor compared to energy consumption for train propulsion, except when driving at low speeds. Vestby (2009) states that, when driving at 70 km/h, energy for comfort purposes may be 19 % of consumption, while it is 7 % when driving at 140 km/h. Vestby (2009) noted that energy for train propulsion depends on:
- Train design: aerodynamics, weight and motor effect
- Railway infrastructure: alignment (vertical and horizontal) and percentage of tunnels
- Weather conditions
- Runtimes and timetable reserves, and how the driver utilizes these reserves

...but the ability to return power to the transmission system when braking ("regenerative braking") can make a significant difference. Newer train types are equipped with such facilities, where it is possible to utilize the motor to reduce speed. Energy will then be fed back to the power network, and may be used by other trains or somewhere else in the system. This will reduce total consumption compared to using conventional braking, that only converts braking energy to heat.

Studies on Britain's mainline railway show savings from regenerative braking of up to 20%, whilst savings of up to 50% have been reported from metros, where there are (of course) more station stops and more trains in the locality wanting to use the power regenerated.

Energy consumption should be, but often is not, considered directly during the train planning process. Passenger trains which are formed of an unnecessary number of carriages, or which run empty, are all using up energy and costing the business money, without providing compensating benefits. Similarly, freight trains which are required to be stopped to be overtaken, can use up a lot of unnecessary track capacity and diesel fuel, as well as losing end-to-end speed.

In recent years, train companies have expended many resources on training and information about energy efficient driving, and achieved a considerable reduction in energy consumption. According to Moen (2005), studies from Sweden and Germany show that up to 20 % of energy may be saved in local train services when the driver accelerates smoothly and avoids braking hard.

The quickest way to get from one station to the next is to use full acceleration up to maximum speed, and then full braking into the station; this gives the minimum runtime. The basis for saving energy through energy efficient driving techniques is that timetables include a little more time than is strictly necessary. The additional time is to increase the robustness of the timetable, so that any delay does not necessarily create more delays; the possibility for energy saving is then in the buffers within a timetable. This means that an "on-time" train does not have to be driven as quickly as possible; a train ahead of time may use the time saved for energy optimal driving.

There are three strategies for energy efficient driving techniques (Moen, 2005). These are: lower acceleration, lower maximum speed and coasting.

The first strategy is to use less power for acceleration up to maximum speed. The motor runs at lower effect, giving less energy consumption.

Another strategy is to reduce maximum speed. This means less driving resistance and lower energy consumption. The saving is largest at high speeds, because resistance increases by the square of speed. As with reduced acceleration, reduced maximum speed will increase runtime. To use lower maximum speed is most obvious as a solution for local trains with short distances between stops.

A third strategy for reducing consumption is to turn power off as early as possible when approaching stations and speed restrictions to coast (roll) as much as possible. Rolling will, however, increase runtime a little compared to driving into the station at high speed with a heavy braking. Coasting (rolling) may be used where there is a longer distance between stations, and where the terrain is appropriate, including down-hill slopes. A similar technique is used by airlines in so-called "green landings". A comparison between these three strategies (Wien, 2006) shows that the energy-saving strategies which have less impact on journey times are lower maximum speeds and coasting.

Drivers with good knowledge of the line have the possibility to adapt speed to the approaching terrain. If, for instance, there is an up-hill slope after a down-hill, the driver may avoid braking, and instead roll up the slope. Then the need for braking and accelerating is reduced, which reduces energy consumption.

Driver training schools, such as NSB's at Sundland (near Drammen) often have a simulation centre for driver training, especially to enhance safety. However it can also be used for energy consumption analysis and training in energy saving techniques (Moen, 2005). In this installation realistic train driving can be simulated when the driver sits in a mock-up cabin containing all the important functions from real trains.

Some railways are now developing Driver Advisory Systems, to provide real-time advice to train drivers about the state of the line ahead (including platform availability) and hence a speed profile which will keep a train in its booked path, enable coasting, and reduce or eliminate unnecessary braking and accelerating. One source in Britain suggested that stopping a diesel High-Speed Train unnecessarily cost £50 each time in fuel etc., so these savings mount up. Writing timetables which minimise the likelihood of this in the first place can therefore provide valuable cost reductions.

10.3 Summary

Whatever the objectives of a railway company or particular project, there are some fundamental underlying economic principles which should give some guidance to the railway planner. Achieving higher line utilisation (hence economies of density), train load factors, higher speeds (to attract customers as well as reducing many operating costs) and shorter turnrounds are key targets, but the underlying circumstances of the operation (e.g. a rural area with scattered population) may simply prevent this. Contrary to the assumptions of many passengers, peakiness creates severe financial, as well as operational, problems for the railway. This means that inter-city operations are always likely to be more commercially-attractive than commuter flows into regional towns, irrespective of the way in which the railway is organised (e.g. public or private) or where it is in the world. However, a specific area of cost which most railways can address is that of energy, and reducing the use of this across the operation may bring substantial savings with little impact on customers.

11 Getting Benefits from Railway Investments

11.1 Cost: Benefit Analysis

Railway plans are generally only going to be implemented if they are worthwhile, which means that the value of the three types of benefits identified in section 2.4 (increased demand/revenue, and/or reduced costs, and/or increased social benefits) must exceed the (capital and/or ongoing) costs of achieving them. As we have seen in chapter 10, relatively few railways are able to operate completely commercially and have projects which can solely be justified on railway financial grounds alone[1].

Cost-benefit analyses are therefore a common method used to analyse government investments. A usual expectation of economic profitability is that profit for the population as a whole is bigger than the total cost of the venture (Finansdepartementet, 2005), because a wider assessment of a rail scheme is likely to include other benefits. Ideally, all activities that are economically profitable should be undertaken (although few, if any, governments have sufficient funds available for this), and capital rationing usually occurs by ranking projects. In cost-benefit analyses, all relevant effects of a project are quantified and compared systematically – and, it is hoped, accurately, although this may be difficult to do, either because of political pressure for (or against!) the project, or because projects may just be really complex.

The costs and benefits of a project must be quantified in a common unit of measurement, usually money. If the calculated sum of all effects put together is positive, the project is economically profitable for society (NOU 1997:227). Together with other analyses (e.g. of political considerations), cost-benefit analyses are an important basis for making decisions about public activities. The analyses are often combined with analyses of goal fulfilment to give a more complete picture of project alternatives. The goal of the analyses is to identify and prioritise the projects to be undertaken.

An economic cost-benefit analysis contains an analysis of costs and benefits to the business concerned, but also includes the consequences of the investment on the wider public economy. In other words, the economic analysis of a project also includes the external effects or externalities of a project. That

[1] Although, obviously, a greater number of railway projects might be financially-worthwhile to government if (for instance) the direct costs of savings to the health service from fewer road accidents were included.

Figure 11.1 Complex Project: Thameslink Project Works: Live Railway, suspended over the River Thames, Central London

means that both positive and negative effects on all involved parties should be included within the decision. A project may therefore be considered to be economically profitable, even if it has a financial deficit, because it has profits not covered by market mechanisms. The economic theory behind Cost: Benefit analysis has been explained in greater detail by others (e.g. Cole, 2001, pp. 246-261 and 264-281).

The transport sector has used cost-benefit analysis as a tool for economic analysis for over 150 years. According to Grøvdahl and Hjelle (1998) the first theoretical contribution to this area may be traced back to the French engineer Dupit, who published a paper on the benefits of public activities in 1844. Cost-benefit analyses were used systematically for the first time in the US "New Deal" in the 1930s. In the transport sector, cost-benefit analyses were used in England from around 1960 and in Norway in work done by The Road Planning Commission of 1964.

In the transport sector in particular, it is now established practice to make economic cost-benefit analyses before investments are made. Danish consultancy COWI (2002) studied the use of cost-benefit analyses in transport infrastructure projects in seven European countries. They found that cost-benefit analyses are used in most countries on a strategic level (e.g. when formulating the Norwegian National Transport Plan), partly to assess project worthwhileness, and partly to prioritize between projects. For instance, in Britain, projects with Benefit:Cost ratios of over 2:1 would be considered good, and expect to be funded; those under 1.3:1 would be regarded as poor and unlikely to be taken forward.

When big projects are to be analyzed, it is necessary to compare costs and benefits which occur at different times. This is handled by discounting the future value of costs and benefits to a reference point in time (usually, the year when the decision to carry out the project is made) with a given calculated discount rate.

However, what may be a bigger problem with rail scheme analysis is that a wide variety of alternative measures may be suggested to solve a problem, and it may not be clear which of them offers the best Benefit:Cost ratio, given their expected success in achieving various outcomes. For instance, Figure 11.2 gives an example of two types of solution for a capacity problem, one involving 'new build' works (NB) but the other upgrading of existing infrastructure (Up). Having defined a 'Do Minimum' case (some schemes may already be committed, and some background demand growth inevitable), packages of different works may lead to all sorts of potential decisions. What matters is the relative increase in revenues for the capital expenditure required (or, more accurately, the net increase in (revenue less operating cost)) i.e. the gradient of the lines shown in blue. However, the capacity required also needs to be taken into account – some (combinations of) works may not provide enough capacity, whilst on the other hand providing capacity well beyond the maximum expected demand levels is unlikely to be worthwhile.

11.2 Scope of analysis

There is a difference between (socio-)economic and commercial considerations depending upon where you set system boundaries, i.e. what is included in the analysis (Figure 11.3). A commercial analysis focuses on income and costs within an organisation. An economic analysis of a railway project includes business economic effects for the train operating companies, and investment and operational costs for the infrastructure authority. But it does not stop there. It also includes how passengers and freight users are affected, for example through reduced travel times and better punctuality. Environmental and safety effects are also included, as reduced air pollution and reduced risks for road accidents when transport is moved from road to rail. In principle, all

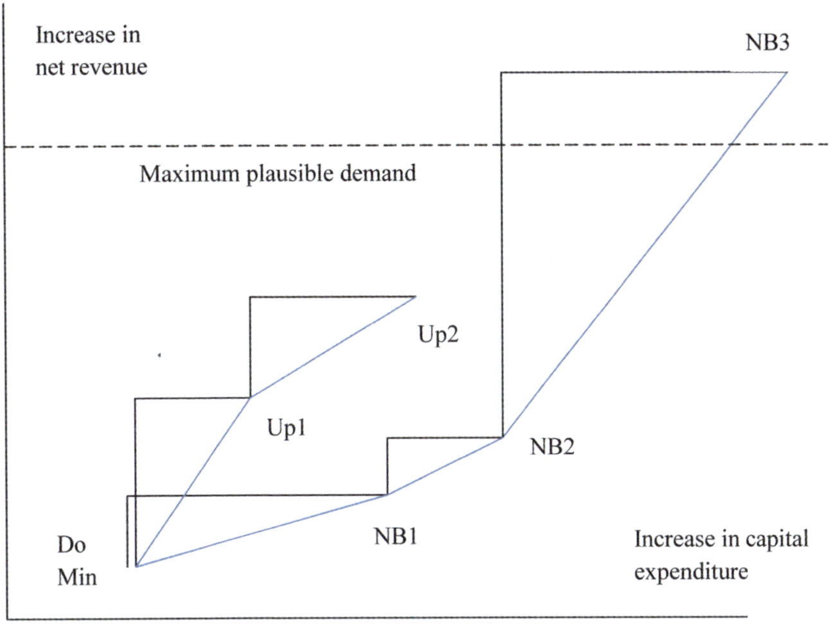

Figure 11.2 Assessing Possible Strategies for Rail Improvements
Points marked "Up" relate to possible upgrades, and those marked "NB" to new build solutions

effects that are consequences of the studied investment should be included. This means that business development and property prices also should be included. In practice, it can be difficult to quantify these, since such things are influenced by many other things than a railway project, whilst some small impacts can be difficult to identify at all. Therefore it is often difficult to define what should be included and not i.e. how to define system borders.

The aim is to put a value on as many things as possible, but there are things that cannot be easily quantified in money terms, for example the conservation of antiquities, which may just be referred to as "unquantified consequences". Economic analyses are mainly carried out before a project is submitted for decision, but sometimes also afterwards. As shown in Figure 11.4, analyzing completed projects is often based on narrower system boundaries.

Economic analyses are a set of tools used as basis for decisions when carrying out projects and investments (Rietweld and van Wee, 2008). However, the analyses are part of a study of consequences, and should not be used as the

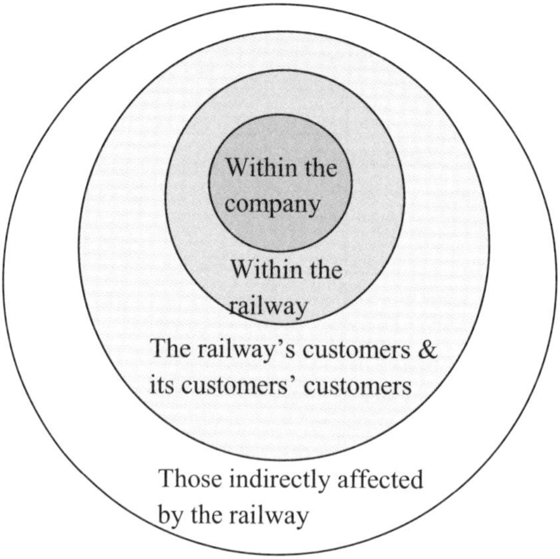

Figure 11.3 System Boundaries in Economic Analysis

only basis for decision. Even so, they are often given much weight, because the analyses seem to give a clear answer if a project is profitable to society as a whole or not. An economic cost-benefit analysis is based on the principle that you can set a (usually monetised) value on all consequences of an activity for the different parties in society.

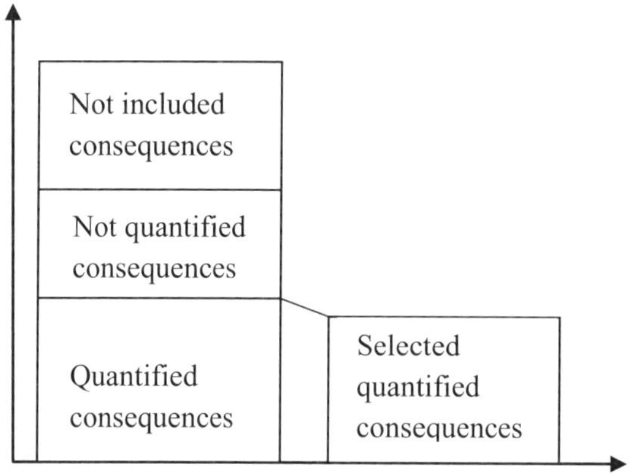

Figure 11.4 What is included in an economic analysis depends on when and how the analysis is carried out

All uses of resources connected to a project must be analyzed, be identified and quantified. This goes for factors like manpower and materials, but also public resources like clean water, recreational areas etc. Such factors may be difficult to quantify, but must be included so that project costs are not underestimated. Because costs for public projects are covered by taxes, a taxation cost is included in the analyses. These add an administrative burden and also reflect a loss of efficiency because resource usage in society is influenced by tax increases.

The cost concept itself in economic analyses is based on a so-called opportunity cost way of thinking. The basis for this is that resources are limited, and when resources are spent in one area, the same resources cannot be spent on something else. In principle, the costs of one project reflect the value of how much you have to give up of other things to carry through a project, and the benefit should reflect how much you are willing to give up (NOU 1997:27).

When the expected benefits of a project are identified, they should be valued in the cost-benefit analysis, in a three-step process:

- Appraising the per-person "willingness to pay" for the effect
- Calculating how many people are affected
- Discounting values of effects to a present value to be compared to the costs

Established practice in cost-benefit analyses is that the benefit given by a project is valued according to what the users are willing to pay for it. If there is a market for it, then price may be used as a measure of the willingness to pay. Ideally you should then make corrections because you often do not have perfect competition, and that some consumers are willing to pay more than they actually do, and this is often difficult. If there is no existing market, you either use "Revealed Preference" (RP) values derived from previous examples, or "Stated Preference" (SP) where surveyors ascertain how much people might pay for something, when trading it off against something else with a known value. However, improvements in econometrics are enabling an increasing number of the wider economic benefits (for instance, the regeneration, employment or business enhancement impacts on a town whose service is substantially improved) to be calculated (see, for instance, Graham, 2007).

Investments in infrastructure, in both roads and railways, mean that transport patterns and transport habits change. Developing a future traffic situation is therefore essential, before calculating the benefits and costs of possible investments. This is done by using a range of transport modelling techniques outside the scope of this book – see Ortuzar and Willumsen (2011) for a thorough treatment. However, in his analysis of usage of cost–benefit analyses, Lauridsen (2000) refers to that there are greater challenges in the way analyses are carried out than in the method itself; he refers to the uncertainty of input data (especially about expected demand) in particular. Further, Flyberg et al. (2003) contend that there are indications to deliberate manipulations to get requested results. Studies also show that decisions often are not in line with cost-benefit analyses, for example when prioritizing between projects. According to Nyborg and Spangen (1996) though, a majority in the Norwegian parliament transport committee used the cost-benefit fraction as an indicator of which projects they wanted to study more closely, but none of them seemed to prioritize *only* from using the cost-benefit fraction.

Økland (2009) has compared the calculation methods used in Norway, Sweden, Denmark and the United Kingdom based on a cost-benefit analysis for the proposed new double track between Oslo and Ski. Variations in results are substantial. The project is profitable from a British viewpoint, but not with the methods used in Scandinavia. Økland's study shows that economic profitability is not a unique concept. By using elements or parameter values from the British calculation method, even railway projects in Norway could appear to be economically profitable.

For railway investments, the trend has been that public authorities cover infrastructure costs, and a question is how much public funding there should be for train services (Peterman et al., 2009). An assessment of the public economic benefit of railways is therefore very important for railway investments. The business perspective is first and foremost relevant for the train operating companies. At the time it was maintained that the income from Gardermobanen should cover both the investment in infrastructure and the operational costs for the train service (Norwegian Parliament document: St. Prp. Nr. 90 (1991-1992)). As NOU (1999, 28) point out, you may ask why a railway in Oslo should be profitable in the narrow business sense, when this happens very rarely internationally[3]. The infrastructure then also was handed over to Government, while the train service itself to Oslo Airport has been commercially-profitable.

[3] Although, theoretically, one can use Stated Preference market research techniques to elicit direct valuations of these by trading them off against other known elements, or use Revealed Preference methods to observe prices (e.g. of houses) which might be affected by proximity to them

11.3 Scheme Assessment: Delivering Benefits

Usually rail construction projects are justified by giving a combination of improved punctuality, more train services and reduced travel times (see Figure 11.4). Improved infrastructure gives higher speed and more capacity. Shorter runtimes and improved punctuality may give shorter overall journey times whilst improved capacity may give increased frequency. Taken together, reduced travel times, better punctuality and increased frequency would be expected to generate more passengers and freight on the railways. Unfortunately it is not always clear to managers or Governments that these improvements require many other actions. In particular it is important to be aware that changes in travel time and frequency implies a timetable change. From experience punctuality improvements often also call for a timetable change. However, rail passenger behaviour is not just changed by a new line; it is also influenced by parking facilities, or an adapted public transport service (e.g. better connections with buses) - all these are marked as "other" in Figure 11.5.

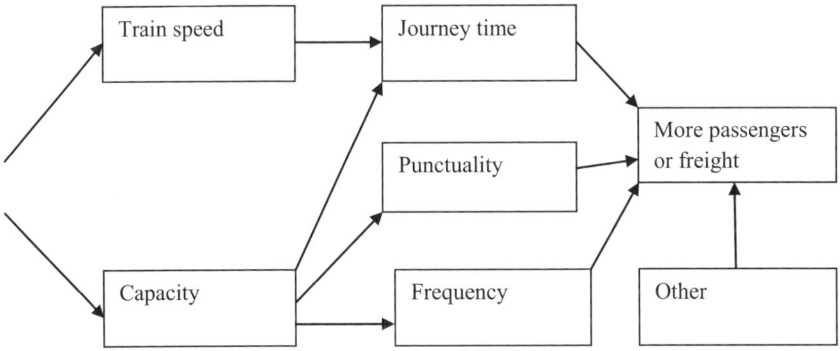

Figure 11.5 Logic underlying Railway Projects

However, as Flyvberg (2007) noted, railway investments have not always achieved their expected benefits. An important lesson from Norway's latest projects is that construction projects alone do not solve system problems. On the contrary, system problems can reduce the benefits of new investments. Long term and consistent focus on maintenance and availability are important, and have up till now been neglected; further reductions in Jernbaneverket's maintenance budget in 2014 reinforced this, although this seems to have been corrected somewhat in the 2016 budget.

Olsson et al. (2010) studied increases in railway delays from 2005 to 2010. They found several factors which separately, but especially taken together, have contributed to an increased load on the railway system. These include increased rates of equipment failure, increased train service levels and increased railway enhancement and maintenance activity. Fewer factors have developed in the opposite direction. The load on the network has therefore increased, but the ability to handle it has not. In future, new tracks, new rolling stock and *increased maintenance* should give improvements. It is a paradox, therefore, that that many of the projects involving new infrastructure in Norway have arguably not yet given any recognizable improvement for rail users; similarly, in Britain, passenger satisfaction with the railway has levelled off somewhat since recovering from the aftermath of the accident at Hatfield in 2001, despite significant investment in the railway (Transport Focus, 2015).

The analysis of causes for increase in delays from 2005 to 2010 pointed also to that railways in Norway have systematic Winter problems. Delays occur to a greater extent in years with harder Winters compared to milder ones. Furthermore, construction work and activities on the tracks are related to increased delays; when construction activities increase, then delay hours also increase.

In practice, it has often been difficult to achieve all good intentions when a new railway is planned. Railways are closely-linked systems. When new tracks are built on one part of a line (for example from Asker to Sandvika), it has been difficult in practice to make the necessary train service adaptations to reduce run times or to increase frequency. This is partly because the sections before and after the new line are not adapted to the new frequency, and partly because a frequency change on one line also influences trains on another. These close links are very clear in the Oslo area, but the principle goes for the railway in general.

Railway projects are big, costly and time consuming. It is therefore common practice to split them in steps, where the railway is decided and built in sections ("parcels"), though in some cases it has been possible to build a new line relatively as a whole. We shall here show examples from four Norwegian railway construction projects. Among other things, we would like to illustrate the effect of section-wise versus united railway projects. All four studied projects have a different combination of planned and actual build strategy. Both planned and actual build strategy can be split into united and section-wise building. Planned building strategy relates to how the building process was intended when the "Main Report" was made (typically one or two years before the project "go" decision was made). Actual building strategy relates to if the projects were decided section by section, or if all relevant sections were undertaken together.

Table 11.1 shows projects with different combinations of planned and actual building processes. "Parcelwise" building means that projects were decided upon or built as a series of sections.

Actual building strategy	Planned building strategy	
	"Parcelwise"	Together
"Parcelwise"	Bergens-banen	Vestfold-banen
Together	Ostfold-banen	Gardermo-banen

Table 11.1 Four different railway building projects and four building strategies

The study of four building projects indicates that section-wise building does not necessarily achieve much of a reduction in travel time. However, on the cost side, it appears that smaller 'parcels' of expenditure may be easier to control. Scheme results summarised in Table 11.1 show that building sections together in one project gives a considerable increase in benefits, in both more passengers and a better train service. At the same time, building projects in sections gave substantial savings in expenditure. In particular, a project planned to be done section-wise, but actually completed as one project, had a large over-run in expenditure.

The study indicates that positive effects of railway developments were maximised when new infrastructure is combined with changes in timetable plans and other production plans (including rolling stock usage). In Britain this was epitomised by the "Total Route Modernisation" carried out on the Chiltern line in the early 1990s. It is often difficult to get the full effect before all sections are built and a comprehensive timetable is made.

Table 11.2 summarizes the impressions from the study. However, there may be instances where substantial benefits can be realised from sub-projects. For instance, the development of TGV Est in France has provided significant benefits for Paris – Strasbourg passengers, even though the final section of the new line is not scheduled to open until 2016; perhaps this is because each sub-section has nevertheless achieved a time saving of perhaps 30 minutes.

Actual Method of development	**Number of passengers compared to "before" situation**	**Train service compared to "before" situation**	**Costs**
Section-wise	Unchanged	Moderate improvements	Controlled
One project	Considerable increase	Large improvements	Over expenditure

Table 11.2 Summary of different development strategies

The section-wise developments have not achieved the planned reductions in travel times – for instance, the project on the Vestfoldbanen and Bergensbanen have prepared for travel time reductions that have not been implemented (yet?). Because of the complexity of train service and timetables in the Oslo area, comprehensive adaptations to take account of a new line section are unrealistic. Any adaptations for one line will also affect services on other lines. Yet these problems are not visualized in the planning stage of these projects. On the other hand, integrated developments have led to new infrastructure being combined with timetable adaptations, for Gardermobanen in particular, but also for Østfoldbanen (Ski-Sandbukta). Section-wise building also provided cost control.

Analyses show that train service is not automatically improved by building new tracks. Changes in travel times are only implemented when timetables are changed. The close connection between getting planned benefits, timetable adaptations and possibly other production elements (rolling stock, maintenance structure, train depots etc.) must be visualized in project planning and followed up during projects.

Increases in passenger numbers have arisen more strongly from integrated developments, partly because those projects have created a momentum to ensure the optimisation of timetable and production plans. With section-wise developments, it is possible that larger changes should be undertaken at intervals of several years, in order to achieve the effects of ready-made projects.

Although only four projects were studied, these four projects represent a major part of Norwegian developments in recent decades. New projects, like the

Lysaker – Asker line, show that it is difficult to see obvious improvements in train service when such a project that is finished.

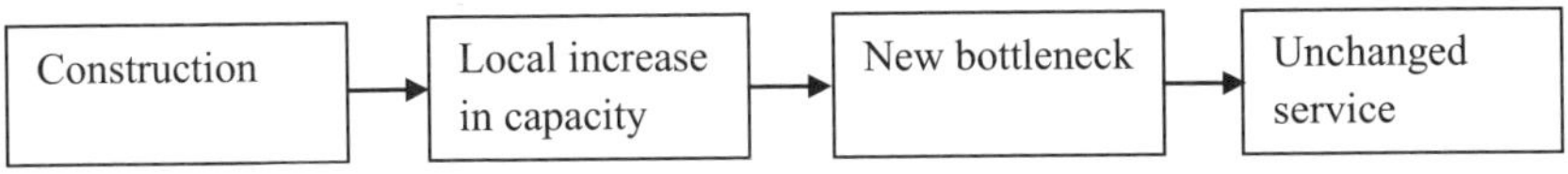

Figure 11.6 Section-wise developments have a tendency just to move bottlenecks

Nyrud (2007) studied the effects of a new double track from Asker to Sandvika the year after opening. The situation in months January to May 2005 was compared to the situation in the same months for 2006 and 2007. The number of passengers had increased, but growth rates had not changed after the opening compared to increase in the years before. In advance it was calculated that development should increase capacity between Asker and Oslo S by two trains per hour per direction. The actual increase was just one train per hour per direction. After development, delays increased (to an average of up to 140 seconds for some trains) and punctuality worsened (up to 30 % worse for some services). This indicates that either the capacity of the line was not as high as calculated, or that it is more difficult than assumed to utilize a capacity increase for punctuality improvements. Figure 11.6 shows that section-wise development of new tracks gives increased capacity locally, but this capacity may often not be utilized to establish a new timetable because of constraints in other parts of the railway system.

We then see a clear tendency that completion of greater parts of a development does not necessarily give a clear improvement in train service. Figure 11.7 shows a large development (project) split into three minor development projects. The purpose of all three is to give improved frequency, travel time and punctuality. Usually the economic calculations are based on improvements in these three factors. Yet experience shows that a timetable change is not made even for quite big singular development projects (Project A in Figure 11.7), such as projects like Vestfoldbanen or Asker-Sandvika. It is also not certain that the next project (development project B) is followed by a timetable change. Section-wise developments then often do not give visible improvements for passengers, especially not in a short term perspective. Sooner or later a timetable change will come, and many of the benefits of the finalized projects may be achieved. In the figure, it is after project C that you may utilize the effect of projects A, B and C. In practice, this was expected to happen in 2012/2015, when the effects of Asker-Sandvika, Sandvika-Lysaker, Lysaker station (and other developments in the Oslo area) could be implemented.

It is also likely that the order of sub-projects will be affected by the difficulty of doing them: one might expect the easy sections to be addressed first. But, as noted above, they may not actually achieve the desired benefits until the difficult (i.e. expensive) sub-projects are completed, which may be never: quadrupling of the lines out of London's King's Cross occurred in 1957, except for the Welwyn flyover and tunnel, which still remain a two-track bottleneck.

The economic analyses for each of projects A, B and C are typically based on step-wise improvements. The actual development at best means an advancement of benefits of project A and B, and at worst a double counting of benefits. For example project C may be justified by getting benefits that at the time were being expected from project A and B.

It is a paradox that even big development projects like Asker-Lysaker tend to *move*, rather than to *remove* bottlenecks. In the case of Asker-Lysaker it is now clear that the Oslo tunnel (Skøyen/Lysaker-Oslo S) is a bottleneck. On the other hand, it has never been realistic to develop projects like the upgrade of the whole Oslo S – Drammen corridor as a single project, not least because the funding cannot be provided all at once.

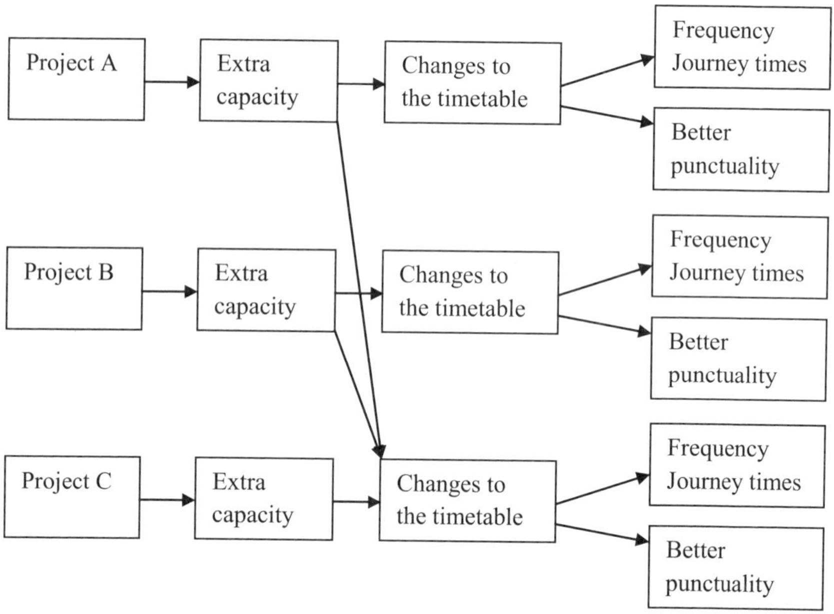

Figure 11.7 Development projects must achieve a critical mass to justify a timetable change

Elsewhere, some projects can only provide limited benefits until complete e.g. platform lengthening at only some locations along a route enables longer trains to be run, but not used by all passengers. Other projects will *only* create their benefits upon completion e.g. gauge clearance to provide a freight corridor able to accept 9' 6" containers from Felixstowe to the North of England was clearly going to be a programme of works over several years, but there are almost no benefits until all works are completed: even if just one overbridge remains too low to accept bigger containers, then no trains can take advantage of the other works already completed.

Railway developments have then often had to be done stepwise. Understanding this is critical, particularly because development projects and production planning need to be done in a more integrated fashion than in the past. Here production planning especially means timetable planning, but also includes other subjects as sidings for trains between journeys, the positioning of maintenance depots, station design and other things contributing to the ability to run more, faster and more punctual trains when new tracks are built.

Experience shows that it has been difficult to implement integrated railway development projects, although it may be possible to do so for new high speed

Figure 11.8 Platform Lengthening Projects enable some benefits to be achieved before programme completion: Wandsworth Common (London) has been extended to take 10-car trains but not all other stations on the line can accommodate them

lines. The tradition of section-wise railway development may be difficult to change, although large-enough sections (such as London – Birmingham, phase 1 of Britain's HS2) are expected to provide visible improvements for passengers.

Big projects have been the main activities for railway improvements in recent years. Increased track capacity is designed to give more trains and better punctuality. However, an alternative way of improving train service is to turn this logic around. Better punctuality gives more capacity because you do not need that many free slots in the timetable to handle delays. An until-now underestimated way of improving punctuality is to improve the reliability of existing infrastructure and rolling stock. This is done by providing more resources for operation and maintenance, by undertaking small projects (such as moving signals slightly, or installing stop boards and requiring train drivers to use them), but also by improving competence, as shown in Figure 11.9.

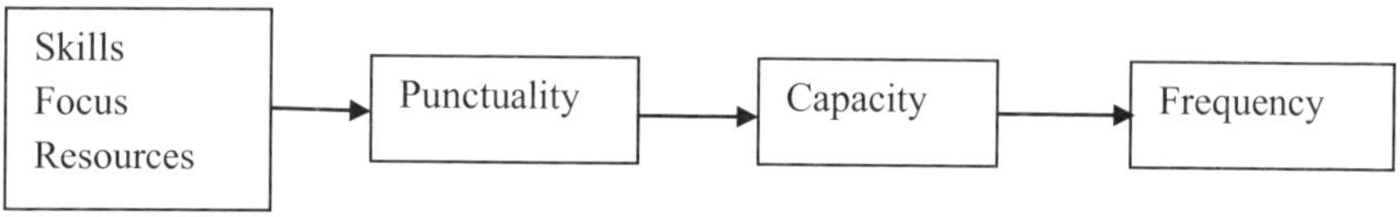

Figure 11.9 Alternative strategy for increasing railway capacity

Figure 11.10 shows our assessment of developments in punctuality work in Norway over the last ten years. Two plusses on data and analysis mean that there are great improvements in data availability and skills to analyze punctuality information. There are improvements in communicating with others (one plus), but not as good as with data and analysis. The largest potential lies in incorporating punctuality considerations in strategy work, and to direct resources and means towards activities that give the best punctuality for money spent.

In Norway, there has been a clear tendency to focus on big projects, both as developments (e.g. new double tracks in the Oslo area), but also for maintenance (e.g. the Oslo tunnel project). This focus, however, may be misplaced, since smaller projects may improve capacity so that the bigger projects are either not needed, or can be postponed. For instance, analysis of station stops at Oslo's Nationaltheatret station suggested that perhaps three extra trains per hour could be run, if operations were of a higher and more consistent standard. The economic value of delaying a project as big as a second Oslo tunnel by five years is very significant.

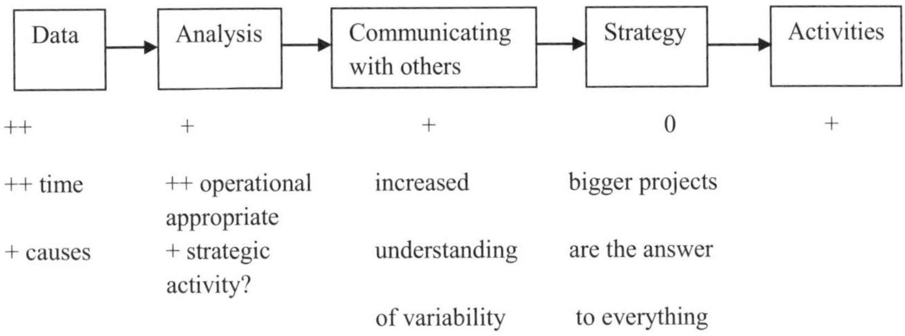

Figure 11.10 Impressions from punctuality work over ten years

Nevertheless, because of the great interest for railways at present, it should be possible to stimulate the railways in Norway and elsewhere. But it is important that not only big and visible projects get attention and are allocated resources. Railway operations are first and foremost the daily work done to make the trains run. And it is only when trains run that they make themselves useful.

11.4 Summary

Railway planning should be designed to achieve specific outcomes that relate to the differing (and potentially mutually-incompatible) objectives of the relevant stakeholders. However, there may be an infinite number of possible projects, and their effectiveness is likely to vary. In order to assess the worthwhileness of these projects methods of economic analysis are therefore needed, and Cost:Benefit Analysis has become the standard approach for this, trying to draw together quantified estimates of all the relevant impacts. However, what is considered relevant does vary, for instance between countries. Moreover, when we examine the actual (as opposed to the planned) outcomes, it becomes clear that some types of project fail to deliver; in particular, care must be taken with capacity enhancement projects that bottlenecks are not merely moved to another location. Attention to smaller-scale improvements (for instance, those resulting from performance analysis) may provide a far better return on effort, and may render some of the larger capacity enhancement projects completely unnecessary. A systems engineering perspective should challenge the planner to consider when the desired benefits really will be achieved.

References

Ackermann, T (1998) *Die Bewertung der Pünktlichkeit als Qualitätsparameter im Schienenpersonenverkehr auf Basis der direkten Nutzenmessung*, Universität Stuttgart, Germany.

Al-Haimi, A A (1991) *Airline Schedule Punctuality Management,* Cranfield Institute of Technology, UK.

Ashton, R and Fowler, A (2005) Human Friendly Rosters: Reducing the Risk of Fatigue, pp. 203-214 in J R Wilson et al (eds.), *Rail Human Factors – Supporting the Integrated Railway*. Ashgate, Hants, UK.

Avelino, F, te Brömmelstroet, M and Hulster, G (2006, November). The Politics of Timetable Planning: Comparing the Dutch to the Swiss. Paper presented to *Colloquium Vervoersplanologisch Speurwerk 2006*, Amsterdam.

Banverket (2001) *Tågtrafiken – Punktlighet och förseningar*. Banverket, Borlänge.

Banverket (2003) *Orsakskoder till tågförseningar* (TFÖR), Banverket Trafikk, Borlänge.

Barter, W (2008) "Will ERTMS give us More Capacity?" *Mod. Rlys.* pp. 84-87, Sep.

Bertolini, L (2008) "Station areas as nodes and places in urban networks: An analytical tool and alternative development strategies", pp. 47-57 in F Bruinsma et al (eds.), *Railway development impacts on urban dynamics*. Physica-Verlag, Heidelberg.

BOB Railway Case (2003) *Benchmarking Passenger Transport in Railways*. Rijswijk, The Netherlands: NEA Transport research and training.

Boge, K (2006) "Votes count but the number of seats decides. A comparative historical case study of 20th century Danish, Swedish and Norwegian road policy", Handelshøyskolen, BI, Oslo.

Casson, M (2004) The future of the UK railway system: Michael Brooke's vision. *International Business Review*, 13, 181–214.

Christensen, T and Egeberg, M (1992) *Forvaltningskunnskap*, TANO, Oslo.

Cole, B and Cooper, C (2005) Making the trains run on time: the tyranny of performance indicators. *Production planning and control*, 16 (2), 199–207.

COWI (2010) *Kunnskapsstatus for høyhastighetsbaner i Norge*. COWI, Oslo. [online]. Downloadable from: http://www.jernbaneverket.no/PageFiles/11538/ Kunnskapsstatus%20for%20h%c3%b8yhastighet%20i%20Norge-2010juli15.pdf. [Latest edn. 7.6.2011].

COWI (2002) *Brug av samfundsøkonomiske metoder i udvalgte lande*. København: Trafikminsteriet,

Coyle, J J, Baradi, E J and Novack, R A (2000) *Transportation*. South-Western College Publishing, Madison, Ohio, USA.

Daamen, W & Hooghendoorn, S P (2004) "Pedestrian Traffic Flow Operations on a Platform", *Proc. Computers in Railways IX* pp. 125-134, WITpress, Southampton, UK

den Brok, M and Vissers, R (1994) VPT, a new systems architecture for planning and control of train traffic in the Netherlands. *Proc. Computers in Railways IV – Volume 2*. pp 19-21, Computational Mechanics Publications, Southampton.

Elliot, R (2001) Maintenance plans for new vehicles. *IMechE Conference Transactions 2001-4. Railtex International Railway Engineering Conference*. Railway Rolling Stock. Professional Engineering Publishing.

EU Commission (2014) Regulation No 1300/2014 "Technical specifications for interoperability relating to accessibility of the Union's rail system for persons with disabilities and persons with reduced mobility", 18/11/2014

Evans, J R & Lindsey, W M (2005) *The management and control of quality*, 6th edn., Thomson Learning, New York.

Fahlén, J and Jonsson, B (2005) Train punctuality in a new perspective. *Eur. Rail. Rev.*, 11 (1), 60–63.

Fiedler, J & Scherz, W (2012) *Bahnwesen*, Werner Verlag, 452 pp. (in German)

Finansdepartementet (2005) *Veileder i samfunnsøkonomiske analyser*, Oslo.

Finansdepartementet (2008) *Veiledler nr 1. Det sentrale styringsdokumentet*. Oslo: Finansdepartementet. [online]. Downloadable from: tp://www.concept.ntnu.no/Publikasjoner/Veileder/Veileder%20nr%201%20Det%20sentrale%20styringsdokumentet.pdf. [Latest edn. 7.6.2011].

Finans- and Tolldepartmentet (1998) *Nytte-kostnadsanalyser, Veiledning og lønnsomhetsvurdering i offentlig sektor*, Oslo.

Flyvberg, B (2007) Cost Overruns and Demand Shortfalls in Urban Rail, *Jnl. Trans. Plan & Tech.* 30 pp. 9-30.

Ford, R and Haydock, D (1992) Signalling and tinetabling. pp. 117-129 in N G Harris and E W Godward (Eds.), *Planning Passenger Railways*. Transport Publishing Company, Derbyshire, UK.

Frontier Economics [supported by the Railway Consultancy] (2005) *Measuring the Determinants of Rail Performance*, report for the SRA and DfT

Gelders D, Galetzka, M, Verckens J P and Seydel E (2008) Showing results? An analysis of the perceptions of internal and external stakeholders of the public performance communication by the Belgian and Dutch Railways. *Government Information Quarterly*, 25 (2), 221–238.

Gibson, S, Cooper, G and Ball, B (2002) "The evolution of capacity charges on the UK rail network". *Jnl. of Trans. Econ. & Pol.*, 36, 341–354.

Glover, J (2013) *Principles of Railway Operation*, Ian Allan, Hersham, 160pp.

Graham, D (2007) "Agglomeration, productivity and Transport Investment", *Jnl. Trans. Econ. & Pol.* 41 (3) pp. 317-343.

Grande, R and Nilsson, R C (1989) «Klart for tog....!» Driftsformer og togmeldinger ved NSB. *På Sporet*, 60, 29–45.

Gunn, H F (2000) An introduction to the valuation of travel-time savings and losses. pp. 433-447 in D A Hensher and K J Button (eds.), *Handbook of transport modelling*, Elsevier Science Ltd., Amsterdam.

Gylee, M (1994) Punctuality analyses – a basis for monitoring and investment in a liberalized railway system. *Proceedings of seminars held at the 22nd European transport conference, P384(9), pp.* 153–165.

Handstanger, A C T (2009) *Scheduled waiting time from crossing on single track railway lines*. Trondheim: NTNU.

Hansen, I A & Pachl, J (2008) *Railway Timetable and Traffic*, Eurailpress, Hamburg (228pp.)

Harris, N G (1988) "The Economies of Massed Reserves for Transport Operators", Trans. Econ. 15 (3) pp. 25-31.

Harris, N G (1992) *Planning Passenger Railways: A Handbook*. UK: Transport Publishing Co. (255pp.)

Harris, N G & Cooper, G (2000) "An Access Rights Database and Validator", Proc. COMPRAIL 00 pp. 203-210, Bologna, Italy (WITpress, Southampton). Available at http://library.witpress.com/pages/PaperInfo.asp?PaperID=4105

Harris, N G & Anderson, R J (2007) "An International Comparison of Urban Rail Boarding and Alighting Rates", *Jnl. Rail & Rapid Transit* 221 F4 2007, pp. 521-526.

Harris, N G, Graham, D J, Anderson, R J & Haojie, L (2014) "The Impact of Urban Rail Boarding and Alighting Factors", TRB 93rd Annual Meeting, Washington DC, USA.

Harris, N G, Mjøsund, C S & Haugland, H (2014) "Improving Railway Performance in Norway", *Jnl. Rail Trans. Plan. & Man.* 3 pp. 172-180.

Harris, N G (2015) "A European Comparison of Station Stop Delays", ICARE conference, Istanbul, Turkey, 2-4 March.

Haugland, H (2006) "TTRA and Capacity Analysis", Vossloh IT Users' Conference, York, 8th Nov.

HEATCO (2006) *Deliverable 5: Proposal for Harmonised Guidelines*. [online]. Downloadable from: http://heatco.ier.uni-stuttgart.de/. [Latest edn. 9.5.2010].

Heinz, W (2000) *Passagerutbyte I tåg. Mätningar av av- och påstigningstider samt ansats till modell för att beskriva samband*. KTH, Stockholm.

Hooghiemsta, J S and Teunisse, M J G (1998) The use of simulation in the planning of the Dutch railway services. Pp. 1139-1145 in D.J. Medeiros, et al (Eds.), *WSC '98 Proceedings of the 30th conference on Winter simulation*, Washington D.C, 13-16 Dec. IEEE Computer Society Press Los Alamitos, CA

Jernbaneverket (2011) *Slik fungerer jernbanen. En presentasjon av trafikksystemets infrastruktur*. Jernbaneverket.

Jernbaneverket (2010) *Slik fungerer jernbanen*. [online]. Downloadable from: http://www.jernbaneverket.no. [Latest edn. 21.2.2010].

Jernbaneverket (2008) *Jernbanestatistikk*. [online]. Downloadable from: http://www.jernbaneverket.no. [Latest edn. 21.2.2010].

Jernbaneverket (2006a) *TIOS – årsakskoder*, Jernbaneverket.

Jernbaneverket (2006b) *Metodehåndbok JD 205*. Jernbaneverket.

Johnson, D (2015) Double-deck Dilemma, *Mod. Rlys.* 72 no. 800 pp.64-67, May

Jorna, R, van Wezel, W, Kiewiet, J and de Boer, T (2005) Analysis and Support of Planning in the Dutch Railroad Company, pp. 203-215 in J.R. Wilson et al (Eds.), *Rail Human Factors – Supporting the Integrated Railway*. Ashgate, Hants, UK.

Kahan, A M (1979) *Railway Capacity Analysis and Related Methodology*. Ottawa/Hull: Canadian Transport Commission, Research Branch.

Kroon, LG and Fichetti, M (2000) *Crew Scheduling for Netherlands Railways "Destination Customer"*. NS Reizigers and Erasmus Research Institute of Management (ERIM), Rotterdam.

Kvaavik B (2008) *Bedre i dag enn i går, men ikke så god som i morgen*. NSB Persontog Drift, Norway.

Lauridsen, H (2000) *Strategisk transportplanlegging og konsekvensanalyser: Erfaringer fra Skandinavia*, Rapportno. 1177/2000, Transportøkonomisk institutt, Oslo.

Lichtberger, B (2005) *Track Compendium*, Eurailpress, Hamburg, 634pp.

Lindahl, A (2002) *Infrastruktur för flexibel tågföring – Kapacitetsanalys av förbigångar på en dubbelspårssträcka*. Stockholm: KTH,

Lindfeldt, O (2001) *Tidtabellskonstruktion, trafikledning och tättidighet på Svealandsbanan*. KTH, Stockholm.

Lindh, C and Widlert, S (1989) *SJ-resenärernas kvalitetsvärdering – med avseesde på information, punktlighet, restid, styv tidtabell och turtäthet*. KTH, Stockholm.

Lumsden, K (1986) *Transportteknik*. Studentlitteratur, Lund.

Lundin, M, Elmquist, A L & Hammarlund, S (2005) "Incitament för ökad punktlighet på järnväg - fortsättningsprojekt", TFK report 2005:3, Borlange, Sweden.

Lustig, D (2015) "Sandy Leaves a Long-Term Legacy", *Rly. Gaz. Intnl.* 171 (5) pp. 64-68, May.

Moen, J V (2005) *Prestasjonsmåling av energiforbruk for tog*. Trondheim: NTNU.

Morvant, C (2015) Challenges raised by freight for the operations planning of a shared-use rail network: A French perspective, *Trans. Res. A* 73 pp.70-79.

Nag, M (2004) *Energiøkonomisering i togfremføring i NSB*. Trondheim: NTNU .

Nash, C and Matthews, B (2009) *European Transport Policy. Progress and prospects*. Brussels: Community of European Railway and Infrastructure Companies (CER).

Nash, C and Shires, J (2000) Benchmarking European Railways – An assessment of current data and recommended indicators. In *Transport Benchmarking – Methodologies, Applications & Data Needs*. OECD, Paris.

NEA (2003) *BOB railway case - benchmarking passenger transport in railways – final report*, NEA Transport research and training, Rijswijk, Netherlands.

Network Rail (2013) *Long Term Planning Process: Long Distance Market Study.* Network Rail, London.

Nordlid, H D (2000) *Bruk av optimering og simulering i kostnadsanalyse og risikostyring for NSB*. Trondheim: NTNU.

NOU (1997) *Nytte-kostnadsanalyser, Prinsipper for lønnsomhetsvurderinger i offentlig sektor*, NOU 1997:27, Statens forvaltningstejeneste.

NOU (1999) *Gardermoprosjektet, Evaluering av planlegging og gjennomføring*. Oslo: Statens trykking.

NTNU (2009) *Kompendium i EVU-kurs BA6004. Jernbaneteknikk. Del 1 og 2*. Trondheim: NTNU.

Nyrud, T (2007) *Punktlighetsanalyser som faktabasert beslutningsunderlag: Analyse av utvalgte tog i rushtid mellom Asker og Oslo*. Trondheim: NTNU.

Nyström, B (2005) *Punctuality and Railway Maintenance*, Licentiate thesis, Department of Applied Physics and Mechanical Engineering, Luleå University of Technology, Sweden.

Nyström, B (2008) *Aspects of improving punctuality - from data to decision in railway maintenance*. Luleå University of Technology, Luleå.

Økland, A (2009) *Samfunnsøkonomi i jernbane – en teoretisk og praktisk sammenligning mellom flere land*. Trondheim: NTNU

Olsson, N (2009) *Sluttpresentasjon PEMRO-prosjektet*. [online]. Downloadable from: http://www.sintef.no/Projectweb/PEMRO/Seminarer-og-presentasjoner/ Sluttpresentasjon-av-PeMRP-1322009/. [Latest edn. 7.6.2011].

Olsson, N O E and Haugland, H (2004) Influencing factors on train punctuality – results from some Norwegian studies. *Trans. Pol.*, 11 (4), 387–397.

Olsson, N, Økland, A, Veiseth, M & Stokland, Ø (2010) *Driftsstabilitet pa Jernbaneverkets nett - årsaksanalyser 2005-2010*, SINTEF, Trondheim.

Olsson, N. and Sætermo, I A F (2006) *Kartlegging av kvalitetsoppfølging i deltakende bedrifter*. [online]. Downloadable from: http://www.sintef.no/project/PEMRO/Rapporter/sammenstilling%20ap%201_4%20.pdf [Latest edn. 7.6.2011].

Olsson, N, Sætermo, I A F and Røstad C C (2002a) *Konsekvensvurdering av anleggsarbeid i Vestkorridoren*. Trondheim: SINTEF Teknologiledelse.

Olsson, N, Røstad C and Veiseth, M (2002b) *Nordlandsbanen – fortsatte analyser*. Trondheim: SINTEF Teknologiledelse.

Olsson, N, Sætermo, I A F and Røstad C C (2002c) *Vurdering av regler for avvikshåndtering ved uregelmessigheter i toggangen*. SINTEF Industrial Management, Trondheim.

Ortuzar, J de J & Willumsen, L (2011) *Modelling Transport*, Wiley, 4th edn. (586pp.)

Pachl, J (2008) Timetable design principles. pp. 9-42 in I A Hansen and J Pachl (eds.), *Railway timetable & traffic. Analysis, modelling, simulation.* Eurailpress, Hamburg (228pp.).

Pachl, J (2009) *Railway Operation and Control*, (2nd edition) VTD Rail, USA, 267pp.

Parsons Brinckerhoff (2014) *Terminal Capacity Research Report*, technical report for British Department for Transport.

Peterman, D R, Frittelli, J and Mallett, W J (2009) *High Speed Rail (HSR) in the United States* Congressional Research Service [online]. Downloadable from: http://www.fas.org/sgp/crs/misc/R40973.pdf. [Latest edn. 7.6.2011].

Preston, J (1993) Does Size Matter? A Case Study of European Railways, *Jnl. Trans. Econ. & Pol.*

Preston, J (2009) Trends in European railways over the last two decades. *Built Env.*, 35 (1), 11–23.

Priemus, H (2008) Urban dynamics and transport infrastructure: Towards greater synergy. pp. 20-28 in F Bruinsma et al (Eds.), *Railway development impacts on urban dynamics*. Physica-Verlag, Heidelberg.

Profillidis, V A (2014) *Railway Management and Engineering*, 4th edn., Ashgate, Farnham, 518pp.

Rietveld, P and van Wee, B (2008) Ex ante evaluation of railway station development projects: Issues still to be solved. pp. 163-169 in F Bruinsma et al (Eds.), *Railway development impacts on urban dynamics*. Physica-Verlag, Heidelberg.

Riksrevisionsverket (1986) *Tågtrafikens punktlighet*. Stockhom: Riksrevisionsverket

Samset, K (2001) *Prosjektvurdering i tigligfasen: Fokus på konseptet*, Tapir Akademisk forlag, Trondheim.

Samuel, H (1961) *Railway Operating Practice*. Odhams Press Ltd., London

Sando, S, Rasten, E & Nilsson, R G (2008) *Norske lok og motorvogner 1.1.2008*, Norsk Jernbaneklubb, Oslo.

Savastano, M (2011) *High-speed Railway Assessment, phase 2. Rail specific planning and development analysis. Appendix 6. Experiences from other countries.*WSP Civils, Stockholm.

Schlaupitz, H (2008) *Energi- og klimakonsekvenser av moderne transportsystemer Effekter ved bygging av høyhastighetsbaner i Norge*. Oslo: Norges Naturvernforbund.

Schüller, N (2011) Global rail traffic makes rapid recovery. *Int. Rly. Jnl.* 51 (2), 20–21.

Seco, A J M and Goncalves, J H G (2007) "The quality of public transport: relative importance of different performance indicators and their potential to explain modal choice", pp. 313-326 in C.A. Brebbia (Ed.), *Urban transport 13 – urban transport and the environment in the 21st century*, WIT press, Southampton.

SIKA (2002) *Tid och kvalitet i persontrafikk*, report 2002:8, Stockholm.

Skartsæterhagen, S (1998) *Kapasitet på jernbanestrekninger. Utdrag av notat 877*. Trondheim: NTNU.

Sone, S (1994) "High-speed, high-density train allocation", pp. 19-21, *Proc. COMPRAIL IV – Volume 2*. pp 19-21, Computational Mechanics Publications, Southampton.

St.prp. nr. 90 (1991–92) *Utbygging og finansiering av hovedflyplass for Oslo-området på Gardermoen med tilhørende tilbringersystem og konsekvenser for Forsvaret*. Oslo: Samferdselsdepartementet

Toutain, J E W, Taarneby, G and Selvig, E (2008) *Energiforbruk og utslipp til luft fra innenlandsk Transport*. Statistisk sentralbyrå, Oslo-Kongsvinger:.

UIC (2004) *UIC Code 406 Capacity,* International Union of Railways, Paris.

van den Berg, J H A and Odiijk, M A (1994) DONS: computer aided design of regular service timetables, *Proc. COMPRAIL IV – Volume 2*. pp 19-21, Computational Mechanics Publications, Southampton.

Veiseth, M (2002) *Punktlighet i jernbanedrift*. NTNU, Trondheim

Veiseth, M (2009) *Forbedring av punktlighet i jernbanedrift – utvikling av punktlighetsprosessen*. Trondheim: NTNU

Veiseth, M & Bititci, U S (2006) "Performance Measurement in Railway Operations – Improvement of Punctuality and Reliability", in Neely, A, Kennerly, M & Walters (eds) "Performance Measurement and Management: Public and Private", 28-28 July, London; Cranfield University pp. 801-808.

Veiseth, M and Olsson, N (2007) *Avgangspunktlighet Alnabru godsterminal*. SINTEF Teknologi og samfunn.

Veiseth, M, Olsson, N, Røstad, C C and Indbryn, M (2003) *PONDUS – Punktlighets Og uNDerveisUnderSøkelse – Oppsummering av et punktlighetsarbeid utført av Jernbaneverket og SINTEF Teknologiledelse våren 2003*. Trondheim: SINTEF Teknologiledelse.

Vestby, S E (2000) *På tur med Signatur. Energibehov ved bruk av krengende togsett på Sørlandsbanen*. Sogndal: Vestlandsforskning.

Wardman, M R (2006) "Demand for Rail Travel and the Effects of External Factors", *Trans. Res. E* 42 pp. 129-148.

Weston, G & McKenna, J P (1990) "The London Underground Train Service Model", *Proc. COMPRAIL II* pp. 133-147, WIT press, Southampton.

Whist, E and Christensen, T (2011) *Universitetet i Oslo Politisk styring, lokal rasjonalitet og komplekse koalisjoner Tidligfaseprosessen i store offentlige investeringsprosjekter Concept rapport nr. 26*. NTNU, Trondheim.

White, P (2009) *Public transport: its planning, management and operation*. Routledge, Oxford, UK.

Wien, I (2006) *Energiforbruk – Avhengighet av ruter og materiell*. NTNU, Trondheim

Wise, R and Baumgartner, P (1999) *Go Downstream – The New Profit Imperative in Manufacturing*. Harvard Business Review, Boston.

Wren, A., Kwan, R.S.K. and Parker, M.E. (1994) Scheduling of rail driver duties, in Proc. COMPRAIL *IV – Volume 2*. pp 19-21, Computational Mechanics Publications, Southampton.

Yuan, J (2008) Statistical Analysis of Train Delays, chapter 10 pp. 170-181, in I A Hansen and J Pachl (Ed.), *Railway timetable & traffic*. Eurailpress, Hamburg (228pp.).

Index of Key Terms